rich AS A KING

Praise for *Rich As A King*

"*Rich As A King* is an entertaining, informative, and very interesting treatment of investment strategy, tactics and wisdom. It is surprisingly exhaustive in its coverage. Its strength lies in three areas. One is the explicit recognition and treatment of the Kahneman-type behavioral decision-making flaws that most of us have, and of organized ways to avoid them. The second is the explicit treatment of market psychology as a relevant variable. The third is unique I think: the use of an extended parallel analysis of the game of chess – a kind of analogy. For those who play the game of chess well, the benefit will be the transfer of knowledge they already have to the field of personal investing. For the rest of us, I am less sure that whatever expertise we have in investing plus the book will make us better chess players. But perhaps learning to play chess well will make us more sure-footed investors."

Michael Spence
Nobel Prize Laureate, Economics, 2001

"Goldstein and Polgar integrate chess and investing strategies in a remarkably entertaining and educational fashion. Chess players who know little about investing, and investors who know little about chess, will gain fresh insights into both. Two very challenging topics are combined in surprising ways to make one very accessible book."

Ken Rogoff
Professor, Economics Department, Harvard University
International Monetary Fund (IMF) Chief Economist, 2001-2003
Chess grandmaster

"*Rich As A King* is a treasure trove of financial tips, brilliantly weaving together the strategic thinking of a chess master with the practical advice of an experienced financial analyst. The authors demonstrate their breadth of knowledge by sprinkling in fascinating insights from the behavioral sciences that help explain why even veteran investors make mistakes with money. The result is a common-sense roadmap that can help investors of all ages strengthen their financial future."

Doug Shadel, PhD
AARP financial fraud expert and author of *Outsmarting the Scam Artists*

"This fast-moving, enjoyable book shows you how to think better, make better decisions, and achieve your long-term goals of 'financial victory' with great certainty."

Brian Tracy
Best-selling author, *Million Dollar Habits*

"Why not make life easier? Apply the systems in this book and become a strategic investor."

Harry Lorayne
NYT Best-selling author, *The Memory Book*

"Susan Polgar and Douglas Goldstein have compared the strategy of chess to investing. As a chess player and investor, I found this fascinating and a great read."

Lewis B. Cullman
Chairman Emeritus, Chess in the Schools, and author of
Can't Take It With You: The Art of Making and Giving Money

"You don't need to be a chess player to appreciate the practical advice of this well-written book by Susan Polgar and Doug Goldstein. Readers of *Rich As A King* will be richly rewarded for their effort to see their finances in a fresh light."

Gil Weinreich
Editor-in-Chief, *Research Magazine*

"With an abundance of wit and wisdom, *Rich As A King* provides one insight after another about chess, investing, and life."

William D. Cohan
Contributing editor at *Fortune*, and NYT best-selling author,
Money and Power: How Goldman Sachs Came to Rule the World

"Chess teaches the basic principles of life. There are consequences or benefits for every decision we make. It is vital that each person consider how today's decisions affect tomorrow's future. We recommend you read *Rich As A King*."

Jim Bob Duggar
Father of TLC's 19 Kids and Counting

"From the open until endgame, *Rich As A King* delivers solid financial advice with fascinating insights from the world of chess."

Terrance Odean
Professor of Finance, University of California, Berkeley

"It is rare to find a readable and interesting book concerning investments. Yet, *Rich As A King* by Grandmaster Susan Polgar and Douglas Goldstein, CFP˚ is such a book. Their story humanizes investment advice. It combines the wisdom of a master chess player and a thoughtful investment advisor. Chess strategies are applied to investment decisions, while recognizing self-knowledge in selecting one's investments. We can enjoy and learn at the same time."

Tamar Frankel
Professor of Law, Boston University, author of *The Ponzi Scheme Puzzle*

"Chess has been one of our most useful thought-tools for nearly 1,500 years. Polgar and Goldstein are cleverly carrying on one of humanity's oldest traditions."

David Shenk
NYT Best-selling author, *The Immortal Game: A History of Chess*

"The ancient game of chess has powerful strategic secrets locked within it that can mean the difference between victory and defeat, success and failure, and I use it as the primary metaphor in my classes on crafting business strategy. Now, Goldstein and Polgar reveal these powerful strategic chess secrets and apply them to the realm of personal finance. *Rich As A King* melds the wisdom of a chess grandmaster and the business acumen of a finance wizard to create a readable and immensely rewarding guide to personal financial security. Powerful and timely, concise and spot-on, a sure guide to financial victory!"

Professor Stanley K. Ridgley
Department of Management, LeBow College of Business, Drexel University

"Douglas Goldstein and Susan Polgar are grandmasters of their craft. The strategies underlying their success are fascinating and apply to many spheres outside of chess and investing – I have adopted many!"

Julie Deane
President, *The Cambridge Satchel Company*,
winner of the Queen's Award for Enterprise

"We do not see the rivals on the other side of our trades, blind to the likelihood that we are the losers. But we see the rivals on the other side of our chessboards, forcing us to ask whether we are likely to be the losers. Susan Polgar and Douglas Goldstein demonstrate in this wonderful book that thinking like a chess grandmaster can help you act as an investment grandmaster."

Professor Meir Statman
Department of Finance, Santa Clara University
Author of *What Investors Really Want: Discover What Drives Investor Behavior and Make Smarter Financial Decisions*

"In *Rich As A King*, Douglas Goldstein and Susan Polgar present a logical, move-by-move game plan for successful financial planning and investing."

Professor Arthur Benjamin
Department of Mathematics, Harvey Mudd College

"Susan Polgar and Doug Goldstein take financial strategy-making to an entirely new level by showing how financial decisions and strategies are like the strategies employed by the chess masters. In entertaining and easy-to-understand prose, Susan and Doug show us the way to achieve personal financial success step by step. This thorough and comprehensive recipe for success will stimulate your thinking and improve your personal financial results. I highly recommend this book to those looking to improve their financial wellbeing."

Henry E. Juszkiewicz
CEO – Gibson Guitars

"Everyone knows that investments can be like a game of poker, but this intriguing system for maximizing profit and minimizing risk when trading stocks employs the strategy and tactics of the greatest game of them all, chess, to help you make decisions that will increase the value of your portfolio. You don't have to be a good chess player to understand the intriguing parallels suggested in this highly entertaining approach to getting rich by playing the market."

Nicholas Wapshott
Author, *Keynes Hayek: The Clash That Defined Modern Economics*
Reuters contributing columnist

"Sun Tzu argued that as much as it was important to know the enemy, know the climate and know the terrain, a master strategist needed to know himself: to understand his own strengths and weaknesses. In *Rich As A King*, Goldstein and Polgar alert their readers to the myriad of psychological inclinations and prejudicial biases that plague most investors. Bad investment choices often arise from a critical lack of self-awareness. Not knowing how to invest comes from not knowing oneself."

Professor Andrew R. Wilson
Department of Strategy and Policy, U.S. Naval War College

"This book is a must read for those who believe that chess is a metaphor for life, and especially for those who want to make sound investments for the long term. The synergy generated by combining the insights of a chess grandmaster with the skills of a professional financial planner is amazing. Careful readers can expect to develop better habits for both investing and for playing chess!"

Professor Hersh Shefrin
Mario L. Belotti Professor of Finance, Santa Clara University, and author of *Beyond Greed and Fear: Understanding Behavioral Finance and the Psychology of Investing*

rich AS A
KING

*How the Wisdom of Chess
Can Make You a Grandmaster of Investing*

GRANDMASTER SUSAN POLGAR
and DOUGLAS GOLDSTEIN, CFP®

NEW YORK

 *rich* AS A KING

How the Wisdom of Chess Can Make You a Grandmaster of Investing

 The authors and publisher are donating 10% of their income from the sale of *Rich As A King* to the Susan Polgar Foundation. The Foundation's mission is to promote chess, with all its educational, social, and competitive benefits, throughout the United States, for young people of all ages, especially girls.

www.RichAsAKing.com

 **bitlit**

A **free** eBook edition is available
with the purchase of this print book.

ISBN 978-1-63047-097-5 paperback
ISBN 978-1-63047-098-2 eBook
ISBN 978-1-63047-099-9 hardcover
Library of Congress Control Number:
2014930596

CLEARLY PRINT YOUR NAME ABOVE IN UPPER CASE

Instructions to claim your free eBook edition:
1. Download the BitLit app for Android or iOS
2. Write your name in **UPPER CASE** on the line
3. Use the BitLit app to submit a photo
4. Download your eBook to any device

Cover Design by:
Rachel Lopez
www.r2cdesign.com

Interior Design by:
Bonnie Bushman
bonnie@caboodlegraphics.com

To our families and friends,
The kings and queens of our lives

Contents

Introduction   xvii

Keys to Reading This Book   xix

*If you want to quickly spot the **Rich As A King** Action Points*   *xix*

If you want a video illustration   *xix*

If you're not an avid chess player   *xix*

If we describe a chess game   *xx*

If you want to get bonus information   *xx*

Part A: STRATEGY   **1**

Chapter I   Avoid These Mistakes and You're Halfway There   3

Hate to lose? Here's why.   *5*

*How to decide whether to sell **this** or **that***   *7*

When to sell an investment… or sacrifice a chess piece   *8*

Where to look if you want to improve your portfolio   *12*

You're losing money because of something you don't see   *13*

How the news causes you to lose   *14*

Why you should walk away from free offers   *16*

What men suffer from worse than women   *18*

Chapter II   How to Achieve Your Financial Goals   23

The system you need to set goals   *24*

Where you should focus your attention first   *25*

How to protect your most important asset   *25*

How castling works   *25*

How to maximize the return on your pieces   *27*

Apply these three core chess strategies to your finances   *27*

The trick to setting goals in personal finance   *28*

How to achieve your STRATegic goals   *29*

Is this your goal?   *34*

Why real-life goals should imitate chess	*36*
How to set up your retirement savings	
by controlling the center of your investment board	*36*
How to protect your core assets by castling	*37*
Develop your fighting pieces	*41*
How to be an active investor	*42*
Using leverage to make more money… and have more risk	*47*
High gear – options trading	*48*
Initiative: Controlling the pace of your investment game	*48*

Chapter III	**The Plan to Get Rich**	**51**
	You need more than tactics to get rich	*52*
	How to control your future	*53*
	Who needs a financial plan?	*53*
	Begin with a "snapshot"	*54*
	Set your goals	*55*
	Determine your risk tolerance	*55*
	Balancing risk vs. reward	*56*
	What will devastate you financially?	*56*
	Let someone else share your risks	*57*
	Set up an asset-allocation model	*57*
	How Monte Carlo can improve your analysis	*60*
	Calculating the average	*60*
	How the same returns can give different results	*61*
	Nothing lasts forever	*62*
	What if you don't withdraw any money?	*62*
	How Monte Carlo simulations work	*62*
	How to determine where to place your money	*66*
	Don't get rooked by scams	*73*
	Four easy steps to doing your financial plan right	*75*
	Do you need to have a financial planner?	*76*
	Step I. Gather your information	*77*
	Step II. Define your goals	*81*
	Step III. Identify barriers to achieving your goals	*81*
	Step IV. Choose an asset allocation model	*83*
	Step V. Choose your investments	*86*
	Step VI. Monitor your progress	*86*

Chapter IV	Computers, Chess, and Money	**89**
	The 3 ways to make the most of computers	*92*
	Get paid for patience	*93*
	Techniques to develop the patience you need to succeed	*94*
	How much money is reasonable?	*94*
	What good financial planning software must do	*96*
	The problem with using a computer to make money decisions	*98*
	How to leverage the power of computers	*99*

PART B: TACTICS — **101**

Chapter V	**Budgeting: How to Use Your Sixteen Pieces Wisely**	**103**
	The attitude that will wipe you out	*104*
	Limit your possibilities	*105*
	Communicating with your spouse about money	*105*
	The 3 T's of a champion	*106*
	Do you love money or hate it? What's your temperament?	*108*
	How fast should you move?	*108*
	4 Reasons <u>not</u> to transfer your credit card balance	*110*
	How to prevent being checkmated by the market	*110*
	How to develop a knack for managing money	*111*
	Can you budget your way to being as "rich as a king"?	*112*
	Helpful hints for a successful budget	*116*
	Use cash instead of plastic	*117*
	Win with tactical finance	*117*

PART C: How the Pieces Move: Stocks, Bonds, and Mutual Funds — **119**

Chapter VI	**Building Your Castle with Stocks**	**121**
	You can own a business	*122*
	Why people buy stocks	*122*
	Is it worth the risk?	*123*
	How to become a market grandmaster	*125*
	What types of stocks to buy	*126*
	Common or preferred stocks	*126*
	Why you need overseas investments	*127*
	American Depository Receipts (ADRs)	*127*
	The easiest way to own lots of real estate	*128*

	Should you buy commodities?	*130*
	Growth or income?	*130*
	Limiting the volatility of your stocks	*131*
Chapter VII	**Strengthening Your Position with Bonds**	**133**
	How bonds are issued, traded, and priced	*133*
	Considerations in buying bonds	*134*
	U.S. government bonds: Why lend to Uncle Sam?	*135*
	The benefit of municipal bonds	*135*
	Zero-coupon bonds	*136*
	Understanding bond yields	*138*
	Premium bonds: What makes them so valuable?	*140*
	Secure or not? Check the rating	*140*
	Junk bonds (a.k.a. high-yield bonds)	*141*
	What is junk worth?	*142*
	"Put junk in the garbage. I want the safety of CDs!"	*143*
	Bond ladders	*145*
	Why build a bond ladder?	*145*
Chapter VIII	**Mutual Funds: Let an Investment Grandmaster Manage Your Portfolio**	**149**
	What are mutual funds?	*149*
	Seven reasons to buy mutual funds	*150*
	How mutual funds lower risk	*152*
	Which fund suits you best?	*152*
	Seven reasons for selling mutual funds	*156*
	Avoid 5 common mutual fund mistakes	*159*
	The best place to look for fund information	*160*
	Should you pay for a mutual fund?	*161*
	How you pay tax on mutual funds' profits	*161*
	Don't pay tax on someone else's gains	*162*
PART D: Getting Rich Using Chess Strategies		**163**
Chapter IX	**64 Strategies to Make You Rich as a King**	**165**
	1. Every move must have a purpose	*165*
	2. Don't feel money is burning a hole in your pocket	*166*
	3. Develop purposefully, and not just for development's sake	*166*
	4. Accumulate small advantages	*167*

5. Make the most of your time 171

6. If you can't explain your choice, don't do it 172

7. Know the purpose of every piece on your board 173

8. Fix a bad investment 174

9. Time is on your side 174

10. Avoid traps 175

11. Take care, even with the small moves 177

12. Sometimes you just need to sell 179

13. How to maximize profits from weak pieces 181

14. Make money by waiting 182

15. Respond promptly to danger 183

16. Be aggressive, but play soundly 184

17. Risky playing will tire you out 185

18. Don't attack a well-protected area 186

19. Never play a risky move 187

20. Don't accept a draw right away 188

21. Castle early because it's a proven technique, but… 189

22. …there are times when you should not castle 189

23. Prepare to attack long before you fire the first shot 190

24. Defend your pawns. They have a great future. 192

25. Double your power 194

26. Playing flexibly vs. sticking to a strategy 195

27. Tactics make you win 196

28. Profit from trading pieces 196

29. Develop during exchanges 198

30. Trade off bad pieces immediately 200

31. How time will make you wealthy 202

32. Don't always exchange a pawn for a queen 205

33. How to hit your target by missing the bull's-eye 207

34. If you blunder, don't give up fighting 207

35. Identify threats 208

36. Answer all _real_ threats 209

37. Don't move your protection 210

38. Get a free piece 212

39. Fork your opponent 213

40. Don't get forked 215

41. *Don't get pinned* — 216
42. *Death traps* — 217
43. *An insurance trap* — 219
44. *The dangerous discovery for bond buyers* — 220
45. *How to react against a killer attack* — 223
46. *What to do when there's nothing to do* — 225
47. *Block your opponent* — 227
48. *Undermine your opponent's plan* — 227
49. *Gain the initiative* — 228
50. *Take your money out of the bank* — 229
51. *Don't look for the most creative way to win the game* — 230
52. *Maintain your concentration* — 231
53. *How to avoid weak pawns in your finances* — 232
54. *Tools to lower fees and limit trading* — 234
55. *Make sure all your pieces work together* — 234
56. *The surprise attack that will wipe you out* — 235
57. *How <u>not</u> to be broke* — 239
58. *Ruined by your own team* — 241
59. *The backup plan you need now* — 244
60. *Buying at the best price* — 248
61. *Don't be a chased king* — 250
62. *Go for a stalemate with the IRS* — 251
63. *How perpetual check can save your life... and your money* — 254
64. *Leverage your strongest piece* — 256
64+. *Don't miss these fabulous free resources* — 258

Conclusion   How to Beat a Grandmaster — 259
About the Authors — 261
    Susan Polgar — 261
    Douglas Goldstein — 262
Index — 264
Don't Miss Out on Any New Ideas — 277
    *How to Get the **Rich As A King** Resource Guide* — 277

Introduction

If a ruler does not understand chess, how can he rule over a kingdom?
—King Khusros II, Persia 580 – 628 CE

This book is designed for people who want to become as *Rich As A King*. If you wish to accumulate substantial treasure (or, more realistically, cash, stocks, and bonds), you need a solid plan (strategy) and the right moves (tactics). Who's better qualified to teach about strategy and tactics than a chess expert? Couple that with a veteran financial planner and you're well on your way to success. Inside these pages, we'll show you how you can apply the wisdom of chess to building wealth.

Not a chess player? Don't worry. Regardless of whether you've ever inched a pawn across the chessboard, you'll understand the ideas and analogies that we use, and you'll have no problem applying them to making money.

When we started putting our research together (taking occasional breaks for a game of chess – Susan won them all), combining the greatest approaches on the chessboard with the best personal finance ideas, we examined how discipline, analytical thinking, and decisiveness on the chessboard paralleled those same traits in the world of investing. We saw that successful investors based many of their decisions on winning chess strategies. We then decided to write this book to share with you what you need to become a grandmaster of your investments and, ultimately, as *Rich As A King*.

Susan Polgar and **Douglas Goldstein**

Keys to Reading This Book

If you want to quickly spot the *Rich As A King* Action Points

Throughout the book, we highlighted specific steps that you can take to get yourself on the path to wealth. Look for the RAAK knight with his notepad.

If you want a video illustration

We illustrated some of the chess and investment concepts in short video clips. When you see the RAAK knight with his video camera, go to www.RichAsAKing.com/videos to watch the related video.

If you're not an avid chess player

For readers who like chess, but may not want to spend a lot of time going over the details of a game or specific tactical moves, we've put a box around the in-depth chess discussions. You can skim or skip those sections if you'd like. Though you may want to refer to them later, you can still learn 100% of the investment ideas without reading these parts. On the other hand, if you enjoy chess analysis, you can focus your attention on the material in the box.

If we describe a chess game

Traditionally, when referring to historical games, chess writers put the name of the player with the white pieces first, followed by the player with the black pieces. You might see a reference to a game like this:

Goldstein vs. Polgar, 0-1, 24 moves, 2013, New York

The notation indicates that Goldstein played white, Polgar black, and Goldstein lost in twenty-four moves. In most tournaments, a player earns zero points for a loss, half a point for a draw, and one point for a win.

If you want to get bonus information

In writing *Rich As A King,* we developed many more ideas than we could squeeze between the covers of the book. We refer to them throughout the text and will direct you to the pages on our website where you can find them.

Part A

STRATEGY

CHAPTER I

Avoid These Mistakes and You're Halfway There

Susan: One of the toughest decisions I ever had to make in my chess career was not which piece to move on the board. Instead, after I had moved to the United States, I was confronted with a test of allegiance. Having spent my whole life representing my homeland of Hungary at the chessboard, I was asked to go to the 2004 Chess Olympiad and lead the American team to its first-ever medals in the sport.

Though my relationship with the Hungarian Chess Federation, once considered a puppet of Soviet controllers, was often tenuous, I had finally achieved recognition from them. In my early years of serious competitive chess (1982 – 1985), the Communist party tried to hold me back by not letting me play in, nor travel to, important international events. However, after the 1988 Chess Olympiad, the whole atmosphere changed. My team, consisting of my two sisters, Judit (age 12) and Sophia (age 14), along with Ildiko Madl (age 19), and I (also 19), defeated the Soviets. Since they had dominated the game for decades, our victory over them turned us into overnight national treasures.

Switching federations to the United States Chess Federation could certainly be seen as unpatriotic. However, I knew that I was not abandoning my roots. Rather, I was fulfilling my desire to popularize chess in the United States and open the door to American women to show them that they, too, could follow their dreams.

What I didn't expect, though, shortly after my announcement, was to hear someone call me by my Hungarian name. "Zsuzsa!" a Hungarian chess fan summoned me. I looked towards him and he continued, "If you play for the Americans against Hungary," he paused and stepped very close to me, "I will kill you." For a moment I thought he was kidding. I looked at him and smiled tentatively. He just stared at me for a moment and then walked away. He didn't smile back. I had thought my decision about switching federations was complicated, but the added element of an attack on me, or perhaps my family, who was still in Hungary, frightened me. I had a hard time assessing the situation. For me, decisiveness was a trait I had worked on building my whole life. But how could I make this choice? What if I made a mistake?

Chess games will always end up being a draw unless one side makes a mistake. Maneuver your pieces skillfully enough until your rival messes up, and you can count on winning. But how do you keep yourself from making a blunder? In investing, too, bad mistakes – as opposed to rough markets – regularly cause investors to damage their long-term chances of financial security.

Chess experts improve their odds of success by studying chess "tactics," the specific moves to make in different situations. The better their recollection of the countless possible board positions *and* the time-tested responses, the more likely they are to conquer their opponent. In fact, winning has little to do with brilliance; plenty of smart people play chess poorly. Triumph on the board comes from having practiced the tactical skills necessary to deal with the obstacles that opponents create.

Likewise, smart investors sometimes fail because they haven't learned the skills that will help them to manage their own money. Many of the tactics that grandmasters use to dominate a tournament also pertain to handling personal finance, and anyone can apply them. By understanding the sixty-four chess tactics in Chapter IX (one for each square on the chessboard), you will make better investment decisions. Why not start by learning those tactics? Since people lose both games and money as a result of making mistakes, we first need to identify the common barriers that stop people from making the right moves. So, stay tuned for the *Rich As A King* tactics later on but for now, learn from other people's mistakes.

Hate to lose? Here's why.

In the fields of finance or chess, regardless of how well you prepare your strategy and plan your moves, if the odds don't roll in your favor, you lose. Interestingly, in both worlds, the amount that people find intolerable to lose doesn't correspond with the amount they hope to win. The fear of losing, known as "loss aversion," trumps the joy of winning in most situations, and this imbalance frequently causes people to make poor choices. Going for the least-chance-of-defeat decision may at first glance seem wise, but this strategy certainly won't make you a winner.

Professor Daniel Kahneman won the Nobel Prize (Economics, 2002) for his ground-breaking work in behavioral finance by describing the phenomenon of loss aversion. Giving the illustration of flipping a coin, he discussed the question of how much test subjects would want to win if losing meant that they'd have to pay $20. "For most people," he said, "when you have a bet with a 50% chance of losing $20, you want to have an equal chance of gaining $40." Kahneman uncovered an astonishing psychological barrier that stops people from advancing. Since the average coin flippers stipulated that in order to agree to play the game, their potential winnings had to equal twice their possible losses, imagine how this stunted their potential to ever get ahead. In theory, a flipper should rejoice if he wins, for example, $21 when he only has to put $20 at risk. Illogically, though, he won't place the bet unless he has the chance to secure a $40 pot.

The disproportionate way in which people regard winning versus losing helps to explain why investors often make decisions based on one of two emotions. According to traditional wisdom, either fear or greed causes people to make an investment move. The flipping study shows that fear motivates people about twice as much as greed does.

What happens when investors' dread significantly outweighs their avarice? They tend to panic when the market drops and they sell. Maybe they started in stocks as long-term investors who thought they could stomach volatility. But when some bad news flashed across their screens, such as the S&L bailouts, Black

Monday, the Gulf Wars, the presidential impeachment, the Russian bond default, the dotcom crises, the terror attacks on the Twin Towers and the Pentagon, the real estate collapse, the banking meltdown, the Japanese nuclear reactor explosions, the European debt crisis, and more, they sold. They suffered from loss aversion, bailing out when economic darkness prevailed.

After the markets recovered, these same investors bought back in, emboldened by their greed. What really happened, though, is that they sold when the market was low, and bought when it went up – a formula for failure on Wall Street. In one twenty-year study[1] that looked at the impact of people chasing market returns, the stock market (as measured by the S&P 500 index) averaged about 8.2% per year, but shareholders in equity (stocks are often referred to as "equities") mutual funds only made about 4.3% on average each year. Investors trying to time the market, selling after it dropped and buying after it already started to recover, caused their own problems. Had they just stayed with their funds when the markets took a hit, they would have almost doubled their returns. As Kahneman summed it up, "The main implication for loss aversion in investing is that you have to think about what you could sustain without changing your mind or without changing course."

In chess, too, the fear of a potential loss outweighs the thrill of winning to such a degree that tournament participants often offer or accept a draw even if they have a superior position – just to be on the safe side. In order to limit loss aversion and encourage the fighting spirit, many high-level chess tournaments now incorporate a system that assigns zero points to a loss, one point to a draw, and three points to a win. In the traditional model, a win earns one point, a draw gets half a point, and a loss gets zero. By making a victory much more valuable than two ties, players opt against acceding to a draw and will instead fight full-guns for a triumph. This rule came about as a result of tournament organizers witnessing how loss aversion caused players to avoid risk and accept the half-point result. For chess viewers and players, the tendency to avoid jeopardy makes the matches rather dull. For investors, the rigid avoidance of risk can cause other problems, not the least of which is that people may not earn high enough returns on their investments because they keep them too safe.

Regardless of how you characterize yourself as an investor (i.e., conservative, moderate, or aggressive), understanding the psychological barriers that cause

---

1   DALBAR, Inc., *Quantitative Analysis of Investor Behavior*, 2013, http://www.qaib.com/, September, 2013

people to make poor decisions should help you formulate your plans logically. Alternatively, if you can't stop yourself from succumbing to the emotional roller coaster of investing, consider one or both of these practical options:

- ♟ Assign some or all of the day-to-day management to a professional or
- ♟ Stay away from risky ventures altogether.

How to decide whether to sell *this* or *that*

Consider another common foul-up known as the "disposition effect," which causes people to err when choosing which stock to sell. Professors Hersh Shefrin and Meir Statman first introduced the concept in 1985 to describe investors' "disposition to sell winners too early and ride losers too long." Imagine you find yourself in a situation where you own holdings in two different companies, Stock A and Stock B, and you need to sell one of them to raise money to pay for your child's college tuition. You bought Stock A for $10 per share. Now at $12, the stock shows an unrealized $2 per share profit on your statement. On the other hand, since you bought Stock B for $13 per share and now it's trading at $9, you have an unrealized loss of $4 per share.

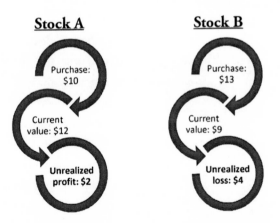

Presuming you must sell one of these two, which one would you select? Should you keep the profitable position or the unsuccessful one? Would you sell Stock A, thus realizing a gain, or would you sell Stock B, locking in the loss? In the end, most investors make the wrong decision and opt to sell the winner, Stock A. This application of the disposition effect leads investors to sell their profitable stocks while holding onto their losers. In fact, though, dumping the losers (since you get the tax benefit of selling at a loss) and keeping the winners (since they are often winners for a good reason – they're better companies) generally makes more sense.

Don't make an unbendable rule for yourself that you will only make decisions to sell based on which stock has outperformed the other, since the winner may not always beat the loser. Rather, stop yourself from making emotional trading choices ("Hooray! I made a profit on Stock A!") without considering the individual merits of each stock.

Professor Terrance Odean (University of California) examined the trading patterns of tens of thousands of investors, looking at millions of trades in different markets. He demonstrated how investors like the feeling of selling at a profit, even when selling a losing position makes more sense in terms of proper portfolio management. If they sell the profitable stock, they can tell their friends, "I made a killing on Stock A!" It certainly makes good cocktail party conversation. Moreover, they can rationalize that as long as they haven't sold Stock B, it can still come around and turn profitable. "Since I haven't sold it, I haven't actually lost any real money," they reason.

Though the joy of selling at a profit might have emotional significance, it can undercut the long-term growth potential of a portfolio. In fact, when studying similar decisions across tens of thousands of self-directed brokerage accounts, Odean found that on average, one year after people sold a winner, it had outperformed the loser (the stock they kept) by about 3.5%. If they had made the statistically rational (albeit emotionally more difficult) decision to hold onto the winner so that it could keep gaining, they generally would have pocketed more money.

When to sell an investment… or sacrifice a chess piece

Chess players, too, make poor moves based on the disposition effect. They may trade off pieces, feeling like they're gaining traction; however, later on in the game, they might find that those trades were merely cosmetic time wasters that set them back strategically.

Consider this real life instance of the disposition effect in chess:

Susan: In my 1996 world championship match against China's Xie Jun, I was playing black in game #8. Towards the end of the game, I had amassed a slight "material advantage," meaning that I had more valuable pieces than my opponent. Specifically, I had an extra rook (a.k.a. "castle"), which is considered to be better than the extra bishop + pawn that she had. In the left diagram below, you can see that I have my two black rooks, while White only has one. Also note that Black has one knight, but White has two bishops (knights and bishops are regarded as about on par with each other, though bishops are sometimes considered a bit stronger). A normal move in this case would have been for my black knight to capture the pawn on square c3 and then for White's rook to capture the pawn on d2, like this:

Polgar: Black knight captures white pawn (Nxc3)

Jun: White rook captures black pawn (Rxd2)

Had I gone for this easy capture of the pawn, the game might have continued on for dozens of more moves, and its outcome would not have been certain. With only a slight material advantage, it could have taken me a long time to chip away at Jun's position. Had I suffered from the disposition effect, I might have disposed of the wrong piece, doing the pawn trade above. So instead of doing that swap, which would have had only a limited advantage, I did the equivalent of selling a losing stock. In the previous investment example, Stock B had gone down in value and, though it might have had the potential to go up, it appeared to be the weaker stock. Likewise, in my game with Jun, I determined that my own rook (on e5), which an amateur would say was quite precious (5 points), was not as valuable an asset as the pawn that was on the verge of becoming a queen, so I sold it. That is, I slid that rook to the right two squares (to g5), allowing Jun's

bishop to capture it. I let my rook go, since at that point it was more of a loser than a winner. In return, my pawn (f6) caught the white bishop. When I made that trade, I heard gasps in the audience. Onlookers were shocked, wondering why I swapped my 5-point rook for a less valuable 3-point bishop. But even though the rook might have succeeded over the long term, it made more sense to dispose of it, losing the material advantage in order to focus on the potential of the advanced "passed pawn"[2] on d2. In fact, Jun realized this a few moves later when she conceded the game. Take a look at how the final steps in my strategy unfolded:

Black sacrifices rook (Rg5)

White bishop captures black rook (Bxg5)

---

2   A "passed pawn" is a pawn with no opposing pawns preventing it from getting to the eighth rank (where it can change into any other piece it wants, except a king).

Black pawn captures white bishop (f6xg5)

Observers whispered their disapproval of the decision to dispose of the underperforming rook. However, just because a piece comes with a great name, this doesn't mean you need to keep it. Consider the fate of some famous, highly valued companies like Lehman Brothers, Bear Stearns, and Merrill Lynch, all of whom used to top the A-list of Wall Street firms. Their ultimate time came, too, and just as you wouldn't want to hold stock in the d1 rook on the chessboard above (because Black would next move its knight to c3), you wouldn't want to have owned shares in those eminent companies. Buying a stock or holding onto a chess piece just because it has a legendary name may lead you to lose the game.

When you have to make a decision to sell, avoid letting the disposition effect blind you. Don't jump to sell shares whose prices have increased while keeping those that have dropped in value. Grandmasters don't do that, and investors shouldn't either.

Rich As A King Action Point:

Pull out your brokerage statements and look at each position individually. Ask yourself, "If I currently had the same amount of cash in the bank as this investment is worth, would I buy this stock/bond/mutual fund now?" Ignore the past results of the specific investment, since the price at which you bought it and the price today are rather arbitrary figures. If you answer yourself definitively, "No, I'd never buy that security today," then sell it now, even if that means disposing of it at a loss. Don't worry about what you would buy with the proceeds. You don't need an alternative investment to buy as a criterion for selling a loser. If an enemy had your king in his crosshairs, you wouldn't start figuring out what other pieces could start an attack on your opponent; you would have only one choice – get your king out of danger. Likewise for this RAAK Action Point, consider the money in each of your investments as if it were a king. Is it well-placed or do you need to move it?

Where to look if you want to improve your portfolio

Imagine if someone summarized your whole financial picture on one page. Wouldn't that be great? Not only would it present all of your holdings, but it would also show you a bit of their history and their relative strengths. On top of that, it would catalog every possible vulnerability for you in an easy-to-read fashion. With all that information at your fingertips, would you make the right investment decisions? Unfortunately, the answer may well be "no." Even with all the information spread out before them, investors tend to only look at, and give relevance to, a small portion of the available information. This is also true of chess players. In a chess game, participants may suffer from what behavioral finance professors call "mental accounting." The players, in this case, focus too much on one part of the board to the exclusion of concentrating on the whole game. While carefully examining all the possibilities for, say, an elegant attack, they might completely ignore the rival bishop perched in the corner of the board. Then, as they complete their maneuver, their opponent swoops in with the up-until-now silent bishop and slays their queen.

Players get a sinking feeling when they accidentally give away a critical piece, similar to how investors feel when they realize that they missed something important because they have spent too much time focusing on just one part of their portfolio. For example, some investors might get so involved with trading their online stock account that they completely neglect the big picture, letting the rest of their money drift in the abyss of low-interest checking accounts and random 401(k) pension plan choices. Frequently, those with multi-million dollar accounts will agonize for days over whether to sell a hundred shares of a small stock rather than review the performance of their money managers who handle the other 99% of their liquid assets. Mental accounting, the tendency to look at one part at a time rather than focusing on the greater whole, leads people to poorly allocate their cerebral resources. In these cases, a wealthy investor might have purchased a small position years ago, and rather than selling the shares, or transferring them over to his professionally traded account, he continues to devote undue time and energy to reading the news, looking at the stock's fundamentals, and tracking the company's trading patterns.

To stop yourself from becoming overly focused on one aspect of your money picture, view yourself, or you and your spouse, as the Chief Executive Officers of your own company, "My Family, Inc." You have different divisions, each of which has certain responsibilities. The checkbook division handles the invoices that your company receives; the bond unit supplies regular income to cover your monthly expenses; and the stock department seeks out new opportunities to help grow the bottom line. Having your divisions set up neatly in front of you allows you, like a chess player who can view all the pieces at once, to analyze your whole board. Anyone who has ever sat in a chess class at Webster University in St. Louis has probably heard the quote, "Look at the <u>whole</u> board!" –SP. Remember those words as you examine the finances of My Family, Inc.

Rich As A King Action Point:

Calculate your total net worth, including all of your assets everywhere (from stocks to bonds, bank accounts to IRAs, 401(k) plans to real estate). Put all of this data into a spreadsheet so you can see your asset allocation. Using this eagle-eye view of your investments, determine whether you have allocated too much or too little to any one asset class. This exercise helps you look at your whole investment board at once without getting sidetracked by the specifics. (Check out the free asset allocation tool at www.RichAsAKing.com/tools.)

You're losing money because of something you don't see

Can you stop yourself from mental accounting, the tendency to look at just one part at a time rather than seeing the greater whole? Can you keep yourself from getting distracted by the small details that seize your attention? If your thought pendulum swings too far in one direction and you only consider yourself a "big picture" thinker, you could easily miss the important facts that are on your statements. As documented in the popular book, *The Invisible Gorilla*, by Christopher Chabris and Daniel Simons, people often suffer from the "illusion of attention," believing that they see an entire scene but actually missing what's right in front of their eyes. The authors, both cognitive psychologists, present cases of how even experts overlook incredibly important hazards. For example, they note how an experienced airline pilot did not see a plane on the runway where he was about to land. And they ask how a veteran nuclear submarine captain could not see a 200-foot fishing boat that was right in the middle of his periscope view screen. Could a radiologist looking at an x-ray just miss seeing a guidewire in a patient's chest? Chabris and Simons explain that people believe that they can pay attention to the world around them, but in fact, they frequently miss obvious impediments because they just don't expect them. If this happens to experts, then surely armchair portfolio managers and amateur chess players alike will also miss critical information, even if *The Wall Street Journal* or some internet site screams the news in a headline. (Take a look at some of Chabris and Simons' fascinating videos at www.RichAsAKing.com/gorilla.)

If someone supplied you with that ideal one-page summary of your entire financial world, could you absorb the whole thing, or would mental accounting and the illusion of attention make you focus too much on one area or simply miss some critical fact? Watch out. The bishop in the corner that you forgot about or just didn't see can be vicious!

Rich As A King Action Point:

Get an extra set of eyes to review your statements. Sit with your spouse, trusted friend or family member, or professional advisor to go over your affairs. Having an objective viewer offer insights helps to ensure that you don't miss a crucial element on your money board.

How the news causes you to lose

When your friends start spewing too many details about their recent barroom conquests, you might raise your hand to stop them and say, "Too much information." It's a pity that people don't behave similarly toward the bombardment of economic news. Many investors hunt for endless minutiae by mining research reports, websites, and blogs. These days, any reasonably savvy computer user can set up a professional-looking website with an impressive sounding name like, "ValueInvestmentResearch.com," and dish out whatever crosses his mind. As such, the viewpoints you find might actually harm your results.

Not all the news is tainted. Certainly many media outlets provide worthy data to analyze. However, sometimes people relate to this information in the wrong way. Suffering from "media response," they feel the need to react, which is too bad, since the low correlation between current events and long-term performance, compounded by a deluge of information, causes stress and often leads to poor financial decisions. In fact, studies have shown that people who make investment choices based on news commentaries perform *worse* than those who make their selections in a news vacuum. Apparently, the urge to "do something" when receiving new facts can cause suboptimal results. People move their pieces even in circumstances when doing nothing would probably be the best tactic. For some reason, doing something feels better than sitting tight.

Chess players who spend most of their time memorizing chess openings may get similarly baffled when trying to apply what they learned.

Susan: Club players who talk about the opening moves of my sister (Grandmaster Judit Polgar) may sound impressive, knowing how she opened in recent games. But if they don't fully understand the rationale behind her moves and if they merely try to copy her, once they are "out of book,"[3] they'll tie themselves up in a complex situation that would require grandmaster-level skill to untangle.

When playing in an important chess competition, players often mistakenly shift their concentration from checkmating their opponent to winning the whole tournament. Such contemplation distracts them from devoting their attention to their next move on the board. Though they may daydream about walking away with the trophy, they need to examine the pieces right in front of them. They must look at each situation on the board as a new problem to solve. If they can't shake the feeling of, "I've got to win this game in order to qualify for my grandmaster title," then they are likely to impair their concentration.

Individual investors, too, must focus on the big picture... but only sometimes. When you run into a store, don't refer to your financial plan as you browse up and down the aisles. Your monthly budget should guide you in determining how much you can spend on the outing. Though you derived that budget from your long-term strategy, keep all of your thoughts of the future within reason. You'll drive yourself crazy if you obsess about tomorrow, and you'll have a hard time concentrating on today's current decisions.

---

3   A game is "out of book" once the players have reached the end of the standard variations that they may have studied in instructional books about chess openings.

When playing chess, don't fixate on winning the game; think instead about which particular move will improve your position the most. Likewise, when shopping, don't get fixated on how this one purchase will affect whether you can retire comfortably; just make sure that you are spending within your budget. And when you are selecting investments, don't get preoccupied with how each choice may affect your ability to pay for your child's tuition; rather, confirm that the type of investment fits into your asset allocation model, and then look closely at the specific security to make sure that it makes sense for you.

Sometimes you must work on your big picture decisions, and sometimes on your tactics. Don't let an outside influence, especially one as powerful as the media, direct your energies to the wrong place.

Rich As A King Action Point:

 If you're a news junkie, commit to limiting the time you spend on financial news on the internet, TV, radio, newspapers, magazines, and blogs to no more than thirty minutes per day for the next week. At the end of that period, ask yourself if the limitation diminished your decision-making capacity. Chances are you'll see that without the normal tidal wave of information, you still made perfectly sound decisions.

Why you should walk away from free offers

If you could tune into the stream of consciousness that a chess player has during a game, it might sound like this: "Inconceivable! She just gave me her queen. Ha! Without a queen, she'll have no chance. I'm going to win and move up to the next tournament round. Here I go, gently moving my pawn onto her queen's square. Yes! I'm removing her queen and dropping it next to the board. I can feel that prize money in my hands. Should I smile? No, that would be too crass. But I'm going to look up at her now. I just have to see her expression. Wait. Why is she smiling? How can she look so smug when she just gave away her queen? Unless she didn't just give it to me.... Oh no! She's going to mate me now. Ugh! She sacrificed her queen in order to trap my king. I thought I was getting it for free, and really it just cost me the game."

When your opponent gives you one of her pieces, don't assume that altruism has gotten the better of her. A smattering of cynicism would help if you asked yourself, "Why is she giving me her queen? What will she get from me in return if I take it?" Similarly, when a business offers you something gratis, figure out the company's ultimate goal and try to find out if you're really coming out ahead. Though "buy one, get one free" may tempt the consumer just like a seemingly helpless queen beckons its attackers, remember that you never get something for nothing. If you see that you can gain a free queen in a chess game, examine what the new position will look like after you take the piece. Will the capture open a pathway for your opponent to strike you later? Likewise, if you accept that special offer for a free iPhone when you sign a cell phone contract, will you have to commit to other expensive services at the same time?

Turning down a free offer defies human nature. As behavioral psychologist Professor Dan Ariely wrote in his best-selling book, *Predictably Irrational*, "We often pay too much when we pay nothing." In his studies, he showed that the possibility of getting something for free overwhelms a person's rational thinking so that a company well-versed in utilizing freebies in its selling campaign can conquer a market. Ariely cited the case in which Amazon started offering free shipping on orders that were over a certain dollar amount. People tended to increase the size of their orders in order to qualify for the benefit. Customers rationalized that if they bought only one more book or a couple of DVDs, they would reach the threshold and get the shipping for that magic price: $0.00. Amazon's executives found this model worked well, except in France. Many years ago, on the French version of the online store's website, customers who bought a specified amount qualified for a huge discount on shipping, paying only one franc (about ten cents). Though it was *almost* free, the psychological difference between a franc and nothing was enough to slow down sales. In fact, when Amazon subsequently dropped the one-franc fee to zero, sales growth in France began to mirror the other countries that had already been utilizing the totally free shipping model.

Ariely further tested how individuals react to a free offer, showing that the almost hypnotic effect of paying nothing will cause people to make the most illogical decisions. He ran a study in a mall in Boston offering two choices: either receive a free $10 Amazon gift certificate or pay $7 for a $20 gift certificate. Irrationally, most people chose the free gift certificate. Whereas they could have profited by $13 (the value of the $20 gift certificate minus the $7 cost), they instead selected the $10 free one.

Given the human propensity to want to get something for nothing, is it any wonder that brokerage firms advertise, "200 free trades," "free investment seminars," or "no annual IRA account fee"? They know that by using that potent word "free!" they will attract new customers. When getting something for nothing, the clients tend *not* to ask, "Do I really need to trade 200 times?" Similarly, they go to the seminars and get sold some program that they surely don't need. And what about the fee on the IRA account? Well, since the owners and employees of the brokerage firms expect to get a paycheck every month, you know the company will find another way to earn the lost income. Making money defines the essence of these firms. If they cut the cost of trading commissions to zero, they'll add fees for advisory services, banking products, borrowing, inactivity, account closing, yearly maintenance, trade confirmations or statements, and more.

Rich As A King Action Point:

Next time you're about to accept something for free, analyze the other side's selflessness. If you can't figure out their motivation, then don't accept the offer. If you do succeed in discerning their motivation for giving you a freebie, then you've calculated the actual cost of the "free" item. Are you willing to pay that amount?

What men suffer from worse than women

People are actually paid to look overconfident and are handsomely rewarded for overconfidence.
—**Daniel Kahneman**, 2002 Nobel Prize Laureate in Economics

"This ship is unsinkable," proclaimed the builders of the *Titanic*. Talk about overconfidence! When individuals believe themselves to be greater, stronger, smarter, or luckier than normal, they misperceive reality and make poor decisions. For example, the vast majority of the population believes that they are above average when it comes to their driving ability, getting along with others, and having a sense of humor. But how could that be? The "average" represents the middle ground, so it's self-evident that most folks can't be better than the average. Moreover, people use random events to confirm their uniqueness; if they buy a stock that then goes up, they'll think, "I knew it was ready to jump." And if the investment drops, they'll rationalize this by saying, "I might have gotten the timing a little off, but I'll just hold on and it will recover." As Dan Ariely explained, "We tell ourselves stories [about what is going on in the stock market] that try to explain what happens. And even though we're just telling a story about a random pattern, all of a sudden we start believing in it. And because we believe in it, we believe in our ability to explain the stock market. ... We say, 'Look at me. I really understand what is going on.' But it's not really understanding. It's just that you can tell yourself a story after the fact."

Overconfident investors tend to trade more actively than others. After all, they feel they have good ideas and a solid grasp of how the market works. However, as Professor Terrance Odean explained, "In general, active trading hurts people. Brad Barber [University of California, Professor of Finance] and I did a study in the U.S. where we looked at 60,000 individual investors. We sorted them based on how actively they were trading, and the 20% who traded most actively on average underperformed the buy-and-hold investors by about 6% per year." Moreover, men's overconfidence dwarfs women's. Not surprisingly, men trade more and do worse than women. In fact, Odean said, "Single men traded 67% more actively than single women ... [and the men] underperformed single women by 1.4% per year."

With the wealth of investment information sites on the web, people develop even greater overconfidence in their abilities, suffering from what behavioral psychologists call the "illusion of knowledge." When studied, groups of informed investors were found to have an increased sense of confidence to forecast the market, which didn't keep pace with the accuracy of their predictions.

Chess players, too, suffer from an illusion of knowledge, believing in their abilities more than the facts warrant. For instance, in *The Invisible Gorilla*, Chabris and Simons describe a study where they asked tournament-level chess players two questions: "(1) What is your most recent official chess rating?" and "(2) What do you think your rating should be to reflect your true current strength?" Given the rigorous methodology used to calculate chess ratings, the two answers should be the same, or at least very similar. However, 75% of the respondents claimed that their actual score underrated their true ability by about 100 points. That staggering difference would be like someone saying that even though he got straight C's all through college, his true grade point average, if the school had properly rated him, would have been closer to an A. The authors conclude that the overconfidence that chess players have in the face of objective evidence to the contrary comes from the "illusion of confidence."

This two-pronged illusion of confidence, which (a) makes people overestimate their abilities as compared to their peers, and (b) makes people respect those who exude confidence regardless of their actual ability, can lead to poor conclusions in chess, in investing, and in life. Stock traders, hyped up by a few profitable trades, often think they have extraordinary insight into the market and as a result make bigger bets on a position than they should.

Doug: Consider the prospective client who wandered into my office in the beginning of 2000. He spoke about the "new economy," which at the time reflected the concept that brick and mortar businesses would vanish and internet-based companies would replace them. He said he had picked high-tech stocks and his portfolio had been making over 100% per year annualized.

Not only that, but the twenty-two-year-old said that he was willing to drop out of school and become a money manager in my firm. When I asked him how long he had been trading stocks, he revealed that he had only started about two months earlier. He had calculated his annualized return by multiplying his actual return by six. Rather than showing the supercilious young man the door for being so brash, I suggested that he reconsider his approach and try diversifying. "Of course I've spread out the risk," the rookie said. "I've got WorldCom, Global Crossing, and JDS Uniphase as my biggest positions. But to really branch out, I've got a big holding in the NASDAQ index." Blinded by his illusion of confidence, he had no interest in listening to the rules of asset allocation. Instead, he ended up learning the hard way when his stocks crashed a few months later.

Though you need a certain amount of confidence for a healthy self-image, you also need to understand your limits. Don't assume you can predict the future of the stock market, and don't hire an investment advisor just because he wows you with his self-assured appearance.

Rich As A King Action Point:

Answer the following questions with a range of numbers, not just a single figure. Write your responses on a piece of paper. Enter the range (minimum and maximum) of numbers within which you are 90% certain the answer lies. For instance, if the question asks for a specific year, give a range of years between which the particular event occurred. If you have no idea of the answer to a question, then expand your range of possible answers in order to feel 90% confident that the true answer lies somewhere between your two guesses. On the other hand, if you think you can give a good educated guess, then choose a smaller range and still be 90% confident. Go ahead, grab a piece of paper, and take the test. Don't turn the page until you have written all the answers. If you don't write them down, this experiment won't work. (Try this test online and get a free PDF version that you can print at www.RichAsAKing.com/overconfidence.)

	Minimum	Maximum
1. John F. Kennedy's age at his death		
2. Year that the Statue of Liberty was dedicated in New York		
3. Number of countries in the world (as of 2013)		
4. Air distance, in miles, between Alaska and Spain		
5. Number of bones in the human body		
6. Average distance in miles from the earth to the moon		
7. Average amount of vegetables an American eats in a year (in pounds)		
8. Length of the Amazon River (in miles)		
9. Year that Beethoven was born		
10. Population of Iceland (in 2013)		

1. 46
2. 1886
3. 195
4. 5032
5. 206
6. 239,000
7. 415
8. 4000
9. 1770
10. 322,000

If you were 90% confident of your answers, you should have missed only one. Most people miss five or more. The fact is that we are too certain about our answers, even when we have limited knowledge about a topic.

If you have the investment savvy and experience of Warren Buffett, or when you reach the chess heights of Grandmaster Garry Kasparov, *maybe* you can justify thinking that you know best. When grandmasters analyze a game they played, they tend to vigorously defend each of their decisions, including the questionable ones. Even the greatest players suffer from overconfidence. In the famous man vs. machine fight, when Kasparov played against IBM's chess computer, Deep Blue, Kasparov seemed to believe that the computer was too materialistic and would not sacrifice a piece. Whereas the human had an intuitive sense for a good move, the cold-hearted computer had no emotions. Finally, even the world chess champion showed his weakness. As can happen to anyone, his overconfidence eventually blinded his understanding of the opponent... and he lost.

José Raúl Capablanca, a Cuban chess player who reigned as world champion from 1921 to 1927, and who was known as the "Human Chess Machine," was once challenged to a game. Capablanca offered "queen odds" to the stranger, which meant that Capablanca would play without a queen. The competitor was insulted, perhaps feeling a little patronized, and he said, "How could you say that? You don't know me. You might lose." Capablanca replied confidently, "Sir, if you could beat me, I would know you."

In our own lives, for those chess players who haven't quite earned the title of world champion, and for those investors who aren't the "Oracle of Omaha," as Buffett is known, a little humility may serve us well in managing our affairs.

CHAPTER II

How to Achieve
Your Financial Goals

A grand duke was marching through the forest with his entourage of hunters when he spotted several trees, each with an arrow stuck exactly in the middle of a large painted target. Amazed, he instructed his men to find the archer who had shot so accurately. They soon found a young boy, bow in hand, who admitted that he was the marksman. "Did you really shoot each of those arrows," asked the duke, "or simply hammer them into the trees?" The boy swore that he had indeed dispatched them himself, and from a distance of one hundred paces. "Then you shall join my division of archers. But you first must teach us your wondrous technique," the duke declared. The boy smiled, "I will do that, sir. First I shoot the arrow at the tree," he began, "and then I paint the target around it!"

Sadly, the boy's system does not work in hunting, in chess, or with money. You can't scramble your pieces around the board and then encircle the enemy's king and announce "checkmate!" And of course, you cannot mark up your monthly statements, claiming that you always hit your price targets. A chess game and a financial plan both require a pre-designed strategy before you make your opening move. First select your target, then develop a strategy to reach it, and finally set your arrow free and execute the plan.

Goal-setting begins with envisioning the conclusion of the journey. Investors, for example, might aim for a comfortable retirement, while chess players target checkmate. Regardless of your wishes, history teaches that the greatest of achievements began with dreams. Just remember Helen Keller longing to communicate, J.K. Rowling visualizing her Harry Potter books being read by millions, or Walt "If you can dream it, you can do it" Disney, who imagined the Magic Kingdom … and then built it in 366 days.

The system you need to set goals

Many unseasoned players cower at the prospect of setting goals. Figuring that only the greatest minds can see far into the future, they ask grandmasters, "How many moves ahead do you think?" since they assume that the "checkmate" goal of the game requires planning every step of the way. In fact, chess masters may occasionally foresee a series of steps going as far as twenty or thirty moves. But that does not mean that they calculate every possible variation of combinations that could take place over those moves. More often than not, grandmasters only contemplate three to five moves ahead. They create "decision trees" in their minds to examine a series of different scenarios – each leading towards checkmate – which may be dozens of moves hence, but they break down the goal into a series of smaller steps.

Susan: In one of my all-time favorite games, I faced the legendary, former women's world champion, Maia Chiburdanidze in the 36th Olympiad in 2004. The game was so complex that by the fourteenth move, I had to think seven pairs of moves ahead, comparing not just one or two possible paths, but five different paths! Each one of those directions allowed for so many possible responses by my world-class competitor that I needed to calculate and compare literally dozens of different variations. With the medium-term goal of gaining the material advantage, I sacrificed my queen on move 15 and was able to turn that temporary loss of material into a gain, pulling ahead by three points, which is a very significant lead. It's always frightening to sacrifice a piece, since a mistake could mean giving your opponent a significant advantage. But I was confident in my analysis and certain that I would reach my goal. In the end, I overcame my fear, followed my plan, and eventually conquered the nine-time-Chess-Olympiad-winner, 2514-rated, 1978-1991 women's world champion.

By setting challenging goals on the board, grandmasters strive for any advantage they can create. If you look closely at their system, you can see common patterns emerge. For example, at the beginning of the game, the formulaic openings that the professionals follow help them to achieve the three main opening-game goals: gaining control of the center of the board, castling, and developing their fighting pieces (which means getting their knights and bishops into the action instead of leaving them in the back row).

Where you should focus your attention first

A newspaper article generally opens with the few critical points that describe an event. The rest of the article then uses that foundation to spell out the intricacies of the story. Likewise, the very first moves of a chess game set the tone for the rest of the contest. By dominating the center of the board, first with the pawns, and then aided by the stronger back-row chessmen, the player ensures that his pieces will have maximum mobility throughout each phase of the game. A knight, for example, in the middle of the board can move to eight possible destinations, whereas when placed on the edge, it can only hit four at most. A bishop covers thirteen squares from the middle, but situated in the corner, it reaches only seven. If the pieces have ready access to multiple squares, the player can fully exploit the power of each piece.

How to protect your most important asset

If countries, companies, or chess players lose their key leader (president, CEO, or king), they may have effectively lost the game. As such, first and foremost, they must shield that critical asset. In fact, chess teachers regularly advise castling as soon as possible, in case the opponent launches an intense offensive that might jeopardize the chance to buffer the king.

How castling works

 Review the diagram below to see how a castling move would normally look early on in the game. The king and the rook move at the same time and cross paths. The king also benefits exceptionally from this because it can move more than its normal single square. (This is move #7 and #8 of the 1992 game between Susan Polgar [white] and Anatoli Karpov [black]. See how in one turn, the white king went from e1 to g1 while the white rook went from h1 to f1, thus protecting the white king behind a detachment of strong defending pieces.)

Is the technique of swapping the king and the rook just a technical chess rule? Certainly not. Consider the Battle of Gaugamela (now known as Iraq) in 331 BCE, when Alexander the Great defeated King Darius, thus conquering the entire known world at that time. Alexander's game plan opened when he raced far to the right of the battlefield with his elite cavalry. With teams of foot soldiers at his side, he resembled a chess king castling early on in the fight. After his troops cleared the center of the field, he personally led his forces to chase the enemy leader, much like a chess king would charge to the center of the board in the endgame in order to engage in the final battle.

Castling offers two key benefits: It keeps the king from getting into trouble, and it also activates the rook by placing it in a strong central position on the board.

Can you win without castling? Famous historical players sometimes abandoned a castling opportunity; however, those games occurred before the development of today's increasingly defensive methodologies. In those days, people would take risks that they wouldn't attempt today. Players enjoyed the romance and gallantry of chess – think *The Three Musketeers* – rather than the precision that characterizes today's tournaments. Look at the current competitive circuit and you will see that the practically-minded master-level player castles in almost every game.

How to maximize the return on your pieces

While beginner chess enthusiasts may thrust their pieces ahead, overly confident simply because they remember how each character on the board moves, they often miss two critical development goals: activity and initiative. "Activity" is defined as the number of squares that a piece controls. The more squares you dominate, the more options you have, and the more you restrict your opponent. You may fully rule some squares, thus giving you the ability to move freely. If your opponent has some activity on the same squares, though, you may only have partial dominion. In economist lingo, the limited supply of squares – no more than sixty-four – means that the demand is high, so you must fight for each one.

In developing your pieces, go after the "initiative," which means staying one step ahead of your opponent. Since chess players alternate turns, one of them always leads the other. The game starts with White going first, but Black may equalize, or even overtake White, within fifteen or twenty moves. If White doesn't constantly reinforce its initiative, it will dilute its first-move advantage over the course of the game. "Initiative" measures the amount of sway that one side has over the flow of the game, so putting your opponent's king in check means that he must react to you instead of furthering his own plans. If you dictate the pace of events, if you attack, or if you constrain your opponent's choices, then you have the initiative. Keep your eye on the goal of gaining the initiative and keeping it.

Chess players must keep in mind the symbiotic nature of the three opening goals (controlling the center, castling, and developing their fighting pieces). If the start of game includes appropriating the heart of the board *without* castling, the powerless king will sit vulnerably in the center, staring at the opponent's venomous queen or rook. Similarly, if a player quickly castles *without* simultaneously seizing terrain in the middle of the board, his king may have temporary protection, but no pawns to capture any terrain (thus leaving the heart of the board available for the opponent to capture). And if a player fails to promote his fighting pieces into the fray, he'll have no offensive team to win the game.

Apply these three core chess strategies to your finances

At the end of the opening stage of the game, you should see three things: (1) Both sides in a vigorous battle for the center, (2) the kings tucked neatly away near the corners, and (3) the bishops and knights actively placed and aiming at the middle of the board, poised to fight. In financial terms, you could compare this to having (1) organized and consolidated your accounts, (2) invested your core assets defensively, and (3) selected parts of your portfolio to place in aggressive investments. Given the importance of all three parts, don't fixate on only one. Follow all of them in the opening of your financial game.

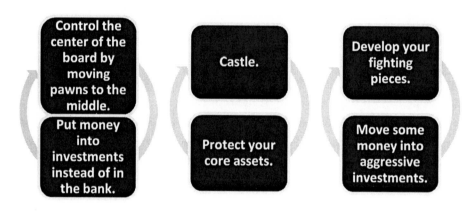

The trick to setting goals in personal finance

Just as chess masters lay out their opening goals of controlling the center, castling, and developing pieces, successful investors must decide on their objectives, too. As celebrated baseball coach Yogi Berra said, "If you don't know where you are going, you'll end up someplace else." All too often, individual investors have no real plan and only find out when they retire that they've ended up someplace that they would rather not be. When a grandmaster endeavors to plan far ahead in the game, she first determines what she wants the piece structure to look like at a certain point in the future and then calculates backwards to determine what intermediate steps she must take to get there.

Though setting goals may sound daunting, don't worry. You don't need to start with audacious plans to accumulate more wealth than Warren Buffet or beat world champion Magnus Carlsen in a blitz game of chess. If "owning your own island" as a financial goal is not reasonable, consider aiming for something more practical, like signing up for a fancy dessert cooking course, enjoying a day off from work every month, or buying a dog. Put a price tag on each idea, a date by which you intend to accomplish it, and then write down the next idea.

How to achieve your STRATegic goals

Give me a stock clerk with a goal and I'll give you a man who will make history. Give me a man with no goals and I'll give you a stock clerk.

—**J.C. Penney**

Regardless of the particulars of your ambitions, make them all STRATegic. That is: <u>S</u>pecific, <u>T</u>ime-bound, <u>R</u>igorous, <u>A</u>ttainable, <u>T</u>empting.

Specific

The "specific" attribute of the goal-setting model refers to the what, why, and how of the objective. "What do I want? I want to retire by age 60 (that's the 'what') so that I can have more time to volunteer teaching chess to kids (that's the 'why'). I can accomplish this by taking an early pension and changing more of my investments from stocks to bonds (that's the 'how')."

If you have an entrepreneurial streak, perhaps you'll write: "What? Start my own website to sell high-quality board games." For "why": "I enjoy designing websites; I'm tired of answering to an annoying boss; and I'm sure I can make enough money to cover my monthly bills through the business." Explain the "how" as: "Before quitting my day job, I will test the idea by registering a catchy web address like FabulousBoardGames.com, look for a distributor for the products, and then see if I can develop a following by writing a daily blog." Make every goal clear, simple, and easy to measure.

Time-bound

For strong chess players, using a chess clock means that they don't have to wait indefinitely for their weaker opponents to make a move. If the challenger deliberates on a situation for too long, he will run down his time and lose the game. Henry Thomas Buckle (an English historian and strong amateur chess player in the 1850s) quipped, "The slowness of genius is hard to bear, but the slowness of mediocrity is insufferable."

Time-bound goals create urgency. They force you to take action now. Though setting a deadline to achieve a goal could seem arbitrary ("Why one month and not six months?" you might ask yourself), think about how the power of external pressure compels you to triumph. Here's an example:

Hernando Cortes tops the list of strict goal setters. In the sixteenth century, the Spanish conquistador led an armada of eleven ships. After landing on the shores of Mexico, all fired up to conquer the mighty Aztec Empire, Cortes ordered his men to burn their own boats. Talk about pressure! The motto, "failure is not an option," must have really meant something to those soldiers. And indeed, by the time the war was over, Cortes had brought large parts of Mexico under Spanish rule and caused the collapse of Aztec ruler Montezuma and his mighty empire.

While Cortes' soldiers watched the flames rising from their ships, destroying their only escape route, they charged themselves up for victory. Similarly, when a chess player hears the ticking away of the precious minutes on his clock he, too, redoubles his efforts. And when you find yourself with a time deadline by which to achieve your goals, you will have your own internal arbiter standing above you also, reminding you that you must reach your target.

When choosing the amount of time to allot, make the deadline realistically far off, yet short enough to maintain momentum. Just as a marathon runner sets a quick yet attainable tempo for his trek, push to achieve your goals on the faster end of your comfort zone. World War II hero General George Patton said, "Accept the challenges so that you may feel the exhilaration of victory." When you challenge yourself to complete a goal in a timely manner, you will certainly enjoy the feeling of success – a victory for your own self-determination.

Once you have chosen the amount of time to allot to your goal, determine how you will measure success. To track the progress of a chess game, you can count which side has more material (pieces on the board), whose pieces are more active, who has the initiative, or whose clock has more time. In the STRATegic goal-setting archetype, choose a metric to measure each goal.

You can easily track your progress with some goals, like cutting down the number of cigarettes smoked each day or increasing the amount of savings deposited in the bank. You can even measure more abstract ideals such as improving your relationship with your spouse. Perhaps you might note the number of hours you spend talking each day or else develop a ranking system based on how close you feel ("1" = falling in love again, "5" = rather be at the dentist). Short-term spending goals, such as buying a car outright for $36,000, lend themselves to easy measuring since you can resolve to squirrel away $1,000 per month for three years. Long-term goals, such as funding retirement, require more analysis, as you will eventually need to convert the lump sum of savings into an ongoing revenue stream that will last throughout all your golden years. Above all, set quantifiable targets and monitor them in order to constantly confirm that you're on the right track, meeting the goals (and sub-goals) according to your timeline.

Rigorous

Chess-playing goal-setters constantly frame and reframe their objectives, always trying to make them as accurate as possible. They rigorously design their future, which means that they carefully and thoroughly map out each step. Unlike the cigar-smoking, eccentric, sometimes peculiar players of yesteryear, today's grandmasters, like Magnus Carlsen, Viswanathan Anand, and Vladimir Kramnik, are all chess "professionals" and not just "players." Their rigorous approach not only on the 64 squares, but also towards their training and lifestyle, includes focusing on, clarifying, and prioritizing goals. And, yet, although they may labor over the chessboard for eight hours a day, they also return home to their families, go to the gym, and pursue hobbies.

Some people imagine the life of an up-and-coming chess master as sitting in a dimly lit room with a gruff Russian coach slamming the table at every mistake. In some cases, this may be true. In fact, the world's oldest tournament-playing grandmaster Victor Korchnoi once noted wryly, "No chess grandmaster is normal; they only differ in the extent of their madness."

Susan: Having a rigorous training model allowed me to become a grandmaster, while still growing up and living a full life. When I was a kid, my parents chose to homeschool me, and then years later, my sisters as well, which was unheard of in Hungary in the 1970s. Though today in the United States lots of people homeschool, in my childhood receiving such permission from the government of a conservative Eastern European communist regime required a great deal of determination. In the end, though I still had to pass all of the regular school exams, I was allowed to study under my parents' tutelage. It's no surprise that most of my education focused on chess. What can I say? I loved it. But that wasn't all. I also studied math and science, and my mother taught me Russian and German. After that, I learned English, Esperanto, and Spanish on my own. I didn't like it when people would say to my parents, "Your girls are so gifted." That belittled the endless hours of work that we did. The "gifts" that we had were two dedicated parents who taught us how to focus. That was how we could learn so much. We set rigorous goals and never took our eyes off the target. Starting in first grade, I used to sit down with my parents and coaches every December and map out the goals for the following year. Whether it meant

finishing a textbook, learning a language, focusing on a new chess opening, and even physical exercise, we wrote down every goal. We then subdivided them into short-term targets, and my father assigned me homework based on these specific aims.

Though the long-term goal from my youth was to become a grandmaster, it was impossible to achieve that in one move. From the opening of my education to the mid-game of training, and finally to achieving the endgame result of becoming a grandmaster, Olympiad, and world champion, we had a carefully planned strategy and every move I made was designed to reach that goal.

Write down your goals and ambitions in the same way that you would present a business plan to a board of directors. Answer questions such as why you chose the goal, how you expect to achieve it, who will help you along the way, what you need to reach it, when you will finish, and more. Make sure you feel confident in answering these queries. Keep in mind what Henry Ford said: "Whether you think you can or think you can't, you're right."

Attainable

If a client, striving to reach the goal of having a billion dollars in the bank, wanders into a financial planner's office and describes her aspiration, the advisor must first consider the whole situation. Oprah Winfrey, for example, should have no problem getting there. But for a minimum-wage earner, having such an unrealistic ambition will just lead to disappointment. If you choose goals that you cannot reach, your motivation will likely falter, causing you to give up the whole goal-setting paradigm. Then, the impractical aims will fade from your mind rather quickly as your commitment level dwindles. That isn't to say that you shouldn't think big. Go for the nice car; strive to own your home; pay for your kids' education; donate more money to charity. Understand the sacrifices that you may have to make and then balance them against your desire to reach your target. If you don't mind giving up discretionary spending today so that you can live out your dreams tomorrow, then record your resolution and get to work. But if you will swiftly slide back into your old routines of spending instead of saving, then reframe your objectives realistically so that you only include attainable goals on your list of ambitions.

Tempting

What tempted you to read this book? Maybe the snazzy cover and intriguing chess/money metaphor grabbed your attention. But ultimately, you wanted to learn the skills needed to reach your goals.

What entices you? Targeting a million dollars in the bank may tempt some folks. Others dream about a fabulous vacation or retirement, while a different group gets excited by realizing that they can use their money to build schools or soup kitchens. Think about what moves you. When you identify a STRATegic goal, consider how you will feel when you achieve it. If you're not drawn to that goal by an emotional rope, then regardless of how well you organize your goal-setting program, the strands of desire will surely snap and your efforts will fail.

Is this your goal?

Your specific goals will never exactly match someone else's. On the other hand, we all want to enjoy some or all of these possibilities:

- ♟ A comfortable retirement
- ♟ Vacations
- ♟ Home renovations
- ♟ Real estate ownership
- ♟ Living debt free
- ♟ Earning more than we spend
- ♟ Buying a car
- ♟ Quality education
- ♟ A topped-up medical emergency fund
- ♟ Owning "big ticket" items like artwork
- ♟ Giving charity
- ♟ Starting a business

Rich As A King Action Point:

Grab a pad of paper and write the words "STRATegic Goals" across the top. If you prefer, use the free online form at www.RichAsAKing.com/tools. Review the above list if you need some inspiration, and then also reflect on your own individual dreams. Make each one you record Specific, Time-bound, Rigorous, Attainable, and Tempting.

You may feel more emotionally or spiritually connected to some goals, such as, "I want to cut my daily TV watching from four hours to one (that's the 'what?') so that I have more time to spend with friends and family ('why?'), and I'll achieve this goal by asking my wife to gently remind me when I've melted into my La-Z-Boy for too long ('how?')." For goals that have a monetary component (i.e., save $2,500 every month), make sure you can answer these questions in the affirmative:

Is it realistic?

Good planning can work well, but it cannot work miracles. Just setting a goal does not mean that you will achieve it. Allow your realistic side to play an important role in determining your goals. Don't organize your financial plan like an amateur chess player who brings his queen out in the beginning of the game. He launches an attack at such an early point in the contest that he has not yet developed any strategy, has no backup support, and will likely lose his strongest piece on the board (or need to waste time to retreat). So temper your hardline goals with a dose of responsibility. A judicious goal-setter allots resources carefully. He won't spread himself too thin, trying to achieve everything all at once. Rather, he'll pursue several goals, attending to each one individually.

Is it flexible?

Goal-driven people learn to negotiate obstacles, changing their course midstream if necessary. With the objective to save $2,500 per month taped clearly to your computer so that you keep it in mind each day, you might feel a bit shocked one afternoon to learn that your child now needs braces... $5,000. Don't despair; just rework your system. Anatoly Karpov held the world champion title longer than anyone in the post-World War II era (1975 – 1985, and again from 1993 – 1999). He attended Mikhail Botvinnik's prestigious chess school at the age of twelve. However, after seeing the boy play, Botvinnik declared that Karpov had no clue about chess and had no future in the profession. Rather than abandoning his goal of becoming a chess champion, though, the young student immersed himself in chess books and advanced so amazingly that he became the youngest Soviet National Master in history. He kept his goal in mind despite the obstacle of his exceedingly critical teacher, and ultimately earned the well-deserved world championship.

Is it resilient?

Can your goal survive changes in the economy as well as in your personal life? No matter which investments you choose, whether volatile stocks or safe bank deposits, anything can happen… economic meltdowns, inflation, currency devaluations, etc. Build in some leeway so that if you suffer a setback, you will have both the time and facilities to rebuild. If you can't bounce back from a setback, then you need to reconstruct your outlook. Consider what happened in 1986….

Susan: The World Chess Federation (known by its French acronym, "FIDE," Fédération Internationale des Échecs) decided to grant 100 bonus Elo rating points to all active female players… except me. Regardless of the FIDE board's rationale (that I had been competing mainly against men, so I didn't deserve the boost in score like the other women who had lower rankings because they competed in women-only events), this unprecedented, unfair – and never again repeated – intervention in the scoring system displaced me from the top spot. I can't begin to describe how painful this was. But I certainly wasn't going to throw in the towel. I charged ahead, and four years later I became the first woman ever to earn the title of "Grandmaster," the highest title in chess, in the conventional way.

Why real-life goals should imitate chess

Grandmaster Garry Kasparov wrote a book called *How Life Imitates Chess*. The title itself teaches an important lesson: When you design your own financial goals, set the same objectives that grandmasters do when they start a game.

How to set up your retirement savings by controlling the center of your investment board

The center of the chessboard consists of four squares. In order to maintain a strong position, make sure you dominate at least two of them. Stationing pawns in the middle of the board is like keeping your best pitcher warmed up in the bullpen. Everyone can see him primed to strike, and the other side feels the constant threat. Likewise, you exert pressure on your opponent with your poised-to-attack pawns in the midpoint of the board. The pawns often don't need to move, since their mere presence intimidates the other side. In fact, both the relief pitcher and the pawns may not actually move for most of the game. If needed, though, they could lead a deadly assault. Likewise, put your retirement planning front and center in your overall financial plan. You'll build it up, making it ever more powerful, until late in your financial game. At that point, being a solid, core asset, it will make all the difference in your winning the money game.

When you start a new job, you can rule over your monetary center by establishing a pension plan and/or an Individual Retirement Account (IRA). You shouldn't need to use them until your endgame (retirement), at which point you will want them to be strong... very strong. According to the Employee Benefit Research Institute, about 40% of couples over the age of seventy-five survive on an income of around $27,000 per year, due to their limited savings. To ensure a more successful retirement than that, set aside monthly savings, perhaps using a mutual fund to diversify your money. Though the specific sum invested may seem rather insignificant compared with the cost of a thirty-year retirement, the strength of savings accumulated with the help of regular deposits and compound interest is astonishing. Consider how much the investment can grow in the future, like a pawn that plods square by square to get to the other end of the board and then transforms into a queen. If you save $100 per month from your twentieth birthday until you retire at sixty-seven, and if you make 6% a year (excluding taxes and fees), you'll enter your golden years with an account worth over $300,000. Won't you feel like a grandmaster then?

How to protect your core assets by castling

Financial rules-of-thumb often prescribe that young people should invest more aggressively than older folks. While this truism holds for parts of a portfolio, soften that strategy with a touch of caution. If you are just starting out, don't invest so aggressively that you neglect to protect your core assets. In this regard, the right insurance policy can help. No one should take an uncompromising stance regarding insurance and say, "I'm too young to die or get sick." Remember, even grandmasters lose games sometimes. If you, as a breadwinner, venture to leave your bed in the morning, you could conceivably face some unfortunate event during the day that stops you from returning that night. Don't wait to see what that might be.

Think about coverage before you actually need it. (How about now? Take a break from reading this book and call your insurance agent to schedule an appointment.) Regard insurance as a critical part of your overall financial plan, since it provides backup financing for you and your family in times of need. For the majority of workers, their greatest assets aren't their bank accounts or investment portfolios. It's themselves, their ability to generate reliable income. If they can't earn because of a disability or death, a well-designed insurance policy can help to fill the financial void and provide much-needed income.

Some people might think that paying insurance premiums is just like throwing money away. In one way, it's true. Ideally, you will pay the insurance company and you won't get sick or die, you won't have a car accident, and your house won't burn down. From that perspective, insurance is a bet you want to lose. On the other hand, proper coverage ensures that in the event of a problem, you won't bear the burden all by yourself, which could potentially devastate you.

Castling is like insurance

Castling, like insurance, moves your core asset – the king – out of harm's way. By positioning it near the corner, you benefit from the two borders of the board, since no pieces can launch an attack from beyond the boundaries of the sixty-four squares, and you've got your own army sheltering your pieces. Castling is so important that in the twelve classical games of the 2012 world championship between India's Viswanathan Anand and Israel's Boris Gelfand, at least one of them, and usually both of them, used castling as a fundamental tool for setting up their pieces. In most cases, they castled early on in the game. A year later, when Anand faced Norwegian challenger Magnus Carlsen, in eight out of the ten games played, both of them castled, and in the other two games, at least one of them did. Like a grandmaster, make sure you have coverage in place before you start setting up an investment portfolio.

Disability insurance

Insurance agents often refer to disability insurance as the "forgotten insurance," because most people don't consider the risk of debilitating illness, especially when they are young. It's more common to associate disability with growing old. Yet according to the Social Security Administration, about a quarter of today's twenty-year-olds will become disabled before they retire. Not all causes of disability are sickness-related. Auto accidents, sports injuries, and "acts of God" can happen to anyone.

A disability, whether permanent or temporary, can affect your cash flow in several ways – by reducing your earning ability, by upping the cost of medications and treatments not covered (or only partially covered) by your health plan, and by forcing you to adapt your home to new conditions. In addition, a disability could spell the end of your home ownership. In fact, the Council for Disability Awareness blames disability for about half of all foreclosures on conventional mortgages. Cover your bases here by making sure you have adequate disability insurance, which in terms of your family and dependents is every bit as crucial as life insurance.

As disability insurance plans tend to vary, research your options. Generally, the maximum coverage for a standard disability policy is up to 60% of gross monthly earned income. Other important aspects to take into consideration are the length of the "elimination period" – the time after the disability occurs until actual benefit payments begin, and the "benefit period," which is the period during which benefits are paid. Sadly, many disabilities do not conveniently disappear after two years or by a certain age, when the disability policies might stop paying, but it is certainly better to have some coverage than none at all.

Remembering to invest in the forgotten insurance is the best way to make sure that a disability does not spell financial checkmate for you and your household.

Life insurance

If you shield your income by buying disability insurance, do you need life insurance too? Ask yourself, if you were to die, would you leave someone in a financial bind? If the answer is "yes," and if you want to solve that problem, start shopping for life insurance.

Which family members should buy policies? If your monthly paycheck fills the well from which your family sustains itself, you should stand first in line. After all, if you were to die tomorrow, who would pay the family's bills? On top of that, though, a spouse working at home to raise the family also has a measurable economic value. The cost to buy all the services provided by a stay-at-home parent who cooks, shops, cleans, and cares for your children could easily approach upward of $50,000 per year in the United States. Insure for that, too, though keep in mind that once the children grow up, the CEO-of-the-home job will probably become much less time consuming and costly, so reduce the amount at that point. As couples get older, they continue to need protection, though the total sum may be lower than while their family was young. They both must feel assured that when one of them is gone, perhaps after having used up their savings due to illness, the surviving spouse can count on the insurance nest egg to pay for unexpected medical bills and general living expenses.

How much life insurance do you need?

The amount of coverage that one needs depends on many factors. Start by considering these three requirements: debt repayment, income replacement, and future obligations. You don't want to leave your family with the burden of paying off your credit card debts, your mortgage, or the cost of the new BMW you just bought. So buy at least enough insurance to eliminate outstanding loans (including your mortgage).

Then, calculate the lump sum that you would need to invest to generate enough inflation-adjusted income, after taxes and fees, to replace your current salary. Add that lump sum to the amount of debt that you want to repay and you're almost there.

Finally, consider future expenses such as college tuition, fulfilling any fiscal promises you made, or moving your spouse to a senior residence, and add those amounts to your running total. Now you have a ballpark figure indicating how much protection to buy.

By using online calculators, or by working with experienced insurance agents or financial planners, you can determine a responsible amount of coverage to purchase. It pays to make a careful calculation of the amount you need because if you use one of the quick calculation methods (such as "multiply your gross income by twenty to get the amount you require"), there's a good chance that you may substantially over- or under-insure. If you over-insure, you will pay too much in premiums, thus taking money away from other expenses/luxuries. If you under-insure, then you leave your family with the risk of not having enough cash after your death.

When working to protect your core assets, keep thinking of castling in chess. Castling, in fact, is the most remarkable step in the whole game because not only does the king get to move more than one square at a time, and not only do two pieces move in the same turn, but the king and the rook (a.k.a. castle) get to jump over each other. In one swift motion, the player deals with all the fundamental protection needs of the principal piece. In buying insurance, make sure that you keep it simple, too. Don't buy all sorts of fancy policies that offer features and riders that you don't require. Rather, buy an insurance policy purely to protect yourself and your family from financial tragedy. In a chess game, if you wanted to protect your king, you would simply castle. You certainly would not try to protect your king by marching it into the center of the board and then encircling it with your pawns, bishops, and queen. Why waste several moves when the basic goal can be accomplished in just one?

For some *Rich As A King* bonus material on insurance, go to www.RichAsAKing. com/bonus. There you will find:

- ♟ The primary goal of insurance
- ♟ Characteristics of term life insurance and permanent life insurance
- ♟ Thoughts on whether you should you buy term or whole life
- ♟ And more…

Develop your fighting pieces

Let's assume that you now control the center of your financial game, having set up long-term savings and retirement plans. On top of that, you've dealt with defense, having carefully planned and purchased solid insurance coverage, like a chess player protecting his king by castling. But there's more. Remember, along with opening the game with the aim of dominating the center and castling, chess experts want to develop their fighting pieces. This is done in two ways: (a) making their pieces active, which means they control key squares, and (b) gaining the initiative, which means they govern the pace of the game.

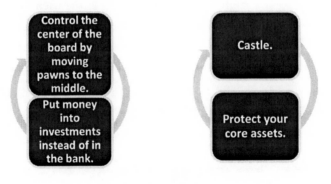

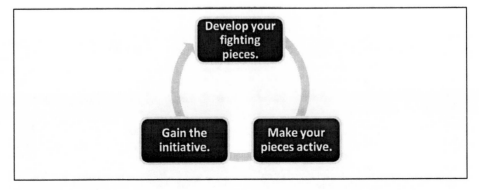

How to be an active investor

For investors, the goal of being active does not mean constantly buying and selling. Churning your portfolio will do you little good, though your broker might benefit from the commissions you pay. In most cases, people who think they have the skills necessary to trade effectively end up drastically underperforming the markets. Instead of trying to add value to your holdings by always moving your assets from one idea to the next, choose investments that give you maximum impact, and then hold them.

Never confuse being an active investor with being a trader. World-class investors may hold a stock, bond, or mutual fund for years... even decades. Warren Buffet, for example, has held shares of Coca Cola for over twenty-five years. He's made billions of dollars from the position. Though he's never sold any of those shares, you can certainly call him an active investor.

Have control over your assets just as a chess player tries to control squares. By making sure that you have actively invested your funds, putting them in the most productive places you find, you can feel confident that your money is working for you even if you don't move it from one investment to another.

Just as a stagnant bishop remaining in the back row, standing behind a pawn, hardly threatens an opponent, motionless money in a checking account doesn't give you much growth or benefit either. However, if you move that bishop diagonally one square, it can remain in its new location for much of the game, wreaking havoc on the opponent's goals.

Stagnant bishops on c1 and f1

Active bishop on b2

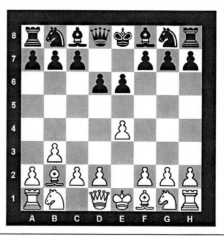

Shifting money from a checking account to a money market fund, interest-bearing bank deposit, or short-term bond fund, could change those dollars from a dormant asset to an active investment. Review each of your accounts to confirm that the selections you have made are still actively productive in their current locations. And don't shuffle around well-placed assets.

To see the incredible stopping power of a well-placed bishop, consider the 1993 chess game: Susan Polgar vs. Vasily Smyslov. To put this game in context, first recall Smyslov's success on the chessboard, which started when he was a teenager, continued through his ascension to become the seventh world champion in 1957 when he beat Mikhail Botvinnik, and went on from there for decades after many of his contemporaries faded from the headlines. His diverse abilities included his remarkable baritone singing voice that nearly got him accepted into the Bolshoi Theater, though he didn't pass the audition... a lucky break for chess lovers. Nonetheless, he would occasionally entertain those who came to watch his chess matches with an aria and he said that he used his music background when playing chess in order to have the pieces harmonize with each other.

During almost half a century of competitions, Smyslov had the opportunity to play and beat the greatest names in chess, including Reshevsky, Ragozin, Geller, Keres, Karpov, Ivanchuk, and more. In 1956, Smyslov's great rival on the board, Botvinnik, described him like this: "His talent was universal – he could play subtly in the opening, go totally onto the defensive, attack vigorously or maneuver coolly. And this is to say nothing about the endgame – here he was in his element. Sometimes he took decisions that were staggering in their depth... The combination of good calculation of variations, boldness, independence, and natural health made Smyslov invulnerable at that time."

Susan: When I played Smyslov in 1993 in Vienna, I placed my white bishop near the corner in square g2, where it stayed for 20 moves. Without constantly adjusting it, nor trying to find a new idea, I just left this well-placed bishop in an ideal spot. The volatility on the board certainly made me reconsider my strategy, but I knew that having a solid asset in the right square would, in the long run, help me to succeed. And when I finally deployed this powerful piece, I was able to chip away at Smyslov's infrastructure, gain a material advantage, and even sacrifice my queen in order to come out ahead

and finally win the game. Though my bishop sat still for the first third of the game, it was well placed to achieve my plans.

With investing, too, moving money around does not lead to profit. It's the proper placement of each asset that will bring you success.

Keep in mind that active money means something different to different people at different times. For example, you might judge money in low-yielding, short-term bank deposits (certificates of deposit – "CDs") as active if you placed it there for a special purpose. Perhaps you intend to buy real estate within twelve months. You will need liquidity, safety, and convenience. Because that CD, regardless of the yield, is providing the maximum impact possible, consider it active. If your long-term strategy, on the other hand, was to continually roll over CDs every six months, you would find yourself actually losing money after taking into account taxes and inflation. Look at the chart below to see how CD investors really performed between 2003 and 2013. If someone had been buying six-month CDs for a decade, would he have been making a smart decision? Was his money active, or was it just dawdling in such low-interest programs that after he paid his taxes and subtracted inflation, he lost money? Was it like a bishop trapped by a pawn?

After tax, after inflation returns of CDs

	2003	2005	2007	2009	2011	2013
6-month CD Rate (%)	1.1	4.5	4.9	0.2	0.5	0.2
Maximum federal tax rate (%)	35	35	35	35	35	39.6*
Inflation rate (%)	1.9	3.4	4.1	2.7	3.0	1.5
Real rate of CD return (%)	-1.2	-0.5	-0.9	-2.6	-2.6	-1.4

Source: Oppenheimer Funds presentation, "Pulse of the Market: The Bottom Line on CDs," 2014.

*Some investors may also be subject to the 3.8% Affordable Care Act surcharge on investment income, raising their net effective tax rate to 43.4%.

Would you have wanted to own a six-month CD paying 1.1% in 2003? If you were in the highest tax bracket, your interest payment would have taken a 35% haircut. Beyond that, with an inflation rate of 1.9% eating away at the buying power of your money, your real rate of return would have been -1.2%. Your $100,000 investment in an insured bank deposit would have only been worth, in real buying power, $98,800 a year later. In 2011, it was even worse. The real rate of return of a six-month CD portfolio was -2.6%. Imagine… losing money with FDIC-insured CDs. It's hard to consider money as active if it loses its purchasing power during the timeframe of the investment.

Beware of illiquid limited partnerships and hedge funds

Here's another example of inactive money: Illiquid limited partnerships or hedge funds, no matter how well they perform, are inactive if you need to use the investment money in the short term. Why? Because you can't access the funds at will. If an unexpected bill or expense comes along, you cannot look to this investment as a source of quick cash. How does this remind you of chess? Activity in chess means having well-placed pieces that give you influence over the maximum number of squares on the board. In money terms, activity means you control your money. One type of control is having easy access to your cash when you need it. To ensure that your money is as active as possible, make sure that you can access it at will.

"Liquidity" is a term that often gets confused with "marketability." You can call money in your checking account "liquid" since you have easy access to it. On the other hand, money tied up in stocks is "marketable," since you can sell your stocks and, within a few days, have access to the cash. But since you don't know how much you will get when you sell, and since you have to wait several days until the trade settles and you actually receive the funds, it's not a liquid investment; it's marketable.

Other, more complex investments are neither liquid nor marketable. Hedge funds, for example, often have restrictions on when you can liquidate them, such as once a quarter or once every six months. Limited partnerships may simply have no market, which means you can't sell them at all. This doesn't mean that these investments aren't active. If you have portions of your portfolio that you wish to lock up in illiquid, non-marketable securities because you think that those investments fit in well with your overall portfolio design, then you are making a controlled decision. Just be aware of the restrictions, and don't get yourself drawn into an illiquidity or unmarketable nightmare.

An illiquidity nightmare

 If you trap your own knight by placing it at the side of the board and set your own pawns on the only squares on which it could land, you paralyze the piece. In this endgame diagram, it's Black's turn, and you can see the clear difference in activity between the two knights – favoring Black. Black's knight has a lot of potential, jumping to c3 or b4, from where it could attack White's pawns on a2 and/or e2. In the meantime, White's knight doesn't have a single legal move. Black's piece is active while White's is inactive.

Grandmasters always look for ways to leverage each move so that rather than limiting their pieces' mobility, they increase it. When challenged by a threatening maneuver, they don't just run away, but strategically move the escaping piece to a square where it will pressure the opponent. Sometimes grandmasters employ a double attack, meaning one piece threatens two. If White were to inch up its pawn on the board below from f4 to f5, for example, to a square where it challenges its opponent's knight *and* king, what can Black do? He can only pull one of them away, allowing White to capture the other. In this case, White has made its pawn hyperactive. Take a look:

The white pawn, protected by its king, threatens both the black king and the black knight. In this case, Black has no place to run. The rules of the game state that when the king is in check, as it is in this situation, the player must save it. Black's king, therefore, must flee to d6 or f6, losing its knight to save itself.

Using leverage to make more money… and have more risk

Just as chess gurus want to make their pieces as active as possible, skilled investors try to make every dollar as productive as possible. Professional financiers often believe so wholeheartedly in their intended purchases that they would like to buy a large number of shares, but they don't wish to move their money from elsewhere to put down the full cash payment. So what do they do? They capitalize a portion of the purchase price with their own cash and borrow the rest from the brokerage firm to buy the shares "on margin." The firm extends credit to the investors, meaning it lends them the money to purchase the extra shares in accordance with both the federal rules (called "Regulation T") and the brokerage firm's own requirements. Margin accounts offer investors the ability to buy many more shares of stock than they currently wish to pay for; it gives them "leverage" (a term the British call "gearing"). When you start to feel like a grandmaster of investing and are ready for the added risks of margin trading, first make sure that you learn all the details. Just as borrowing money can leverage your profits, it can also magnify your losses.

High gear – options trading

Even though there are times when options make sense for personal portfolios, think of using them as being akin to bringing your queen out early in the game. It's normally considered a bad idea and you'll most likely waste valuable time or even lose the piece, though for some players in certain situations, it could improve their odds. Perhaps the most powerful piece on the board will guarantee their victory. However, one mistake and they're doomed.

As both margin and options entail a great deal more risk than standard investment strategies, and since many people end up losing painfully when they get involved in them on their own, these approaches to increasing your money don't make it to the list of *Rich As A King* Action Points. Just as you shouldn't start betting on a game of chess against a grandmaster, don't get involved in risky investing until you have the equivalent of a 2500+ Elo rating as an investor, meaning that your skills match those of an investment professional. (The "Elo" system of ratings, developed by Hungarian-born physicist Arpad Elo, calculates the relative skill level of players. Earning the "grandmaster" title requires a rating of at least 2500. Garry Kasparov held the highest rating ever counted by FIDE from 1999 until 2012, when Norwegian Magnus Carlsen claimed that title with a score of 2864.)

Initiative: Controlling the pace of your investment game

Though statistical studies of thousands of historic tournaments have shown that White wins a little more than half the time, experts debate the reason for the imbalance. It would seem that since White goes first, it gets the "one up" on Black, known as the initiative. On the other hand, no chess game ever ended before starting because the player with the black pieces announced, "Since I've got black, I'm just going to quit now." Regardless of which side of the board you play, you have an almost equal chance to win. In any event, though, the pendulum swings, and a participant in a tournament will get to play both colors. So rather than focusing on what the flip of the coin brings you at the start, direct your energies to playing the best game you can. Interestingly, Bobby Fischer noted, "The turning point in my career came with the realization that Black should play to win instead of just steering for equality." He didn't seem to think that playing with the black pieces was a significant disadvantage.

Similarly, many people make the mistake of assuming that since the big institutional investors have such a huge advantage on Wall Street (their own analysts, large sums of money, and many years of experience), it doesn't even pay for regular families to have their own portfolios. That kind of thinking, like resigning from a chess match because you have the black pieces, will stop or limit you from ever succeeding in developing a logical, long-term portfolio. Everyone has the chance to do well in the money world, so don't give up.

When handling your money, strive for the initiative. In chess, having the initiative means controlling the pace of the game; in money, having initiative means taking charge of every step of your investing. You have many tools at your disposal to gain the lead. For instance, you can decide how much money to save and spend each month. Let's say your savings strategy calls for a $500 monthly mutual fund purchase. Though the fund may have good years and bad, you can put this self-payment at the top of your priority list, thus ensuring that you maintain decision-making power.

Moreover, with either mutual funds or individual stock purchases, you can gain the initiative by selecting your own asset allocation, meaning the percentage of your investments in different asset classes. Assume you've put together a plan with a 50/50 split between stocks and bonds, and the stock market jumps up. You can sell some stocks and buy bonds to reset your account to your desired allocation. Though it's true that the size of your pie will change depending on the markets, which is something that you can't influence, you can certainly choose how you will react.

Along with taking the initiative to regulate your own big-picture issues, such as the amount of savings you will put away and your portfolio's asset allocation, you can also take charge of your specific investment choices and, more precisely, how you trade them. Placing an order can involve more than simply asking your broker to buy or sell shares. Your instructions can often influence how much you pay or how much you receive when your order gets executed. Get a list and explanation of all of the different types of qualifiers you can use when entering trade orders by going to www.RichAsAKing.com/bonus.

CHAPTER III

The Plan to Get Rich

It is better to follow out a plan consistently even if it isn't the best one than to play without a plan at all. The worst thing is to wander about aimlessly.
—Grandmaster Alexander Kotov (1913 – 1981)

"Blitz" chess games, where each player has only a few minutes (up to five minutes per side) on the clock, don't allow time for the two sides to develop long-term, in-depth strategies. Short games are mostly about quick pattern recognition and tactics. One of the world's top players in the early 1900s, Richard Réti, once said, "Those chess lovers who ask me how many moves I usually calculate in advance, when making a combination, are always astonished when I reply, quite truthfully, 'as a rule not a single one.'" It's not that he lacked the ability to think ahead. After all, he was the first player in eight years to defeat the world champion José Raúl Capablanca using an opening that was later eponymously called, "The Réti Opening" (moving the knight to square f3), and subsequently in 1925 he held the world record for playing twenty-nine simultaneous games while blindfolded. Remembering so many games at the same time without seeing or touching the pieces, and developing and playing out strategies to win those games, demonstrates mental acuity beyond the capacity of most human beings.

The reason why Réti didn't need to plot every step of the way was because he could recognize the patterns of typical chess games. Having studied tens of thousands of games, a grandmaster rarely finds a completely new situation unless he's playing against another superpower. In fact, the importance of remembering patterns was documented by the 1978 Nobel Prize winner in Economics, Herbert Simon. He posited that stronger players perform better because of their ability to analyze "the position into larger perceptual chunks, each consisting of a familiar sub-configuration of pieces." In other words, a chess expert does not need to recalculate the power of each piece with every move. Instead, he recognizes how different patterns appear on the board.

When shown a game setup, grandmasters can memorize the whole situation in a matter of seconds. Compare this to a novice who barely recalls the placement of the two kings. However, if you *randomly* station the pieces around the board, the chess expert will hardly recall their locations any better than the beginner will. Chess pros rely on pattern recognition, looking at what Simon termed "chunks" of information. Short-term memory works more efficiently when it recodes information into units of perception that mean more than each of the individual parts. By parsing the data into recognizable chunks, people can more easily see and understand what is in front of them. With professionals in all fields, experience helps them see the patterns in all types of information. Investment advisors can often understand a brokerage statement with a brief look, whereas the client might have to spend hours reading it. This is similar to a doctor studying a patient's chart, a patent attorney reviewing a patent application, or a teacher looking over a lesson plan.

You need more than tactics to get rich

Strong "tactical" players excel at pattern recognition and quick decision-making. On the other hand, some players have a more "strategic" predilection. They look at the big picture, the long term, and the end goals. Grandmasters must perfect both their tactical and strategic skills. Likewise, successful investors must also use their dual abilities to make crucial money decisions on a regular basis (tactics) as well as map out and keep track of their long-term plan (strategy). Though many people make a series of tactical investment decisions throughout their lives, believing that they don't need an overall approach, they sometimes slip. They make one bad choice that they can't unwind, and then they end up on a dismal path. In chess, once you touch your piece, you must move it. And with money, too, if you commit to an illiquid investment, or you get emotionally tied to an idea, you may end up getting stuck. Like a chess player who follows his plan but then makes one mistake and loses the game, the investor whose tactical decision causes a significant loss could also lose the financial game. As international master and *New York Times* chess columnist Israel Horowitz pointed out, "One bad move nullifies forty good ones." So leave tactical moves to the hustlers in the parks and get started on your big-picture plan. Here's how....

How to control your future

Although you cannot influence many events, you can control enough of them to prepare a more comfortable future for yourself and your family. Stop to consider: Do you have a financial plan? Does it coordinate your short-term needs with your long-term goals? Does it balance withdrawals against anticipated streams of income? And if an unfortunate incident should alter your flow of incoming funds, can your plan serve as a tool to help you restore balance to your economic life?

A financial plan is like a set of blueprints for a house. No builder would begin construction without a master plan. He would not stockpile bricks, concrete, and electrical wiring without first studying his inventory requirements. Chess professionals function in the same way. Whether deciding in which tournaments they want to participate or whether they construct the pattern of the game by considering the opening, middle, and endgame strategies they will use, they've got a plan in mind. They won't advance even a single pawn if that move doesn't fit into their strategy. In fact, in order to dominate a game, grandmasters often look for positions that will stop their opponents from following their plans. Grandmasters know that if their adversaries don't have plans, or can't stick to them, this inequality will lead the better planner to victory.

Who needs a financial plan?

If you ask the average person whether he has organized his finances, odds are that he will stop to think about whether he has balanced his checkbook and paid his bills. If he has, he'll probably answer in the affirmative. But that's like asking a chess player if his pieces are set up on the right squares at the opening of the game. You can't get past the first step if you haven't structured the very basics. In other words, just being organized does not mean you have a financial plan.

A solid plan involves a total review of your lifestyle, a reasonable listing of your aspirations, an honest understanding of your earning potential, and a complete accounting of your assets and liabilities. A plan done too casually – say, promising yourself that you will save more in the future or spend less tomorrow – tends to lose urgency and is easily forgotten. Committing figures to paper after careful consideration, however, will help focus your thinking and enable you to integrate the various aspects of your financial life.

Begin with a "snapshot"

Newsflash – 2005: Susan Polgar breaks the world record for the highest number of simultaneous games of chess played.

Susan: I remember walking around the room looking at each of the 326 chessboards. As I stepped from one board to the next, my first assessment was to determine which assets I had and the value of each one. In other words, not only did I get the basic count of how many pawns, bishops, knights, and rooks I had, but I also calculated the value of each one and determined how well they were placed in relation to those of my opponent. What could each piece do to improve the overall situation? Was one piece worth more than another? When reviewing a single board, I gave all my attention to that board, forgetting the previous or the next. I had to focus on what assets I had at hand and how I could best use what I had to further my goal – to win.

When putting together your financial plan, start by listing all of your assets. These might include a business, your home, other real estate, cars, collectibles, jewelry, stocks, bonds, cash, trust funds, and bank accounts. Determine the value of each position, understanding that an illiquid family-owned business may not have the same worth as a similar investment that you could easily sell. Add to this list your salary and any other sources of money coming into the household. Continue by recording a summary of general expenses, mortgages, and other liabilities. Take note of any imminent decreases in family income (such as an upcoming retirement, anticipated lay-off, or company downsizing) or soon-to-occur major family expenses (like needing to buy a larger house, a new car, pay for a vacation, or tuition expenses). Complete the assessment by directing your attention to retirement funds and pension plans – Social Security, IRAs, 401(k) plans, etc. Note any personal insurance policies you have that will provide income in the future. (Feel free to use the questionnaires designed to help you focus on your details at www.RichAsAKing.com/tools.)

Set your goals

Why do financial planners spend a great deal of time helping their clients express their objectives as explicitly as possible? They know that if the plan can't help someone to specify and achieve his goals, he won't follow it. When you begin your plan, jot down your short-, medium-, and long-term aspirations (such as buying a car, traveling, or retiring early) and estimate the amount of money you will need to cover those expenditures. Differentiate between realistic goals and impractical wishes and follow the STRATegic – Specific, Time-bound, Rigorous, Attainable, Tempting – modeling system from Chapter II.

Determine your risk tolerance

Many people avoid thinking about risk and hope that by putting the subject out of their minds, it will disappear. But it won't. In fact, those people who shy away from investing because of the word "risk" and instead hide their money at home or deposit it in low- or non-interest-bearing bank accounts that purport to be "risk-free" subject themselves to inflation risk – which means that they lose the buying power of their dollars over the years.

The inflation monster

Young children fear the monsters that lurk under their beds or at the top of the stairs. Their parents check every night and announce, "I don't see anything; the coast is clear!" before bedtime. However, as any self-respecting child knows, just because you can't see the monster, it doesn't mean it doesn't exist. You can extend that lesson to inflation: Just because you don't see (feel) inflation, it doesn't mean it's not hiding around the corner.

An investing TIP

Inflation can erode your portfolio's real value. However, there are tools to use to minimize the negative effects of inflation. Purchasing real assets (like real estate) and inflation-adjusted debt securities (like U.S. Treasury Inflation Protected Securities, TIPS) may help to protect a portfolio's purchasing power during periods of inflation.

Buying a diversified commodities fund during a period of high inflation might help to hedge your potential losses. But these finds also entail high levels of risk.

Balancing risk vs. reward

As you set the parameters for your financial plan, be honest with yourself about how much risk you can comfortably stand. Keep in mind that if you lack sufficient cash inflow to fully cover your current budget, you will have to acquire the extra funding elsewhere. You can work harder and increase your income, or you can let your money work harder and increase your investment income. Investment selections (ranging from volatile high-flyers to ultraconservative short-term CDs) reflect investors' willingness to absorb risk. Generally, the riskier the product, the greater its *potential* for gain – and loss. Every investor needs to balance the chance of losing money against the possibility of a profitable outcome.

When both establishing and monitoring your plan, constantly revisit the question of risk. Judging your "tolerance for risk" means asking yourself: What would I do if one of my investments became almost worthless overnight? What if my portfolio dropped 20% in value? Would I wait for recovery? Would I sell out? What would be my time frame for making these decisions?

It helps if you avoid euphemisms. In fact, "risk" is sometimes simply a more acceptable way of saying, "you might lose money." Wall Street participants have their own jargon, with plenty of synonyms when they don't want to say the word "lose." You might hear about a market "correction" or "adjustment," or perhaps an analyst will talk about hitting a "short-term trough," "reaching a support level," or a "cyclical variation." People use these expressions to make losing money sound more palatable. When you want to understand your own tolerance for risk, don't ask yourself if you could survive a 20% drop in your account. Try using more specific figures: "How would I react if my account lost $30,000 in a week?" That's what risk really feels like.

What will devastate you financially?

Always hope for the best, but prepare for potential problems. In designing a plan, include a risk-management component. Start your thinking with a "What if…" scenario. What if your child was about to get married? Or you had an opportunity to enter into a business? What if the price of the computer system you were considering for your company increased dramatically? What if your house burned down? What if you lost your job, or became disabled? What if you died? Or the opposite – what if you lived well beyond normal life expectancy? As the science of geriatrics advances, people are living longer than ever before. In fact, top gerontologists predict that human beings will soon live well into their nineties and pass the 100 mark. Exceptionally long life expectancies call for a whole new view on financial planning.

Let someone else share your risks

In Chapter II, we looked at the "how" of buying insurance; now consider the "why." While stocks, bonds, and cash may comprise a considerable portion of your portfolio, and you could sell your assets if you needed money, this wouldn't address all the possible worst-case scenarios. Having proper insurance coverage could mean that you and your family would suffer much less and sustain far fewer hardships in the event of a catastrophe.

How much risk would you like to take with your future? If you lose a chess match, you can always come back next year. But the stakes are higher in your personal financial tournament. If you lose your ability to work, your health, or your life, you have no second chances. When you pay the premium on your insurance policy, you are giving up this cash. But in the event of an unfortunate occurrence, you (or your family) collect a payment.

Set up an asset-allocation model

Your asset-allocation model clearly illustrates the different asset classes in your portfolio. To make it accurate, begin by recording all your current resources such as your home, business, collectibles, stocks, bonds, and cash.

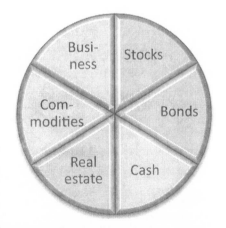

Present your portfolio in the form of a pie chart, with the different investment categories that you own depicted as slices of the pie. Often, seeing a pictorial representation of assets enables a viewer to understand where he is over- or under-represented. For a customizable worksheet, use the "Net Worth (Assets and Liabilities)" worksheet at www.RichAsAKing.com/tools.

Asset allocation pundits preach the mantra of "not putting all your eggs in one basket" in order to mitigate the risk that you might over-expose yourself to a poor investment. They know that divvying up your money has the added benefit of strengthening your overall position.

 How can allocating your assets benefit you financially?

Take a look at a chessboard to see how diversification can make you stronger.

Here a bishop, with the power to glide down the board, raises the level of threat against the opponent. However, every cunning bishop has one major flaw: it's stuck on its one color. You can never take a bishop that starts the game on a white square and use it to capture or even threaten an enemy on a black square. A player who diversifies his fighting assets, though, will pair up his white-square bishop with his black-square bishop and create a mighty force on the board. Like tag-team wrestlers, pilots and co-pilots, or stocks and bonds, having two complementary parts working together can fortify your situation.

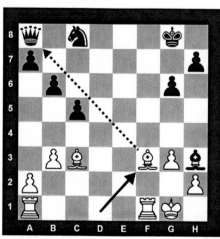

Now look at this model of a diversified chess position. By pairing up both bishops, the white player not only establishes a strong defense, but she also sets up a game-winning offense. The black bishop on the right side of the board, h3, threatens to capture White's rook on f1. But worse, Black can checkmate White if he brings his queen from the upper left corner, a8, to the square facing the white king, g2. The white king would have no place to go, and also could not capture the black queen, since it would be protected by the bishop on h3.

The good news for the player with the white pieces, though, is that she need not run away from the attack on her rook. Her pair of bishops can both defend and counterattack. She can move the bishop on d1 up to f3, thus stopping the checkmate threat and at the same time attack Black's queen. Once the bishop moves to f3, it enjoys the protection of the rook on f1.

If Black wants to protect his queen, he must move it to the right, to square b8. However, fleeing like that will lead to an immediate loss, since White could then move her bishop to d5… checkmate!

Where could the black king run in this situation? White's two bishops have eliminated most of the escape routes, and the rook has closed off column f, completely locking in the king.

In this illustration, in fact, White's bishops have proven to be even more valuable than Black's queen. Much like an investor might allocate some assets to stocks and some to bonds, White developed both her white-square bishop and her black-square bishop. Using both together, she was able to protect herself against checkmate and ultimately win

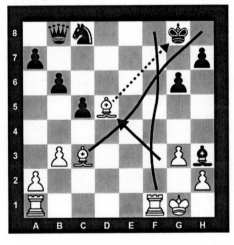

the game. The two bishops stationed on different colored squares, plus the rook on f1, worked together as a team. The white-square bishop could cover the squares that the black-square bishop couldn't touch, and vice versa – and with the backup investment being held in reserve – the rook, White virtually "cornered the market."

Even though diversification in investing means using several asset classes, your money isn't spread out haphazardly; the different asset types work in tandem and create a team. Both in chess and investing, diversification is one of the most important and powerful tools available.

Now that you have an accounting of your current assets, are aware of your incoming cash flow and your debts, understand your insurance policies, established your goals, and considered your tolerance for risk, it is time to actually get started creating a target asset-allocation model.

How Monte Carlo can improve your analysis

 *Doug: My brother, a professor of aeronautical engineering, once asked me how I make financial plans for clients. I told him that I use a statistical modeling system called a Monte Carlo simulation. "That's interesting," he noted. "I use Monte Carlo, too." With a specialty in computational fluid dynamics, he researches air particle movement. For example, he'll look at how air flows over the cutting edge of a wing and then design a plane to optimize the airflow. Monte Carlo simulations are used in many areas of study when you're dealing with a massive body of data, like air particles or stock prices, and when you don't know where any one of those data-points will be at any one time. Instead, you know in general how the data-points move and based on that knowledge, you need to make some decisions.*

Unfortunately, numbers don't always reveal the whole truth. We all want to make investment plans based on very solid statistics, but we can all easily get fooled. Let's look at the model of using "average annual return," a very frequently utilized metric on Wall Street. It's reasonable to rely upon averages and quite simple to calculate them. However, what you learn from that calculation could mislead you.

Calculating the average

The most common statistic people use to judge an investment is its return – how much money the investment made. If the asset was held over a period of years, they look at a number known as the "average annual return." To calculate this figure, they examine the returns for each year in the series, add them up, and then divide by the number of years. In fact, when people refer to an investment that averaged 6% over the last two years, they usually don't mean that it made exactly that amount each year. Rather, it might have produced 4% in the first year and 8% in the second for an average of 6% per year.

Averages sound simple, but can actually be deceiving. Let's say that a client has a $100,000 portfolio, and he estimates that he'll make 6% on it, or $6,000 per year. Furthermore, each year he plans to take a fancy vacation with his family and will use this $6,000 to cover the costs. Assuming he nets *exactly* 6% per year, he'll have enough money to pay for his goal. But in the real world, investments don't always work the way we wish. Let's assume that during the first few years of this withdrawal plan the portfolio returns are low, whereas the later years produce high returns. This sounds more like the reality of the stock market – some years can be great, and some years poor.

Take a look at the chart that follows (p. 63). Example A shows a series of ten years' worth of returns that could be the performance of a typical stock portfolio. The account started with $100,000. The average annual return was 6%, and the investor withdrew $6,000 per year. Strangely enough, the initial capital ended up being cut in half by the tenth year! Why? Because even though the portfolio was averaging 6% over the ten-year-period, that wasn't the amount it grew every year. During the first few years, the market value of the portfolio went down, and worse, since the investor withdrew $6,000 each year for vacation expenses, his total net worth decreased substantially by the end. By the time the market turned around and started going up, he was working with a much smaller principal sum. In fact, by the time the bull market was making impressive gains, the investor had less than $37,000 – and he was still withdrawing his yearly allowance.

How the same returns can give different results

Now take a look at Example B. Here, all we did was take *exactly* the same yearly returns as shown in the previous set of figures and run them in reverse. In other words, the first year's return in Example A becomes the final year's return in Example B. Naturally, the average annual return on the bottom line (6%) remains the same, since we're using the same numbers, but just presenting them in a different order. The surprising results show that even though the average annual return is exactly the same, and even though both situations include the yearly $6,000 withdrawal, the person in Example B finishes up with over $111,000, which is more than twice the sum of money that the first person had at the end of the period. What caused the difference? Think of the expression "adding insult to injury." The *injury* to the portfolio in this case is that the market drops. The additional *insult* to the account is that the client continues to remove principal on a yearly basis. When the market eventually moves up, there is not much principal left to grow. In Example B, on the other hand, in the first few years with a strong market, the account benefits from large returns on an ever-increasing amount of principal. Having great returns on a small amount of money is nice, but it doesn't net you too much (Example A), whereas a big portfolio in a strong market will net you considerably more money (Example B).

Nothing lasts forever

Imagine how much worse it would have been if person A had been caught in a bear market and didn't even average 6%, or if his portfolio wasn't well enough diversified and he owned a few unlucky stocks. Making projections where the market grows 10% or 15% or more can create beautiful charts and compel people to make lavish retirement plans. But the reality is that most people don't enjoy returns like that every year. And not only is an investor's average annual return usually significantly lower, but if the yearly returns don't come in a favorable order, even a strong average annual return may not help your bottom line.

What if you don't withdraw any money?

The chart on page 64 is a replica of the one on page 63, with only one change. The second chart shows what would happen if the client did not withdraw $6,000 every year. In this case, both Example A and Example B end up with exactly the same sum. If you don't withdraw money from the account, regardless of whether the good market returns or the bad market returns come first, the final outcome remains the same.

Avoid making "average annual return" assumptions because you can never know whether the market's return will resemble Example A or Example B. In fact, there are an infinite number of possible returns that the market might produce. Instead, employ Monte Carlo simulations to consider how different possible returns in the portfolio will affect the principal. Can the order in which you make your yearly returns affect the long-term bottom line? As we saw, the answer is absolutely "yes," so design your portfolio to take these different possible market scenarios into account.

How Monte Carlo simulations work

(Go to www.RichAsAKing.com/videos if you want to see a video explaining Monte Carlo simulations.) The Monte Carlo simulation (MCS) is an analysis tool

**A comparison of two portfolios with the same
average annual return but different outcomes:**

Initial portfolio value = $100,000, Withdraw $6,000 per year
Average annual return = 6%

Example A			Example B		
Year #	Return	Value of account	Year #	Return	Value of account
		$100,000			$100,000
1	-15%	$79,000	1	30%	$124,000
2	-9%	$65,890	2	24%	$147,760
3	-5%	$56,595	3	22%	$174,267
4	-4%	$48,331	4	12%	$189,179
5	-3%	$40,881	5	8%	$198,313
6	8%	$38,152	6	-3%	$186,364
7	12%	$36,730	7	-4%	$172,909
8	22%	$38,811	8	-5%	$158,264
9	24%	$42,125	9	-9%	$138,020
10	30%	$48,763	10	-15%	$111,317
Avg. Annual Return	6%		Avg. Annual Return	6%	

that deals with uncertainty. It calculates the probability of meeting specific future targets. Investment professionals use MCS to put order into a large body of data (such as capital market results) so that they can help their clients make practical decisions (e.g., how much money can I spend yearly?). By using computer-driven MCS programs to analyze answers based on mathematical probabilities, you can greatly improve your chances of following the right road to success. In the average annual return charts, you saw the wide range of possible returns, based on two numerical configurations, for an investor who wanted a yearly $6,000 income stream. However, you would need a lot more than two sample cases to estimate the probability of future success.

**A comparison of two portfolios with the same
average annual return but different order of yearly returns:**

Initial portfolio value = $100,000, No withdrawals
Average annual return = 6%

Example A			Example B		
Year #	Return	Value of account	Year #	Return	Value of account
		$100,000			$100,000
1	-15%	$85,000	1	30%	$130,000
2	-9%	$77,350	2	24%	$161,200
3	-5%	$73,483	3	22%	$196,664
4	-4%	$70,543	4	12%	$220,264
5	-3%	$68,427	5	8%	$237,885
6	8%	$73,901	6	-3%	$230,748
7	12%	$82,769	7	-4%	$221,518
8	22%	$100,978	8	-5%	$210,442
9	24%	$125,213	9	-9%	$191,503
10	30%	$162,777	10	-15%	$162,777
Avg. Annual Return	6%		Avg. Annual Return	6%	

How can a Monte Carlo simulation help to test multiple possibilities? Imagine taking a fish bowl and filling it with ten slips of paper on which you have written various stock market annual returns. Then draw a slip, note the result on a chart, and throw the paper back into the bowl (as this same answer could be a possible return for a future year, too). After repeating this nine more times, you will have a string of figures that represent one possible market future if you invested over a ten-year period. You could then ask, "If I had achieved that series of results, would I have reached my goals?" You would then mark down if the answer was "yes" or "no," and then repeat the fish bowl drawing. If this exercise is repeated numerous times, a pattern might develop. For example, you might see that in seven of the trials, you had enough money to pay for your goals but in three of them you failed. A pattern based on relatively few samples (say ten or twenty) hardly provides statistically significant information. That's where Monte Carlo simulations fit in.

MCS programs determine – based on very large numbers of tests – the probability of achieving certain outcomes as a result of choosing particular investing paths. In our fish bowl paradigm, a Monte Carlo simulation might examine hundreds, thousands, or even millions of possible market scenarios. With a database of historical asset returns, MCS programs can look at specific asset allocations (i.e., 30% U.S. stocks, 25% foreign stocks, 40% corporate bonds, 5% cash) and simulate how that specific account might do over a period of time. Plug your actual allocation into the system, or test any model you want, and have the computer analyze thousands of possible financial lives for you without you having to make a single investment. Then check all the various outcomes and decide which way you want to invest. Knowing how your future might look on all those different possible paths could help you to make wise decisions.

Each Monte Carlo simulation represents one possible future for you. By looking at all of them together, you might realize that in most of the tests, for instance, you will run out of money by the time you're seventy. Or the MCS report might point out, "If you continue spending the way you are spending today, and if your asset allocation is kept in the current position, you have a 55% chance of success." That would mean that had the computer run 1,000 trials of your life (based on your specific holdings, income, expenses, etc.), 550 of them would have had you being able to pay all your bills for your whole life; but 450 of them would have had you running out of money before your death. "Success," for the purpose of MCS, is defined as having enough money to pay the bills every month until you die. Once the program gives you a figure for your probability of success, decide if you can sleep at night with those odds. Generally, people feel reasonably secure with a 70% to 80% chance of success in their financial plans. Of course, as they get older, they tend to look for an even greater probability of success.

Monte Carlo simulations not only help aeronautical engineers design planes and investment professionals create financial plans, they have also become a core part of the engine of chess software. Imagine the power of a computer being able to play out each possible move in thousands of different iterations. It can then measure which path has the greatest odds of success and then follow that course.

How to determine where to place your money

For a basic idea of which asset allocation fits best, investors often cite general guidelines based on age brackets, with more aggressive designs for younger people and more conservative ones for older folks. However, don't rely too much on asset allocation generalities. Use these models as starting points in a Monte Carlo simulation, and then adjust them until they meet your needs.

Tournament-level chess experts use asset allocation theory as well. For example, chess champion Magnus Carlsen employs a variety of different opening strategies – diversifying his approaches – which mitigates the risk that his opponent might have great expertise in one or two of them. On the other hand, when Garry Kasparov was competing in the 1980s and '90s, the boards looked different. For years, Kasparov would often use the same opening plan (the Najdorf variation of the Sicilian defense). In place of diversifying his opening strategies, he trained himself to become so proficient that it was nearly impossible for anyone to beat him. Unless you intend to totally fixate on one particular investment that you can truly control, follow the Carlsen model rather than the Kasparov approach and use an assortment of investment categories in your portfolio instead of just one.

Asset allocation is the art of balancing your different holdings to enable you to meet your changing monetary needs while keeping in mind your personal tolerance for risk. And so, when you actually sit down to do your periodic reviews, keep in mind the most important variable in the situation: You! Look at the recommended range of equity allocations for each stage in life in the following pages and, assuming that you can emotionally handle the risk, test the numbers using a Monte Carlo simulation. You can find some financial planning software online or else sit with a Certified Financial Planner™ professional who can assist you. Use the following percentages of your money to have in stocks only as a guideline, since everyone has a different situation.

Twenty-something: Go for it!

> *Concentrate on material gains. Whatever your opponent gives you take, unless you see a good reason not to.*
>
> **—Bobby Fischer**

Young investors may lack experience, and they may have limited resources, but they do have time. If you are an average investor in your twenties, chances are that you have finished with your schooling and are now beginning your career. Saddled with debts from credit card expenses, student loans, mortgages, or car payments, you may also have the responsibilities of a new family. With your retirement way beyond the horizon, start putting away a set sum of money on a periodic basis. Make a target for yourself of saving 15% of your income every month. If you can manage this, you're well on your way to becoming as "rich as a king."

With time on your side, build up a portfolio of growth-oriented stocks. Skip the income-producing investments for now since they usually have less potential for growth and you, being gainfully employed with an expectation of many more employable years ahead, do not need dividend or interest checks to replace a salary. While having an aggressive portfolio of stocks and mutual funds makes sense, even putting 75% to 95% of your long-term savings in equities, keep in mind that wild investing schemes or penny-stocks rarely become economic superstars. Do you believe you will discover the next Google or Apple and become a high-tech billionaire? Don't let yourself get overconfident. Consider the wisdom of Vasily Smyslov, "In chess, as in life, a man is his own most dangerous opponent." As an investor, learn from his comment and don't plough money into high-risk investment schemes thinking you know best. Your overconfidence could be dangerous to your portfolio.

The beginning of your career is like the opening of the game... very unpredictable. If you were playing white and did the standard e4 opening (moving your king's pawn up two squares), your opponent might counter with one of the seven or more typical responses (Caro-Kann, French, Sicilian, King's Pawn, etc.). Since you don't know which move he'll make, you cannot yet imagine the whole scope of the game. Similarly, in dealing with your money, you cannot put into place a full-fledged, long-term plan since you lack even the basic information you would need to know about your future career (which people usually change about six times during their lifetime), your income needs, your family structure, and more. After ten years, though (such as after the first ten or fifteen moves of a chess game), you may begin to have a better view of your future and then be able to make a reasonable financial plan. Grandmasters follow formulaic openings and you should too with your investment approach. When you're in your twenties, make sure you make the standard moves: set up a bank account, establish credit, maximize your 401(k) and/or IRA contributions, and buy aggressive investments.

Susan: The setbacks that investors face when they try to aggressively grow their portfolios remind me of when I was making my run to earn the grandmaster title. Like people who buy high-growth stocks with the aim of becoming wealthy, I used some very hard-hitting strategies in order to win the title. Though the aggressive moves didn't always work, I could never have won enough games to qualify for the title if I hadn't pushed myself to the limit.

My battles weren't only on the board, though. The political machinations behind the Hungarian Iron Curtain were trying to suppress my ambitions. As I mentioned earlier, being a woman in a male-dominated sport, I was at the receiving end of one of the most discriminatory and arbitrary decisions of the World Chess Federation (FIDE) when they granted one hundred bonus points to all women players except me! That's like the government saying that the tax rate for everyone is 35%, but you have to pay 65%. As if that wasn't bad enough, another equally painful incident took place in the same year (1986). Although I was the top-rated seventeen-year-old player in the world at that time (of either gender), and I had qualified from the Hungarian National Championship to enter the "Men's Chess World Championship," I was not allowed to compete, as it was for "men only," I was told. Though they tried to crush my spirit, I just used these setbacks to regroup and fight back even harder.

Young people have time to recover from painful falls and they possess the strength to keep pushing. As such, they should normally invest aggressively. They need to realize that if they buy stocks and the market dives, that's the time to keep looking for more growth opportunities rather than run away. Unfortunately, some new investors feel shell-shocked from the market crashes. As a result, they may never put their assets into investments that have enough growth potential.

Thirty-something: Focus on wealth-building

At this point, you may be getting married, having children, buying a home, purchasing a larger car, and then even a second one, and advancing in your career. If you have kids, perhaps even handling a single-parent household, you have additional expenses: childcare, school tuition, building up a college savings account, the cost of extracurricular activities, and camp. Remember to stick to the budget you worked so hard to devise.

You still want to focus on growth, since with many income-earning years ahead to insulate you from occasional losses, you can afford to continue taking on a moderately aggressive risk profile. It's appropriate to continue to add to the growth section of your portfolio with high-quality stocks and perhaps some global and domestic mutual funds. If you have the tolerance for risk, you could easily allocate 65% to 90% of your investible assets into equities. At the same time, place some of your resources into intermediate-term bonds and CDs to save for "big ticket" items that you will need, especially if you have a growing family.

Don't confuse "aggressive" portfolios with "wishful" ones. Let's say you're a fan of the one-time world chess champion (1960 to 1961), Mikhail Tal, whose brave moves were often called "magical." Though he clearly rocked the chess world with his daring, sacrificial style, his methods lacked longevity. Could he have succeeded in the long term? Ultra-forceful players make interesting moves, look clever, and entertain audiences. But in the end, the very aggressive players tend to peak early and then vanish from the limelight. Mikhail Tal, for example, was world champion for only one year. In comparison, more conservative players like Vladimir Kramnik and Anatoly Karpov, known for their positional[4] and pragmatic styles, have reigned over the highest circles of chess for decades. In describing his own style of playing, Karpov said, "Let us say the game may be continued in two ways: one of them is a beautiful tactical blow that gives rise to variations that don't yield to precise calculation; the other is clear positional pressure that leads to an endgame with microscopic chances of victory.... I would choose the latter without thinking twice. If the opponent offers keen play I don't object; but in such cases I get less satisfaction, even if I win, than from a game conducted according to all the rules of strategy with its ruthless logic."

Today's top players compete aggressively and don't avoid a fight. Certainly, the research available to them now allows them to set up solid defenses that would have been virtually impenetrable to the assaults of a hundred years ago. By playing conservatively, they have literally been able to stay in the game much longer than their more uncompromising counterparts. And the #1 tool

---

4   Positional vs. tactical chess: The purpose of playing positional chess is so that the tactical moves that you make later in the game will have a greater chance of success. Positional players think more in terms of controlling squares, developing pieces, and preparing multiple strategies to back each other up. Tactical players, on the other hand, look for how they can "fork" two of their opponent's pieces, how they can ambush the other player into a losing position, or how they can force the enemy into a series of moves that will eventually lead to checkmate. Professional chess players need expertise in both positional and tactical skills.

they have used to improve their game is information. By strengthening their fundamental knowledge of the game, they have slowly crushed their opponents, leaving no place for themselves… except on top. While the Soviet Union used to own the greatest databases of chess games, anyone can access that same information on the internet today. Likewise, whereas the big brokerage firms used to have a virtual monopoly on investment research, you can obtain almost all of the data with a Google search. If you want to build your success over the long term, therefore, first continue to garner the best intelligence in the world of investments and, second, don't take needless chances, no matter how magical the moves might appear.

Forty-something: Growth and income

As you enter your forties, you make an unsettling observation: Prices keep rising. It costs twice as much now to go to the movies as it did when you were a teenager. And you need to consider whether you want to drive to the theater at all since gas prices have shot up, too. If you have children, you see that teenagers no longer want to wear hand-me-downs, and new sneakers cost five times the $30 you used to pay. At this point, you start to worry about college tuition payments and bills for weddings. In addition, your parents, who have always been self-sufficient, might need a bit of extra support. While reviewing your asset allocation, you observe changes in your personal priorities. With more immediate expenses looming, it's time to begin moving a piece of your portfolio into more conservative investments. Start shifting some assets into dividend-paying stocks and a selection of bonds and CDs. Consider setting up a bond portfolio with a variety of maturity dates (called a "bond ladder" – more on this in Chapter VII) to benefit from the liquidity of short-term bonds and also to capture the higher interest rates available on longer-term instruments. Check with your employment benefits representative to confirm that you are participating to the maximum possible extent in your retirement programs. Although you want to add current income to your household budget, you do not want to shortchange your retirement nest egg in the process. Therefore, don't start withdrawing any money from savings and still try to maintain a solid percentage of your investments in growth investments, perhaps anywhere from 50% to 80% in stocks and stock mutual funds.

In your mid-forties, you are right in the heart of the "mid-game." Lots of pieces are on the board, you've won some battles and lost some, the pressure of defense and offense weighs heavily on your shoulders, and you need to keep your eye on the target, not letting one bad move ruin all the work you have done so far. If you prepared well in the opening of the game, you now have a strong foundation for managing your mid-game. If you have fallen behind a bit though, you still have time to catch up, so don't get discouraged.

Fifty-something: Safety first

In your fifties, some of life's pressures may have eased. Hopefully you have a high level of job satisfaction and can stop putting in so many late hours. Your children may be in college, or married and beginning families of their own. Is your account size diminishing as you pay the tuition and wedding bills for which you've been saving over the past couple of decades? Don't worry, that's why you saved the money.

Review the will you wrote when you were younger. If it doesn't reflect your current situation, revise it. Also, set up an appropriate trust if your lawyer suggests it, and draw up some powers of attorney and a healthcare proxy, too… just in case.

Your portfolio may have grown nicely during the years, but now as retirement looms, consider becoming a bit more conservative with your assets to ensure that they'll be there when you need them most. On the one hand, if the stock market crashes, you won't have as much time to wait for the recovery as you had in your thirties and forties. On the other hand, though, you shouldn't cash out all of your investments on the day you retire. In fact, a large portion of your savings should stay invested for decades after you hand in the key to your boss. So even though you may have hit fifty, continue to view yourself as a long-term investor. Look at maintaining an asset allocation model that has anywhere from 40% to 65% of your money in a broadly diversified portfolio of quality stocks or stock funds. While this may seem high, it's important to keep enough growth in your portfolio to keep pace with inflation as well as to enlarge your retirement savings, but without as much risk as before.

If your financial plan shows that you will have problems in the future, take advantage of "catch-up contributions" to your 401(k) and IRA. To encourage savings among 50+-year-old citizens, the government allows you to put an extra $5,500 into your retirement plan on top of the $17,500 normally allowed (as of 2013). If you can find the cash to bolster that retirement plan, see if you can also put aside $1,000 extra in your IRA, too.

Sixty-something: Prepare your portfolio for retirement

As you enter your sixties, you look around and wonder if you are getting old. But you feel fine. You've become a pretty good tennis player, a better-than-average chess competitor (you can sometimes beat your grandchildren), and you're considering traveling to the Galapagos. No, you aren't getting older; you're getting better.

You may have decided to work for a few more years or maybe cut down to three or four days a week. But as long as you remain employed, keep making contributions to your portfolio. You definitely plan to make the break and retire during this decade, but you aren't sure exactly when. In reviewing your portfolio, check that you have the critical amount of capital saved up to afford a secure future. While you need to think about growth investments to combat inflation, putting anywhere from 25% to 50% of your assets in equity-based products, you should lean more toward safety. At this point in life, you can't afford the risk of gambling on a big idea that may turn sour. Re-evaluate your diversification among different sectors, checking that you are not too heavily invested in any one industry. If you have a number of insurance policies whose premiums have jumped in price, consider if you still need them all. Carefully consider keeping and/or buying long-term health insurance, since a prolonged illness could decimate your retirement savings. Again, review your will, trust documents, healthcare proxies, and powers of attorney. Do they still represent your wishes?

Once you actually retire, you have even more decisions to make: Do you wish to live in a smaller home, a larger one, or stay put? In the same town or in a new locale? Think about which activities you wish to engage in — volunteer work? Travel? A new business? Maybe you might begin to write a book or sort through your old photographs. Stay busy. Make sure that you not only retire *from* something, but also that you retire *to* something. Now's your opportunity to help others, to have fun and catch up on all the things you've always wanted to do.

Seventy-something: How to set up your accounts for the endgame

You've worked. You've saved. You've invested. And now you're retired. Congratulations! It's time to enjoy yourself. But remember the wisdom of Grandmaster Emanuel Lasker, who said, "The hardest game to win is a won game." In other words, just when everything looks fine, you can easily slip.

The golden years, much like the endgame of chess, do not allow much room for error. In fact, the last part of a chess game is much more technical than strategic. Don't start researching novel combinations with only a few pieces left on the board. At this point, each piece represents a higher percentage of your net worth than it did at the beginning of the game. When you started the match with sixteen pieces, each one was about 6% of your assets. In the endgame, where you might only have four of your own pieces on the board, each one is 25% of your stable. So don't start taking big risks when the stakes are so much higher. Lower your equity allocation to 10% to 30% of your overall investment pool. Hopefully, your opening and mid-game practices have set you up so that now you just need to follow the well-known technical patterns of the endgame to take down your opponent. And just as you should not pursue out-of-the-box approaches to entrapping your opponent's king, don't start looking for never-heard-of-before methods to get rich. Leave those types of gambits, which often fail, to people still in the opening or mid-game of their financial life. After making it this far, don't risk the pieces you managed to keep or the funds you managed to save. Follow the words of chess great Rudolf Spielmann (1883 – 1942) who advised, "Play the opening like a book, the middle game like a magician, and the endgame like a machine."

Don't get rooked by scams

Unfortunately, con artists target senior citizens. The FBI catalogues common frauds perpetrated against people who grew up in the 1930s, 1940s, and 1950s, a time when being polite and trusting was considered a virtue. Regrettably, these deeply engrained traits also make those generations easier marks. Moreover, older people tend not to report scams because they don't know whom to tell, are too ashamed, or don't even realize that they have been swindled.

Rip-offs come from many different angles, including healthcare and health insurance fraud, counterfeit prescription drugs, funeral and cemetery shams, anti-aging products, telemarketing cons, internet deceit, investment schemes, reverse mortgage and life insurance rackets, and more. Sadly, not only do strangers harm seniors, but people close by hurt them as well.

Doug: Not long ago, an elderly client told me how she had lent the Visa card that was linked to her brokerage account to her son to use for the day. She forgot about it, since she rarely used that card herself. It took her almost a year to discover that he had been using it to steal money from her on a regular basis by withdrawing funds from a cash machine. He would take only small amounts, so that she wouldn't realize that the changes in her portfolio were due to withdrawals. She would just assume her stocks and bonds had dropped a little in value. Another woman's nephew, who was a lawyer, told her that he was investing her money with a major, international investment house. He even printed false statements with the logo of the company on it. When she asked for her money back, he told her the investment house had gone out of business. And yet another client kept lending money to help a sick friend pay for medical care. Half a million dollars later, he finally said to himself that something is very wrong here... and then the sick friend disappeared.

Never blindly jump to capture an opponent's chess piece, since he may intend to sacrifice it in order to get a much larger compensation from you. Stop and think about the whole plan and why he's giving you something for free. Unlike in chess, where the rules prohibit consulting with your coach or computer, in the financial world, you have a lot of people upon whom you can rely before you make a move. Keep these steps in mind to protect yourself:

- ♟ Double check with trusted family members, lawyers, accountants, financial advisors, and other professionals before you commit to any major deals.
- ♟ Regularly inspect your credit report for suspicious activity. Get it for free every year from each of the three credit rating agencies. Go to www. RichAsAKing.com/credit for further instructions..
- ♟ Never do business over the phone unless you initiate the call.
- ♟ Make sure people don't crowd around you when you withdraw money from an ATM.
- ♟ Be wary of all links and websites that someone emails you. If you get an email from your bank, for example, that asks you to click on a link, don't! Instead, log into your account the way you normally do and see if any messages await you there.
- ♟ Never respond to emails that ask for your account information.
- ♟ Review your bank and brokerage statements on a regular basis, and ask your financial advisors questions if you don't understand why the balance changed more than you anticipated.

Even if you're in your seventies, don't get overconfident when your financial plan shows everything in the black. Continue to play each and every move carefully. Retain the majority of your money securely in a variety of income-oriented investments, but keep your guard up against the dangers of inflation by maintaining some of your money in equities.

The main issues to think about include paying for health care and maintaining your lifestyle. Hopefully, you can also focus on charity, vacations, and family (though don't give away or lend so much to your kids that you end up jeopardizing your own financial safety). And though you may not like to think about it, it's your responsibility to organize your affairs so that someone can handle them for you in the event of serious illness or your ultimate checkmate.

Four easy steps to doing your financial plan right

"When you see a good move – wait – look for a better one."
—Grandmaster Emanuel Lasker (1868 – 1941)

Although many people carefully design plans, some stop at the preparation stage and never enter the implementation stage. Even worse, they may have a plan, but they act impetuously and disrupt it. Very often the deviation does no harm, and during the next review session, they can resolve any problems. But occasionally the losses that result from a spontaneous action cause considerable damage. Remember these points when creating and maintaining your financial plan:

- ♟ **Avoid unrealistic expectations.** Don't think you can increase the value of your investments in one year by 30% by simply "taking a chance." Just as a grandmaster doesn't jump to take an opponent's unprotected piece, knowing it might be a setup to a trap, don't let a fast-talking salesperson with a "get-rich-quick" scheme draw you in. Remember, if it sounds too good to be true, it probably is.
- ♟ **Don't confuse your financial plan with your actual investments.** The plan is the blueprint for your financial program. Base any updates to the plan on actual changes in your life. The investments, on the other hand,

are the specific stocks, mutual funds, and other assets in your portfolio. They are the individual chess pieces that need to move in tandem to get you to your final destination. Make adjustments to your investments based on analyzing how well they do their tasks and meet their goals. Don't buy an asset just because you like the company, think it's the "right" security to hold, or because it's what you've always owned. Own only those assets that will help you achieve your goals.

♟ **Don't forget your goals.** A financial plan enables you to measure your actual success against your planned returns. Although the two may not be identical, they should move in tandem. When comparing your plan versus the actual results, use specific numbers to avoid subjectivity in your review. "It seems to be OK," is not an ideal answer to the question, "Is your financial plan on track?"

♟ **Avoid putting your plan on the shelf and forgetting about it.** A financial plan is a dynamic document. It changes as your life progresses and as the economy shifts. Keep it close at hand and in your thoughts when you make financial decisions.

Don't think that only wealthy people need to do planning. Though they certainly require a well-designed approach, it's just as important, if not more so, for a family where every penny counts. As Estonian Grandmaster Paul Keres (1916 – 1975) noted, "The older I grow, the more I value pawns." Even small sums of money carefully placed can eventually lead to significant growth. After all, many grandmasters have triumphed in tournaments by promoting a lowly pawn to a queen. Having a concrete plan serves as a guideline toward greater freedom and opportunity, no matter where you are on the financial board. So don't make the mistake of waiting until a crisis arises before determining your future moves. Get started today.

Do you need to have a financial planner?

Working with a professional does not mean giving up the management of your assets. Advisors help you interpret your situation, needs, and aspirations. Think of them as coaches; they assist you in seeing different sides of the issues and present you with varying choices, but you make the call in the end. In chess, even the world's greatest players have trainers. Though a player might perform better in tournaments than her coach could, she may get emotionally tired or lack the same analytical tools that he has. On the other hand, she might have certain traits that he lacks, such as bravery, decisiveness, and the ability to think quickly under pressure. She would follow the Hannibal battle approach: "We will either find a way, or make one," whereas her coach might be less of a combatant and more of a Ben Franklin type of philosopher: "For life is a kind of chess, in which we have often points to gain, and competitors or adversaries to contend with, and in which there is a vast variety of good and ill events, that are, in some degree, the effects of prudence or the want of it." The coach/player connection, much like the advisor/client relationship, blends different skill sets that together can lead to a winning combination.

Three-time world chess champion, Russian Grandmaster Mikhail Botvinnik noted, "Chess mastery essentially consists of analyzing chess positions accurately." This applies in the world of investing, too. Don't fret over who actually performs the analysis, you or your advisor. Having professional input can only help you master your own financial game.

RAAK Action Point – How to get started

You can read books on investing, get inspired to save, and even subscribe to *The Wall Street Journal*. Similarly, you can solve chess puzzles all day until you're a whiz. But in either case, until you make a financial plan or play in a tournament, your moves won't matter. Follow these steps in order to get on the path to becoming as "rich as a king":

Step I. Gather your information

Download a free online system called "Financial Snapshot" which you can use to organize your information at www.RichAsAKing.com/tools

Personal information

- ♟ For each spouse: Name, date of birth, target retirement age, health status, life expectancy.
- ♟ Dependent children: Names, dates of birth, health status.
- ♟ Other dependents (parents, siblings, etc. who rely on your financial support): Names, dates of birth, health status, summary of their situation.

Income

- ♟ Work income for each spouse: Description of all work income sources, gross/net income, expected yearly increase (will it keep up with inflation?), bonuses – fixed or variable (if your salary changes monthly, use a conservative average annual estimate), employment status (self-employed, regular employee).

- ♟ Special income sources: Description (inheritances, royalties, trust distributions, gifts, child support, etc.), amount (net or gross), one-time event or multi-year, linked to inflation, taxable, if it will go into savings or if it will be spent.

Taxes

- ♟ Current tax bracket.
- ♟ Future anticipated tax bracket.

Inflation expectations

- ♟ When planning for retirement, or any long-term goal, account for the fact that inflation whittles away the value of your savings. Just to give you an idea of the effects of inflation, what would have cost you $100 fifty years ago would now cost $761! That increase represents about a 4% annual compounded rate of inflation.

- ♟ What number should you use in guesstimating future inflation? It's very hard to tell. Since past performance is no guarantee of the future, you may not want to use 4%. Over a longer-term view, inflation has averaged closer to 3.5%. But in the recent past, inflation figures have been painfully high. In 1980, the number topped 13%. Therefore, it may be prudent to make a cautious inflation assumption and choose a slightly higher figure rather than hoping that inflation will stay low forever.

Savings plans

- ♟ Tax-deferred: Description (401(k), 403(b), IRA, SEP, etc.), start and end dates for the savings program, annual contribution, how it's invested, how much your employer matches (if at all).

- ♟ Taxable: Description, start and end dates for the savings program, periodic contribution, how it's invested.

Investments

Make a line item for each investment that includes the following information: Description, where held, type of investment (stock, bond, mutual fund, bank deposit, annuity, and sub-category, if applicable, including domestic, global, large cap, small cap, etc.), trading symbol (many software programs will automatically update the value of your securities if you supply the symbol), taxable/tax-deferred, cost basis (what you paid for it), current value.

Special assets

If you own any valuables that you would sell to raise capital to fund your retirement (or any other goal), write them down. If you wouldn't sell a certain possession (such as your engagement ring), then don't include it as part of the plan. Special assets could include real estate, a boat, a business, a collection (coins, art, stamps), and a vacation home. Jot down a description of the item, whether (and when) you plan to sell it, cost basis and current value, anticipated increase in value over the time held.

Residence

If you own your castle, even if you don't ever plan on selling it, record some basic information. Many people enjoy the comfort of knowing that as a last resort, they could always sell their house to fund their retirement, so list it as a resource. Record the following information: whether you currently own the property or plan to buy it in the future (when?); hold forever or sell it (when?); purchase/sale date; cost basis (add in the cost of major renovations); current value; anticipated increase in value (will it increase at the rate of inflation?); mortgages (first and second, length of loan, average interest rate, original balance, current balance, pay period {monthly, quarterly, yearly}, and anticipated balloon payment).

Life insurance

Gather information about all of your life insurance policies. Sometimes people forget to include their veteran's policies, deals through work, life insurance on their mortgages, and old contracts on which they no longer have to pay premiums. Write down a description or title of the plan, the type of policy (term/whole/ universal), start and end dates, death benefit, premium type (annual renewable, fixed) and amount.

Loans

Apart from mortgages, record any other loans (including credit card debt) you might have, and include these details: description, current or future loan, start and end date, length, average interest rate, original amount, payment period (monthly, quarterly, yearly), whether you will make a balloon payment early.

Expenses

Divide up your expenses into categories such as basic living (pre- and post-retirement), education expenses, and special expenses. List them by name, start/ end date (one-time expense or multi-year expense), amount in today's dollars, and whether the cost will increase by inflation (or more – U.S. public college tuition has been increasing at about 8% per year).

Retirement benefits

⚖ The majority of elderly people who receive Social Security rely on it for more than half of their income. If you don't know what you'll get, order a benefits statement from www.ssa.gov/mystatement. Along with other useful information, that document tells you what monthly income you can expect to receive from the government one day. It also has a huge warning on the first page letting you know that, "in 2033 the Social Security Trust Fund will be able to pay only about 75 cents for each dollar of scheduled benefits." Depending on how you think the government will resolve this issue, you might want to assume that you will not receive as much in monthly payments as listed on your statement. If your spouse earned considerably more than you, find out about "spousal benefits," which may be higher than your own social security account would provide. Even if you're divorced, as long as you were married for more than ten years and haven't remarried, you may be able to collect a higher amount based on the contributions your ex-spouse put into the system.

⚖ If you will get any other fixed monthly pensions, record them in the "future income" section. Note the age at which you can begin collecting the estimated benefits, whether they are linked to inflation, and whether your spouse will continue to receive money after your death.

Gather your information – conclusion: If you need a way to organize all of the data above, download a free RAAK Financial Planning worksheet at www.

RichAsAKing.com/tools. Remember that grandmasters don't just show up at a world championship match and start playing. They gather as much information as they can long before the game. They understand their own strengths and weaknesses and have advisors and coaches help them to analyze their position.

Step II. Define your goals

"You can't target what you can't see," said best-selling author and motivational speaker Brian Tracy. All too often, people start investing with no particular goal in mind. When that happens, their investments lack focus and these individuals change strategies frequently. It's not that they don't achieve their goals; they just don't have any.

In the 2012 world chess championship, where Israel's Boris Gelfand nearly unseated the reigning champion from India, Viswanathan Anand, viewers criticized the play as boring. In the first twelve games, ten were draws, and in the final four blitz games, three were draws. When asked about why the players agreed to a tie in the games instead of playing longer rounds for the crowd to enjoy, Gelfand said they were in a battle to win the championship, not to entertain the viewers.[5] Both players had their target in front of them, and weren't distracted by what other people thought their goals should be.

In defining your STRATegic goals (Specific, Time-bound, Rigorous, Attainable, Tempting), don't let your parents, boss, or friends dictate your direction. Don't count on CNN or Fox Business to tell you what to do. Think about your specific desire, write it down, and then figure out how to get there. The low-tech and easiest action step here is to grab a pen and paper and just start writing. If you'd like to try our free RAAK STRATegic Goal-Setting tool, go to www.RichAsAKing.com/tools.

Step III. Identify barriers to achieving your goals

Fabulous! You've put pen to paper and recorded your first goal. Is it attainable? As Abraham Lincoln said, "A goal properly set is halfway reached." So you're halfway there, having set the target. The second half of the process is to make sure your ambition jives with reality. Here's where it helps to get some outside advice, whether from a friend, family member, or professional advisor. Let's say you've set a rigorous goal to retire at age fifty-five. You've calculated that you'll need $4 million in savings to achieve the lifestyle that you want. You divide that amount of money

---

5   http://www.haaretz.com/news/sports/israeli-grandmaster-gelfand-loses-world-chess-
      championship-1.433386 (5/30/12)

by the number of years until your desired retirement age. Now look for the barrier. If you're fifty-one today and you earn $100,000 per year, there is no way you can sock away a million dollars a year for the next four years. On the other hand, if you're twenty-five with a great income and you can figure out how to save $60,000 every year, then you could very possibly reach your $4 million goal if you average a 5% return on your money over the next thirty years.

Susan: When I play, I always have goals that I know I can achieve. However, I realize that something might surprise me. Right at the beginning of the game, I'm already considering what endgame structures I want. I then choose the opening strategy that is most likely to get me there. If my opponent creates a counter-attack or has a clever defense, in most cases I've already considered it, studied it in similar historical games, and created my own response.

If any of the following barriers to success apply to you, determine if you need to adjust your objective, or devise a strategy to deal with the obstacle. Only list the hurdles here, not the solutions. You will find the solutions later when you do the actual analysis in the plan. Or, possibly, you will find that as you foresee each stumbling block, you might come up with an idea for how to fix it. That's exactly the point of thinking about each of these impediments. By understanding the hindrances that might stop you from achieving your aims, you can take the necessary steps in advance to mitigate or completely eliminate them.

- ♟ **Goal**: Fund a college education account for a child who will start in five years.
  Barrier: You cannot save enough on a monthly basis to accumulate the capital to pay the full tuition.
- ♟ **Goal**: Go on a vacation next year to Thailand.
  Barrier: Though you can afford the cost of actually staying in Thailand, the airline tickets for you and your family might break your budget.
- ♟ **Goal**: Buy a Land Cruiser for your twentieth anniversary.
  Barrier: You don't have enough savings to pay cash, you don't want to finance it, and since it only does about 15 to 20 miles per gallon, filling it up would probably set you back over $5,000 per year.
- ♟ **Goal**: Become a professional tournament chess player.

Barrier: You need to have enough time to devote to studying chess in order to get to a professional level. On top of that, will you have the resources to manage the business side of your career choice, including getting health insurance, setting up a pension plan, and putting aside a significant enough emergency fund to support you in lean times?

Just because something might impede your ability to achieve your goal, you don't need to toss aside the aspiration. Rather, recognize the risk as part of the planning process.

When your opponent opens the chess game by moving his pawn to the middle of the board (e4), he's created a barrier for you. You can't move your pawn to f5 because he'll just capture you. Does that mean you have nothing to do? No. You just need to consider your options more carefully.

Chess experts spend years studying moves from old chess matches to understand which barriers one player imposed on the other. Armed with this knowledge, they can make robust plans to deal with these eventualities.

Step IV. Choose an asset allocation model
Your asset allocation model shows you what percentage of your portfolio you have invested in the various asset classes. Consider everything: your home, other real

estate, business, collectibles, stocks, bonds, and cash. Look at your portfolio in the form of a pie chart, with the different investment categories that you own depicted as slices of the pie. Often, seeing a pictorial representation of your positions enables you to understand where you are over- or under-represented.

We spoke earlier about using a Monte Carlo simulation to test various asset allocation models and investment scenarios. For a quicker, albeit weaker system, you can use simple rules like, "The percentage of your portfolio in bonds should equal your age." Focus a lot of energy on determining what asset allocation you need because that decision will have a huge impact on your long-term success. Unfortunately, people spend an inordinate amount of time on security selection, but overlook the importance of asset allocation. According to one often-quoted study[6] on the topic, more than 90% of the return of a portfolio is attributable to the asset classes in which it is invested as opposed to being attributable to the individual positions in the account. Why do people spend so much time picking individual investments instead of thinking about their overall asset allocation? It certainly doesn't make much sense.

Your whole future could change based on your choice of whether to put 0%, 20%, 50%, or 100% of your money in stocks. In the same way, the flow of a chess game depends completely on the first moves that the players make. Which of the 1,327 named opening variations (such as the "Réti Opening," "Caro-Kann Defense," "Ruy Lopez," "Queens Gambit," "English Opening," "Philidor Defense," etc.) will they select? Some openings would be considered "flank openings," where the action happens on the sides rather than the middle. Others are called "open games," which start with the traditional white pawn advance (e4) and black pawn advance opposite (e5). And there are "closed games," where the queen's pawns begin the advances. Depending on the opening combination, the game might be slow and positional, or filled with vigorous tactical battles, or somewhere in between.

All great chess games today start with one of the known chess variations. It's not because the players can't come up with anything original. Rather, they are using the research that has been done by the chess masters who came before them. It's often not until the twentieth or thirtieth move or sometimes even later that the players begin to go "out of book," which means that they deviate from the known systems. Likewise with asset allocation: You can tell a

---

6   "Determinants of Portfolio Performance," Gary P. Brinson, L. Randolph Hood, Gilbert L. Beebower, 1986.

huge amount about a portfolio by looking at its division of asset classes. With so many time-tested approaches to investing, it's prudent to use the known models and not try to search for the unique. Don't think that "unique" is an attractive quality in investments, even if investment marketers try to sell that feature to you. There is no evidence of a correlation between uniqueness and profitability.

When selecting an opening to use for chess, a player will think very carefully and then stick to the original model unless some fundamental change occurs on the board. Constantly changing strategies are as much of a hallmark of inexperienced chess players as they are of novice investors. It's not always easy to maintain only one approach, but if you want to succeed, commit yourself to keeping on track.

Susan: As a surprise opening in my game against Maia Chiburdanidze (2004 Olympiad), I decided to use the "English Opening." This was considered a shock to the onlookers, and to Chiburdanidze too, because I rarely used that opening. As part of my pre-game preparation, I carefully researched the English Opening so I would have an in-depth understanding of how Black could counter White's hard-hitting attacks. I prepared responses to those possibilities, and then committed myself to the strategy. Even when she made the correct moves to try to thwart me, I didn't abandon my approach. She was forced to spend a great deal of the time on her clock trying to counteract my well-researched plan, but because I held on steadfastly, she was not able to recover once I got a material advantage.

I'll admit that it was a little tense playing against her, since her championship record was so impressive and there was so much at stake. Like me, she used to compete in the men's competitions, traveling the globe and picking up medals on most of her stops. But with all of my preparation beforehand and my determination during the game, I was confident that I would succeed. It's that attitude of determination and steadfastness that I've found in other successful chess champions, and in people from so many backgrounds, from educators and doctors to martial artists and investors.

Regardless of whether you will use a Monte Carlo simulation to find the optimal asset allocation, in which case you will need some special software (or a financial planner who can help you), or whether you choose to design an asset allocation model based simply on how much exposure to risk you want, understand your own tolerance for risk as well as your long-term goals. Unless you see the whole picture, you will have a hard time sticking to your plan during rough periods. Consider these questions:

♟ How much time do you have until retirement (or whatever goal you are targeting)?

♟ How much does your money need to increase in order to be able to pay for that future expense?

♟ If the market drops, would you add more money (buy when it's cheaper), hold on and wait for a recovery, or sell (get out now before you lose it all)?

To test your own risk tolerance to finish this step of determining your asset allocation, use the free online RAAK Risk Tolerance calculator at www. RichAsAKing.com/tools.

Step V. Choose your investments

When you get to the stage of actually committing to the purchase of an investment, you have two choices: Either do it yourself or hire a professional to do it for you. Whichever approach you choose, though, you still need to take an active role. Read the chapters in this book about stocks and bonds, and about using mutual funds and money managers. There are pros and cons to both approaches, so don't get sucked into the hype that either "you can't do it yourself – you need an expert" or that "every penny you pay an expert is money that you don't get to use for your retirement." Not only do you have many choices, but you can also mix and match. Use professional management for one part of your portfolio and handle a different section on your own.

Step VI. Monitor your progress

Once you've put everything into place, from creating your plan to buying the specific investments, your job isn't done; you still need to keep an eye on the big picture. Depending on your cash flow needs and the types of investments you own, you might have to watch your accounts hourly or daily, or you might determine that a monthly review is sufficient. Traders must always keep their finger on the pulse. Long-term investors, on the other hand, shouldn't have many changes to make in their accounts. The reason to read statements at least monthly is more of a good housekeeping issue than an investment issue. If keeping an eye on the swings in the value of your account encourages you to trade too often, be careful. Overtrading often makes you underperform the market significantly. But you should check that no important news has developed about one of your positions, that your debit/credit card and checkbook usage is within the parameters you set for yourself in your budget, and that your overall asset allocation is what you intended. Frequent reviews of your financial statements could take as little time as ten or fifteen minutes. Every twelve months, if not more often, compare your investments to your written plan to make sure that you are still following the path. If not, consider whether your plan or your investments need reforming.

Susan: With the threat from the Hungarian chess fan who said he'd kill me if I played for the Americans still looming in my mind, I had to make a difficult decision. In fact, I had been planning on not playing against Hungary in the Olympiad. I didn't wish to compete against my colleagues from my homeland. Moreover, from a purely practical vantage point, I knew that by playing against the Hungarian team, potential endorsement income that I got from Hungary was at risk. And unfortunately, my family was not much help because they were divided in their advice to me. I thought of my new American teammates and my dream to put America on the map in women's chess. I had struggled so hard to bring in fabulous coaches and sponsors, including Garry Kasparov, I had switched federations from Hungary to the United States, and I knew that if I didn't play for my team, our chances of winning a medal were significantly reduced. So I made the tournament-changing decision, switching from my original plan after very careful consideration, and I played first board in the match against Hungary.

CHAPTER IV

Computers, Chess, and Money

W hen Lockheed Skunk Work's lead engineer Kelly Johnson coined the phrase, "Keep it simple, stupid," he was not questioning his team's intelligence. Rather, he wanted them to create a fighter jet that field mechanics could repair in combat conditions with only a handful of tools. Unfortunately, people tend to misinterpret the wisdom behind the "KISS" acronym and confuse simplicity with carelessness. In other words, they'll follow the path of least resistance rather than seek the most efficient solution to their problem.

With simple financial planning, for example, people love to get a "red light" or "green light" after entering a few bits of data into a computer. They know that either they'll make it or they won't. In today's sound-bite world, a snappy result satisfies people who don't want to invest the necessary time or effort to get a correct result. Overly simplistic calculators usually ask for variables like current age, retirement age, income, expenses, pensions, and assumed return. With only those figures, you can create a long-term cash flow model that might look pretty good. However, as we saw in the previous chapter about Monte Carlo simulations, an average annual return assumption has little to do with the reality of investing. In fact, we saw how

two people with exactly the same average annual return and the same spending habits could end up in dramatically different situations after just a few years.

Rudimentary plans often ignore or downplay game-changing factors. Consider these economic risks along with the comments below, from investors who didn't realize that financial planning needed to go beyond penciling a few numbers onto a spreadsheet:

- ♟ **Inflation**: "Buying groceries costs a whole lot more this year than last year."
- ♟ **Volatility**: "Everything was going fine, but the stock market crashed six months before I planned to retire … and that was five years ago and I'm still working."
- ♟ **Longevity**: "Instead of exercising and eating healthy, I should have eaten more donuts and watched more TV. Now that I'm turning 85, I've almost depleted my assets. Who knew I'd live so long?"
- ♟ **Interest rate changes**: "The banker told me an 'adjustable rate mortgage' was the best deal. I didn't realize that when interest rates moved up, my monthly payments would become higher than my salary. I'm lucky my parents let me and my family move in with them."
- ♟ **Political risk**: "All the politicians touted the creation of the European Union as the greatest step of economic unity in hundreds of years. Now it turns out that half of the member countries can't even pay their own bills. How can I diversify internationally if the whole continent is on the verge of collapse?"
- ♟ **Death**: "My husband always earned well and took care of the money matters. Only after he got killed by an uninsured drunk driver did I find out that the payments on our life insurance policy stopped four years ago. Now I need to spend my children's college savings just to cover monthly expenses."
- ♟ **Health risk**: "My parents used to assure me that my sister and I would receive a hefty inheritance, so we didn't save that much. But after they got sick and moved to a nursing home, I realized that they were burning through over ten thousand dollars a month. And to make matters worse, they had a reverse mortgage on their house, so when they sold it to raise capital, they got almost nothing. Now while I am helping them, I need to increase my own savings, too."
- ♟ **Pension risk**: "With my husband out of work for over a year, we can't put aside savings. I was hoping we could rely on Social Security, but now they're saying they'll only be able to pay about 75 cents for every dollar we were promised."

Susan: Sometimes you lose a game. Later, when you analyze what happened, you realize what you could have done differently. On the other hand, some situations are absolutely beyond your control. In 1993, I played a critical candidates' match against Nana Ioseliani. Neither of us could get a decisive victory, but ultimately I was eliminated. Even though I never once trailed in the match, the prize was awarded to her because of a drawing of lots. Imagine such an important game being decided randomly!

Some people argue that the inherently arbitrary nature of the markets makes it impossible to plan, but they're wrong. They just don't know the type of planning they can do. Back-of-the-napkin plans cannot deal with market shifts, interest rate changes, and personal tragedies. Likewise, an amateur chess player might not recover if he lost a tournament on a coin flip. However, more carefully designed algorithms that can process the ambiguities of the markets, just like higher level players who can handle the uncontrollable setbacks that occur, can help you to make solid plans that will work for you in many situations. To make such plans, you'll need some advanced software and some know-how. So the moral is, instead of following the mantra of the Lockheed engineer to always keep it simple, try this idea instead: KISS: Keep it sophisticated… *sometimes.*

The 3 ways to make the most of computers

It's not that I'm so smart, it's just that I stay with problems longer.
—Albert Einstein

There are three things you need to effectively leverage the computing power available today: Patience, a realistic outlook, and a good computer program.

Doug: I get calls all the time from people whose first question is, "Doug, which stock should I buy?" I know they don't like my answer when I tell them that I'm not a prophet and can't predict the next hot stock. I then start asking them questions about their time frame, their other investments, their

investment experience, their goals, their family situation, and more. As you can imagine, this conversation extends for much longer than they might have wanted. However, without getting a complete understanding of their financial situation, how can I give a recommendation? That would be like going to a physician and saying, "Doc, my left arm hurts. Can you fix it?" When he tries to listen to your heart, you stop him and say he should only examine your arm. No doctor would agree to that since pain in the left arm can be connected to a heart attack.

Get paid for patience

All too often, people's plans fail because they don't invest the time required to analyze the complete situation. Just like a good chess player wouldn't move a piece until he has examined the board, don't make an investment until you've thoroughly studied your circumstances, and that takes time and patience. For sure, spending five minutes entering data into a financial planning website won't yield a particularly useful result (no matter how colorful the charts are). People who rely on these types of analyses are really just dressing up providence in the clothes of a financial plan, and luck hardly makes for a solid strategy.

Counting on fate doesn't make for good chess either. In 1896, Emanuel Lasker was set to play against Wilhelm Steinitz. They were the top contenders of their generation and, to this day, are still considered among the strongest players ever. Legend has it that before the match began, Lasker received a box of cigars with instructions to, "Smoke these cigars during the games. They will bring you luck." He lit one up before playing, found the quality unbearably poor, and he tossed it. After Lasker won the match (becoming world champion), the gift giver said, "My cigars brought you luck, didn't they?" Lasker replied, "Of course they did." The man asked, "Did you smoke them all?" Lasker replied, "Not me! I gave them to my opponent and he smoked them. And this brought me luck and victory." Lasker didn't rely on the "good luck" cigars to spin the wheels of fortune for his success, and you shouldn't count on the fates either.

In order to succeed in building wealth, you not only need to have the patience to be a long-term investor, but you need the endurance to gather the information, enter it all into the computer program, and take the time to understand the results. The trait of patience is perhaps one of the most important skills you can develop on your way to becoming "rich as a king."

Susan: In 1984, I became an "International Master," which is one step away from the highest ranking in the chess world ("Grandmaster"). For the following few years, I was the #1 woman player in the world. However, with all of the roadblocks that the Hungarian government put in my way, I never knew when the next opportunity to play in an international competition would arise, but I kept training anyway. Having the patience to work every day, never knowing what the results will be is hard enough, but as a teenager, the agony of waiting was emotionally draining, too. I knew that I needed to have patience not only on the board, but off the board as well. In the end, I got my grandmaster title the way that the men had to earn it.

Techniques to develop the patience you need to succeed

If you're ready to start achieving financial freedom, then you'll need to make sure that you have the patience to actually create the plan… and then execute it. Copy these words of Benjamin Franklin on a card and stick it in your pocket to remind yourself, "He that can have patience can have what he will." To get "Four techniques to make you a better investor," go to www.RichAsAKing.com/bonus.

How much money is reasonable?

> *You can't always get what you want.*
> —**Mick Jagger**

When using computers to calculate your long-term cash flow (how much money you'll have coming into your bank account versus how much money will flow out), you might make slight alterations in the plan assumptions to satisfy your goals. For example, if you increase your hypothetical allocation to stocks, your potential returns could increase by several percent per year. Over decades of saving and investing, the amount you accumulate in the riskier model could amount to tens of thousands, hundreds of thousands, or perhaps millions of dollars more than in a safer model. Once you see these huge numbers, the optimist in you might surface and convince you that you should take on the added risk. Then you might say to your spouse, "Wouldn't it be great if we had $4 million when we retire in 25 years? And that's such a long time away that we can surely ride out the ups and downs in the market." But can you? Is it really such a long time? And will the market make those returns?

When you enter assumptions into the computer, satisfy two levels of realism: (1) your own ability to handle the risk without bailing out if the market drops, and (2) the reality of the investments (i.e., the stock market doesn't grow at 12% every year). When putting figures into your plan, consider using the tailored assumptions below, even if they seem rather conservative. Remember, you'd rather have more money than you need in retirement than not enough.

♟ **Inflation**: Though the "consumer price index" (CPI) has ranged from just below zero to the high teens in the past hundred years, in the past two decades the inflation rate has been around 3%. Given the ongoing uncertainty in the economy, build into your plan an inflation rate of at least 3% to 4%.

♟ **Returns**: When using a Monte Carlo simulation to test future market returns, the computer will generate random returns for how the securities markets might perform. To curb your confidence, instruct the software to cut off some of the return every year. In other words, if the computer program generates a random return of 10%, you can have the simulation credit you with only 8%. Whether that 2% difference comes from investment fees or just underperforming the average, you are making your plan more reasonable and more capable of withstanding the unknown future. The more money you allocate to stocks, the higher you should make your adjustment to anticipated returns. So if you test a 100% equity allocation, consider knocking off 2% to 3% every year from the returns that the computer credits you. On the other hand, if you plan to invest only in bank deposits and money market funds, it's reasonable to make a smaller adjustment of half a percent.

♟ **Pensions**: Depending on the source of your pension, whether government or private, realize that the life-long pensions of your parents' generation may no longer exist in the future. Even if the corporation has promised you a fixed monthly payment, their guarantee may not be worth too much. From municipalities to private corporations, and even the U.S. Social Security system, no pension is truly fail-safe. Do you believe the politicians will all band together, forget their special interests, and find a solution to make sure that you will get 100% of the Social Security pension that you were promised? Or do you think it's more likely that there will be lots of lobbyists, haggling, and compromising and you will end up with only a fraction of what you've been expecting? Use a moderately conservative approach, anticipating the shrinking of the government's coffers, and plan to receive 50% to 70% of what you see promised to you in your Social Security statement (which you can order at www.socialsecurity.gov/mystatement).

♟ **Spending**: Some pundits suggest that your expenses will drop after you retire. Perhaps. If you choose to change your spending habits, then you can lower your monthly budget. However, when people stop working, they often choose to travel, shop, fix the house, and more. Rather than using less money, they consume more. On top of that, healthcare expenses normally rise as people get older. Instead of feeling that life gets easier, you might find yourself like a chess player in a competition. Every game she plays poses progressively harder challenges because as she moves up in rank, she must face tougher and tougher opponents. For each game, therefore, she must prepare more than she had for the previous match. Similarly, when you test your future spending models, consider testing post-retirement expenditures equal to, or perhaps slightly higher than, pre-retirement. Add in extra health costs, too, which can vary widely depending on where you live and what type of insurance you have. By the way, don't be too quick to count on an inheritance from your parents. They will face similar retirement expenses and could easily deplete the nest egg that they were saving for you.

What good financial planning software must do

Now that you're patient enough to gather all the necessary information, and you've committed to believing in the real world of investments (where markets can go down, as opposed to the fantasy world where everyone makes money all the time), you've got to use the right software to help you make wise decisions. Many software packages exist, and you might find it tricky to differentiate among them. If you work with a planner, he'll probably have a software system he prefers. But regardless of whether you do it yourself or work with a professional, look for software that includes the following to make sure that you will get meaningful answers:

♟ **Retirement planning or financial planning**. Though the difference between retirement planning and all-inclusive financial planning may seem slim, people often plan too much for one target. If you focus excessively on how you can retire, you might forget that you've got a lot of years until then. Obviously, the less money you spend today will mean the more money you'll have tomorrow. But is that what life is all about? Find a balance that allows you to maximize your average lifestyle from now until the end of the plan. Look for software that doesn't only focus on retirement, but that can help you develop a cash-flow model that covers your whole life, including short-, medium-, and long-term goals.

♟ **Investment expenses, inflation, and taxes**. The program you choose should allow you to make adjustments for fees, inflation, and taxes. Look at the financial costs associated with your portfolio and incorporate them into your plan since those expenses build up over time.

♟ **Life expectancy**. Some software programs assign an "end date" for the plan. Since you don't know how long you'll live, using a standard actuarial table gives you a starting point as an estimate, but probably shouldn't be the actual number you use for your plan. When an IRS longevity table says, for instance, that a seventy-year-old has a life expectancy of another seventeen years, that's just an average. Half of all seventy-year-olds, in fact, will likely live beyond that. If your parents and grandparents lived to one hundred, you certainly don't want to have a document that assumes you'll die at eighty-seven. Make sure that the software you use allows you to plan for a death date for both you and your spouse that makes sense given your health, genes, and lifestyle.

♟ **Social Security**. With the variety of employment experiences that you may have had, sometimes staying at home with the kids, sometimes working part-time, sometimes having high-paying or low-paying positions, your government pension may be significantly different from the assumed average that the computer algorithm uses. It's best if you can enter into the system the actual figures that you receive on your Social Security statement – and adjust them downwards if you suspect that the whole system might default in part (or completely).

♟ **Residential real estate**. How will the program account for the mortgage on your home, or the second mortgage? What about selling the property and paying a tax? Real estate deals are notoriously complicated, so make sure that the computer program you use takes all of the variables into account.

♟ **Monte Carlo simulation**. Since no one can predict exactly what the market will do over time, choose a program that incorporates a Monte Carlo simulation. It allows you to test thousands of different market possibilities to see how you would fare in each case. Relying on a program that doesn't use Monte Carlo would be like playing chess against a computer that only had one game programmed into its memory.

Holistic financial planning requires that you think about how you want your life to turn out. A grandmaster can't guarantee how the endgame will look. Rather, she knows the general direction she wants to follow and then develops a strategy to stay on that path. As she gets closer and closer to her ideal set-up, she'll begin to think further down the line. She's always looking to improve her position step by step rather than to find the shortcut to winning the game – which rarely exists.

People often misunderstand this concept and end up taking huge risks in order to try to achieve unlikely returns. Think about how you would like your financial board to look at varying steps in your game and then, with the least possible amount of investment risk, develop a strategy to get you there. Instead of identifying your maximum risk tolerance and positioning yourself to reach it, figure out how you can achieve your lifestyle goals with the least amount of market exposure. When you meet an investment professional, don't ask, "How much money will I make?" Rather, ask him if he can help you frame, and hopefully reach, your goals.

The problem with using a computer to make money decisions

No matter how scientifically minded you might be, you're still a human being. If you believe you can completely separate your decision-making from your emotions, think about coming home one day and saying to your spouse, "Honey, we have no more money, but let me show you why that is just a statistical anomaly."

The psychological pressures that weigh on you when handling money make it impossible for you to completely rely on a computer to handle all your affairs. Computers are great for simulations, keeping budgets, researching companies, and even for practicing trading (using simulation accounts). They don't get tired, and they never feel afraid.

On the other hand, computers don't understand your tolerance for risk. Though they can run sophisticated questionnaires and assign a risk-tolerance level to your profile, they don't feel the worry building up inside you when the market starts tumbling. They don't see how spouses and partners view their investment accounts differently, nor can they sense one person's need for security versus another's high tolerance for risk. Moreover, no matter how many news stories you enter into their databases, they still won't predict the collapse of Communism, a banking crisis, or even the amount of earnings that a company will announce this quarter.

How to leverage the power of computers

The world of money, like the world of chess, is filled with people who have dreams and emotions. Computers are the tools we use, but the human soul wants more. It wants to be creative, impressive, and elegant. We all want to feel good, try something new, and find beauty. We look for ways to boost our self-esteem, achieve greatness, and earn the respect of others. Try telling that to a computer. A chess computer runs millions of calculations, determines whether one sequence of tactics has a slightly higher point value than another, and then makes a move. When a computer is playing chess, it's playing a different game from human chess. Humans lost this race against computers a long time ago. But that's OK. Do you feel bad that you can't run faster than a sports car in the Indianapolis 500?

In the chess world, computers are best used for training. You can find resources like games databases, instructional chess videos and articles, software and analytical engines, and innumerable related websites. Be aware, though, that training with computers might make you focus too much on *repetition* and *memorization* as opposed to *understanding*. In fact, beginners often waste their time staring at screens. They learn tricks without comprehension. They may play positions over and over again, getting good at one track, but that is more like a video game than a match of intelligence.

Use computer chess programs to help practice endgame tactics, check a specific line of thinking, or hone your skills at acting under pressure. But these programs should not be a substitute for playing with others. Similarly, refer to the internet to research investments, and take advantage of financial planning software to guide you in your decision making, but do not replace yourself as the ultimate decision maker.

PART B

TACTICS

CHAPTER V – BUDGETING

How to Use Your
Sixteen Pieces Wisely

It is not enough to be a good player... you must also play well.
—Siegbert Tarrasch, Grandmaster

Navy Sea, Air, and Land (SEAL) teams change the reality of the world through their hundreds of life-threatening missions each year. While the Pentagon plans and the politicians preach, the SEALs perform. Just as this well-prepared, crack commando team excels on the battlefield, you have to go beyond the planning stage and start making moves too. And the #1 move in your current money situation that you can regulate is your spending. Though you can talk about making changes and plan for great things, if you don't police your cash flow, you can wipe yourself out. In a rather short period of time, you can usually evaluate your financial health based on the amount you spend. Like a chess move, cash flow is a definitive figure. As Grandmaster Emanuel Lasker pointed out, "On the chessboard, lies and hypocrisy do not survive long." It's the same with your budget. If you spend $10,000 but only have $5,000 coming in each month, you will perceive the imbalance very soon.

The second part of this book is all about tactics. In Part A, we covered planning. Now let's get to the actual tools required to implement your strategy. In the same way that the SEALs plan their adventures before executing them, and just as world champion chess players develop strategies before moving, draw up a financial plan before you make any investments. But the plan alone is not enough. What's next is making it happen.

Would you like to be as successful in your endeavors as the SEALs are in theirs? One way to succeed at this might be to make sure you play chess. It turns out that the Navy SEALs trainees who play chess are *three times as likely to succeed* in becoming Navy SEALS as their non-chess-playing mates.

The attitude that will wipe you out

There's a story about a fellow who jumps off the Empire State Building. When he's halfway down, a guard sticks his head out of the window and shouts, "How's it going, buddy?" Flying past, the man yells back, "So far so good!" Though many people use the "so far so good" approach to manage money, stay away from it. As the joke suggests, if you follow this line of thinking to its logical conclusion, you'll hit the ground with a thud.

Following the "so far so good" method, some amateur chess players like to bring out their queen early in the game. Having this powerful piece battle the weaker ones early on can create an ostensible advantage. However, this benefit quickly vanishes when the opponent develops his pieces and begins maneuvers that allow him to conquer the whole board. In Josh Waitzkin's *The Art of Learning*, he explains that as a young player, he won a lot of games with a wandering queen. His coach, however, taught him to stop that routine. He chased Josh's queen around the board in practice games, always putting the youth on the defensive. For a long time, using his queen against lesser players had worked, but "so far so good" didn't help Josh dominate the chess circuit when he played against better opponents.

 *Doug: When I first started working for a Wall Street firm, I figured that since I was pretty good at math, I could make money trading options in my own account. In the beginning, I started trading calls and puts on Pepsi. I made money at the outset, and started increasing my investments from hundreds of dollars to thousands. At that point, I lost. I turned to my mother, who was my business partner at that time, and she*

laughed at me. "It's a good thing that you lost now," she said. "I hope you'll learn the lesson that just because you make a few good trades, it doesn't necessarily mean that you're any better than the next guy. It could just mean that you were lucky."

If you can pay your bills each month, but cannot manage to put aside savings, you may be operating your budget on a "so far so good" basis. But if you want to become as "rich as a king," start dealing with your budget more actively.

Limit your possibilities

At the opening of a chess game, you have ten possible pieces that can move – the eight pawns and the two knights. Even players who haven't studied the traditional openings can often think of a reasonable move. Likewise, your monthly budget should only have about ten general categories. With relatively few possibilities, deciding where to spend your money should not grow into a monumental task. That being said, after noting fixed expenditures such as rent, loan payments, etc., coordinate each of the remaining areas so that one doesn't overtake the others. Just as you probably wouldn't start your game by moving one specific pawn up square by square, don't let one particular expense in your budget outshine the others. Allot an hour or so each month to reviewing last month's outflows and for planning the following month's expenditures. If you're on your own, block out the time so you don't get distracted. If you're married, do this exercise with your spouse. A couple should not have one person making all the spending decisions and simply informing the other one what to do.

Hammer out the details together, lest the efforts of one of you get torpedoed by the other's spending. Should you call your better half every time you want to buy a sandwich? Probably not. Rather, develop an approach that works for your family situation. The two fundamental parts of the system to determine are the means of communication and the division of labor.

Communicating with your spouse about money

In the same way as a chess player will not make a move without knowing the location of each of the pieces on the board, neither should a couple make financial decisions without having all of the facts. When you work with your spouse, be sure that you not only gather all of the information about your accounts, but that you speak honestly and clearly about your own fears and desires.

 *Doug: A husband came into my office a few minutes before his wife for the appointment in which we were going to discuss the financial plan that I had prepared for them. He asked me if they could afford to buy her a new car for her upcoming birthday. He explained that she didn't like her old car and was always concerned that it might break down at night. When his wife joined the meeting, we started going through the written document page by page until we got to the section about trade-offs, which is basically a grid that allows clients to state whether they would be willing to give up on one thing in order to get another. Though the issue of the car wasn't on the page, coincidentally the wife said, "I'm nervous that we won't have enough money for retirement. In fact, I was thinking we could sell my car now and invest the money since I don't really need a car." I could see the husband was shocked, but he didn't say anything. He realized that rather than him making all the plans, guessing what his wife wanted, it was important to start talking to her and actively listening to her ideas.*

When starting the dialogue with your spouse about finances make sure to be particularly sensitive, since money pushes a lot of emotional buttons in people, including fear, anxiety, guilt, and anger. The role of money in marriage ranges from enjoyment and security to status and domination, so strive to understand how both you and your partner view it.

For a list of opening questions you can use to start the conversation with your spouse, go to www.RichAsAKing.com/bonus.

The 3 T's of a champion

Just as a board of directors steers a company, or a world champion chess player has a team of advisors and coaches to guide her, you and your spouse must work together on the "big picture" items. Learn together, review together, develop goals together, and plan together. Separately, though, you can each assume the handling of certain tasks. For example, someone must oversee the savings, check the credit card, bank, and brokerage statements, pay the bills, and maintain the budget. You can both do these tasks together, or only one of you can undertake these particular responsibilities, and then review them as a team in the periodic get-together. These day-to-day operations represent the tactics, as opposed to the strategy, of dealing with your family's wealth. Successful tacticians have these three qualities – the "Three T's": Time, Temperament, and Talent.

Susan: When I was four years old, I played in the Budapest Girls' Under-11 Championship. I was probably the smallest kid in the room. My problem was that as soon as my opponents moved, I wanted to respond immediately. I could hardly wait for my turn since I quickly saw the answers to their threats... or at least so I thought. My father, who was coaching me at the time, told me I literally had to sit on my hands so that I would spend at least a little time thinking of the moves to make. I imagine how funny I must have looked jamming my hands under my legs, popping them out to make a move and push the button on my clock, and then returning them, lest I accidentally move without thinking. My father's lesson to use time wisely paid off that day. I walked away with the gold medal, winning every one of the ten games I played.

When Garry Kasparov briefly worked with the U.S.A. Women's 2004 Olympiad team, he advised the players to always leave ten minutes on their clock. Since they started the game with 90 minutes to play, he said they should pace themselves so they would not end up, as so many players do, darting around the board with only one minute left. In making your monetary decisions, too, don't spend huge amounts of time on smaller choices, thus forcing yourself to make fast decisions when time becomes short. Handle money moves like a grandmaster handles chess moves. Purely technical responses shouldn't take much time. New challenges, on the other hand, deserve greater contemplation. Amateur players tend to spend too much time in the wrong places. They don't realize that most choices are technical, almost common sense. Only a few situations in a game normally require heavy analysis, the type that wears down the time on their clocks. The tactical money manager, too, must budget time wisely. Understand that "petty cash" is called that for a reason, and that if every small receipt doesn't correspond to your spreadsheet, perhaps being off by a few cents or dollars, don't spend a lot of time dealing with it. On the other hand, when more major issues arise, like renegotiating your mortgage or buying a car, that's when you need to invest the time. It's funny how people will literally spend hours choosing a $50 pair of jeans, but when their broker calls them to buy a new mutual fund, they'll make a hundred-thousand-dollar decision in a short phone call. In deciding which spouse will handle what task, consider who can properly allocate the appropriate blocks of time to the various responsibilities.

Do you love money or hate it? What's your temperament?

No one seems to hate *having* money, though lots of folks find *dealing* with it too onerous. Some dislike the responsibility, while others feel frazzled when they have to make specific monetary selections. Alternatively, for many individuals, handling money comes naturally. They like numbers, have no problems separating their emotions from the facts, and don't get bogged down in the details. What's your temperament? Do either you or your spouse have an easier time when it comes to pulling the trigger on an investment choice?

How fast should you move?

Sometimes you might get tempted to take the obvious choice, since (a) it looks pretty good at first glance, and (b) you don't feel like spending the time carefully analyzing it. That's human nature, but not necessarily a great tactical approach.

In some chess situations, too, you might feel that a certain move looks pretty good and that you don't need to spend time analyzing it. For instance, take a look at this board. If you were playing with the black pieces, you might capture White's rook on d3. After all, it has no protection. But not so fast.… If you make that move, look what would happen:

The board looks like this:

Then Black captures the white rook:

And with the next move, White checkmates Black:

Chess wisdom teaches the importance of taking time to consider all of the implications of a move. In particular, if you think you've found a free piece, beware. It could cost you the game.

In deciding who in your household should handle certain tactical decisions, think about who has the temperament best suited for handling these types of processes. For example, think about which one of you is able to see beyond the "free" deal that just arrived in your mailbox to the cliff from which you might fall later if you accept it. One standard free deal that you see all the time that, more often than not, can hurt you down the line is the credit card balance transfer. A new company offers to let you transfer your high-interest debt from an old card to the new card where your interest rate will be 0%. Sounds like getting a rook for free, right? The two situations are similar because later on, this loan deal will likely do damage to your wallet, just as taking that apparently "free" rook will set you back strategically. Here's why:

4 Reasons <u>not</u> to transfer your credit card balance

♟ The low transfer rates eventually expire, normally after six or nine months. You will then pay a higher rate, sometimes above the rate you had with your old credit card company.

♟ During the honeymoon period of 0%, if you're late, even by one day, you lose the 0% deal and go back to paying ultra-high rates.

♟ The small print… and who reads that?… states that the 0% only applies to the transferred balance, but every new purchase you make on the card will be charged at rates that can range from 8% to 28%.

♟ If you keep transferring balances every half year, you can damage your overall credit score, which could make it hard to borrow money for big-ticket items such as homes and cars.

To avoid making emotional decisions, reaching for the first free deal that comes your way, you need the wherewithal to step back from a situation and carefully deliberate your options. That's hard to do, though, especially in this era when people expect decisions at the speed of a tweet.

How to prevent being checkmated by the market

In his best-selling and controversial book, *Blink*, Malcolm Gladwell argues that people's first impressions often trump researched decisions. He opens the book with an exciting account of how a larger-than-life, noseless Greek statue known as the *Getty kouros* was bought by the J. Paul Getty Museum for $7 million. Naturally, the curators brought top-tier experts to examine the piece before they acquired it. Though the museum purchased it based on the authentication of the professionals, a number of those who looked at it said they had had a strange feeling about it. On first glance, many felt the statue was a forgery. In fact, one well-respected Greek museum director commented, "Anyone who has ever seen a sculpture coming out of the ground could tell that that thing has never been in the ground." Gladwell points out that the first reaction of the people who recognized the artwork as fake was better than the analysis of the people who studied, examined, and concluded the piece was genuine.

Though Gladwell's theory has garnered a lot of support, many people have misunderstood him. They have presumed that he meant you should always make decisions based on your first impression. Yet that's hardly the lesson. He purports that you *can* develop intuitive judgment, meaning the ability to make correct choices in the blink of an eye, by experience, training, and knowledge. Combine those three components and you will have the talent necessary to make money choices in a Gladwellian blink.

How to develop a knack for managing money

Winning is not a secret that belongs to a very few. Winning is something that we can learn by studying ourselves, studying the environment, and making ourselves ready for any challenge that is in front of us.
—Garry Kasparov (World Chess Champion 1985-1993)

Knowledge: Since you've made it this far in the book, you're certainly on the right track to increasing your knowledge of investing. Developing an understanding of basic money management does not require a PhD, and you don't need to dedicate years of your life to studying every aspect of corporate finance before you buy a stock. Likewise, just because you meet someone with a fancy title or a bunch of letters after his name, don't presume he knows how to always pick a winner.

Training: Chess players who want to improve spend a lot of time not only playing and reviewing their games, but trying to solve chess puzzles. These brainteasers might entail figuring out how to checkmate your opponent in three moves, or they might involve calculating the steps to winning a game with only a bishop and knight. In investments, too, if you want to learn about stock trading, go to one of the many free online stock trading games. You get a mock account with faux-money and can buy and sell all day. This "paper trading" will give you a sense of how the motions feel without your having to risk any real money.

Experience: Though you can hit the books and practice the trades, ultimately there's no substitute for attending the "School of Experience." People often find that the switch from paper trading to actual trading, where real money is at stake, changes their whole approach. They might have been rather cavalier when trading virtually, and therefore they made a lot of paper profits. But with their hard-earned savings on the line, they find themselves unable to generate the same profits and often end up losing. There are two important lessons to take from this: (1) It's probably a bad idea to trade your own stock portfolio, even if you have practiced on online stock trading games, and (2) If you're going to try, start with a small amount of money that you can afford to lose.

If you truly want to garner investment experience, try leveraging the know-how of others. Seek mentors or licensed financial advisors who will take the time to teach you. If you go to an investment or insurance salesman, avoid hiring one who tries to push a specific agenda on you. Even if he offers reasonable programs, this won't help you develop your own talent. When interviewing advisors, let them know at the outset that you want someone with the spirit of a teacher who will invest the time in you to help you understand.

Having the time, talent, and temperament to make investment decisions will not guarantee wealth. However, without at least a sampling of each one of these, you've got almost no chance. In the short term, though, there is something that you can do that really will make a difference in your financial world: budgeting.

Can you budget your way to being as "rich as a king"?

In the same way that a chess player can't move for his opponent, you can't tell the stock market what to do. However, you can decide how much you spend. You can choose whether to buy a hamburger or a house, a coffee or a car, a Valentine necklace or a vacation. And over the long term, the individual decisions that you make every day will really add up. People constantly seek some type of talisman to help them prophesy the markets and turn them into millionaires. They will pay a lot for a newsletter, a hedge fund, or some special advice because they want more information and counsel. They should realize that most millionaires built their wealth by being careful spenders and savers, not by getting a windfall.

Grandmasters of money have better financial habits than amateurs. Rather than trying to live a rich-looking lifestyle, they're willing to sacrifice now in order to build a rock-solid economic foundation. You can look rich by borrowing against your house and maxing out your credit cards, but who does that impress? Billionaire Sam Walton, founder of Walmart and Sam's Club, was known for driving himself around in an old pickup truck. He didn't try to impress anyone. Could you change your habits and copy Walton's habits?

♟ Could you brown-bag your lunch and save $50 per week? Invest the money in a stock mutual fund from the day you start working at age 20 until you retire at age 60 and you could have over $1 million (assuming a 10% average annual return, net of fees and taxes).

♟ Could you purchase a used car? As you drive a new car off the lot on the day you buy it, its value decreases by about 20%. Why let your money evaporate like that just for the pride of owning a new vehicle? Imagine how many hundreds of thousands of extra dollars you might have later in life if you just save and wisely invest that difference now.

 Relatively small moves in current habits can lead to tremendous benefits down the line. Chess masters have long known this secret, always looking for one small "discovery" tactic that can improve their long-term position. Here's a great example:

You're white, and it's your turn. What would be a smart tactical next move for you?

How about moving your pawn from e5 to e6, threatening both the black pawn (d7) and the black rook (f7)? Though you might correctly note that the black pawn could just capture your pawn, look closely and see that by moving your pawn up, you open an attacking line from your bishop (g3) directly to Black's king. Since Black must take evasive action to protect his king, this allows you yet another turn to then capture his rook.

This tactic, known as "discovered check," makes your small pawn move a very powerful step. Skilled chess players constantly seek small gestures that can swing the game to their benefit.

Which of these small moves can you make today to save a little bit now and enjoy a huge return later?

♟ Could you stand being a little less fussy about brand names, borrow books from the library instead of buying them, and wear extra sweaters indoors in the winter rather than reaching for the central heating switch straight away?

♟ How about renegotiating your cell phone bill or not letting your kids spend so much on theirs? If you make them pay for everything over a certain amount – perhaps $25 per month – they'll learn to watch their cash flow, too.

♟ While you're talking to providers, what can you do to lower your internet/cable fees? Look closely at the bill. Surely you don't need all the services they provide. When you call them, your goal is not to speak to the sales department representative, but rather to the person in the "retentions department." Say something like, "I'm unhappy with the service and I'm shopping around. What can you offer me to stay?"

♟ Take a close look at your shopping habits. Do you get drawn into buying "family pack" sizes of potato chips even though you don't need that quantity? Does fancy wrapping tempt you to buy a more expensive product? Before you leave the house, know exactly how much you want to spend and what you intend to buy. Once you've bought what you planned, go home.

♟ How can you lower your grocery bill? People frequently overspend on grocery shopping by 10% to 50%. By cutting out some packaged products and junk food (which could be a topic for another great book called *Fit As a King*), you could save hundreds of dollars a month.

♟ Can you give yourself a time limit in the store? Put a half hour on your parking meter and you won't have time to browse leisurely.

♟ Can you be patient? When you spy a great deal, wait forty-eight hours. If you think about it for two whole days, and still want/need the item, and if you can't find something at home that you're just as happy with, then check your budget. If you can afford it, go ahead and buy it.

♟ Are you able to give yourself some spending freedom? Make a "miscellaneous items" line on your budget that allows you a certain amount to spend each month on nonessential or impulse purchases.

♟ Can you be accountable? Keep a "money diary" to record the cash that comes in, when it comes in, and the amount, date, and reason you spent it. This exercise may keep you from making a purchase that you can't readily justify.

♟ Can you continue to improve your spending habits? As you become better at thinking and dealing with money, refine your system to track everything. There are two parts to the procedure: (1) the spreadsheet that shows how much you have spent, and (2) the budget that shows how much you are allotting for specific purchases during the month.

Regardless of whether you implement all of the suggestions or just some of them, a rigorous determination to stick with specific and achievable goals will guide you towards success. If you keep a money diary for a week and then quit, stop shopping efficiently, or neglect your savings targets, you could lose the whole financial game. Try to maintain the outlook of six-time U.S. Chess Champion Walter Browne (who has also won hundreds of thousands of dollars as a professional poker player) who explained, "I feel that everyone is good. In this way I give every game my best effort. The moment that you let up is the time that you can be hit by the sucker punch."

Susan: From a very young age, I decided that I didn't want to play only in women's tournaments. I wanted to test my skills against the top male players, so I signed up for those competitions. That was a shock to the old boys' club. It turned out that when men lost against me, they always had a headache or something like that. In fact, I once joked in an interview, "I have never beaten a completely healthy man!" If you sit down at the chessboard or manage your money, you need to take full responsibility for your actions. I often feel of one mind with the heroic Florence Nightingale. She said "I attribute my success to this – I never gave or took any excuse."

Helpful hints for a successful budget

♟ Use the envelope system.

1. When you have a list of all the places where you spend money, divide it into categories such as food, gas, clothing, entertainment, charity, education, etc. Take a plain, white envelope for each grouping and write the category name on it.

2. Fill each envelope with the amount of money that you will spend on that category for the month.

3. Use the envelopes to make the respective purchases. That literally means you take your food envelope with you to the grocery store. When the money is gone, you're done for the month. That's it.

4. In the beginning of the next month, empty out envelopes that might have extra and save that money.

5. Refill the envelopes for the new month.

♟ Save your receipts. As you start the process of gaining your financial freedom, you might find it daunting to watch every expenditure. However, with practice it will become a habit for you to request a receipt, even when "just" buying an ice cream at the neighborhood kiosk. If a storeowner refuses to give you a receipt (even though the law obligates him to do so), or if you forget to ask for one, record the expenditure yourself, and put the slip in with your other receipts. Then, by reviewing the numbers either weekly or monthly, you can better understand where you spend your money.

♟ Track your expenses. When you first begin a budget, keep close tabs on your spending for at least three to six months.

♟ Add details to your written budget. Make separate listings to subdivide some of your expense categories. The more exact you make your budget, the better tool it will become. You might find it difficult to cut spending in an entire category (e.g., entertainment), but if your budget is detailed you can focus on specific areas that need trimming (e.g., sporting event admissions, movies, etc.).

Use cash instead of plastic

The ubiquitous use of credit and debit cards has led today's consumers to forget about planning and saving. People love to own things, and their Visas or MasterCards have become the ticket for providing them with everything. But at some point, they have to pay for those goods, and they end up paying a lot more. Not only do they pay interest on their credit card debt, but they suffer from a phenomenon known as "credit card premium," which causes them to spend more when shopping with plastic than with cash. A Dunn & Bradstreet study found that people spend 12%-18% more when using credit cards than when using cash. And McDonald's found that the average transaction rose from $4.50 to $7 when customers used plastic instead of cash.

By using actual money, you force yourself to plan better and you regularly see the consequences of your spending habits. Unlike a credit card statement that you view once a month, you see the contents of your wallet every time you pull it out. The pain of watching your funds diminish can suffice to keep you on track and curb your impulse spending. And if all of that is not enough to convince you to try paper money instead of credit, studies now show that people who pay cash, not credit, for groceries end up selecting healthier foods. Those who used credit ended up making unplanned, impulse food choices that often included "vice products" like candy, cookies, and sugary drinks, whereas cash spenders were more likely to stick to their shopping lists.

Win with tactical finance

Most beginner and even medium-level chess players should focus their training predominantly on tactics. Tactics are the execution of the strategy, in the same way that budgeting is the implementation of the financial plan. In fact, you could substitute the words "managing money" for "chess play" and the wisdom of American Grandmaster Samuel Reshevsky would aptly apply: "No matter how much theory progresses, how radically styles change, <u>chess play</u> is inconceivable without tactics." The failure point for many players comes when they want to spend too much time on strategy, since they like the artistic side of it, but they aren't sharp or alert enough in the implementation of actual tactics. Along with this, many players work on their tactical moves but neglect to observe the movements of their opponents. Managing your income and outflow, the cornerstone of fiscal responsibility, requires you to plan each move you make very carefully, and to keep an eye on what's going on around you constantly so that you can adjust your moves accordingly.

Susan: When I was growing up, I saw a lot of chess players fail because they spent too much time on strategy. I liked both tactics and strategy, and my father always had me work on both, saying that I needed to develop a "universal" style. Although you need to have a good strategy in a game, you will never win without tactics.

PART C

How the
Pieces Move:
Stocks, Bonds,
and
Mutual Funds

CHAPTER VI

Building Your Castle
with Stocks

Fame, I have already. Now I need the money.
—Wilhelm Steinitz (World Chess Champion 1886-1894)

W hile talking about his career, the very practical chess champion Wilhelm Steinitz captured the essence of how people misunderstand stock picking. Mediocre investors often go for the glamour of buying celebrated stocks, equating fame with money. If they can brag about their portfolio of renowned equities to their friends, they'll envision themselves as being like popular money managers whose names grace the pages of *The Wall Street Journal*. Even professional investors suffer from the vice of pride, and will often buy shares of big-name companies just before reporting time. By engaging in this "window dressing," the managers can tell their constituents, "See, I also owned the hot stocks," even if they only bought them one day before the end of the quarter, when they needed to announce their holdings. Though cosmetic moves like these might make you sound like a talented investor, in the end your results will tell the whole story. This chapter is for people who don't care about the fame, but rather for those concentrating on the second part of the Steinitz quote: "Now I need the money."

Rich As A King is structured not only to present an in-depth understanding of how personal finance works, but also to serve as a practical guide with a step-by-step approach to gaining financial freedom. The first part of the book explained planning, the second part covered tactics, and this third section focuses on the specific moves you can make now. The discipline of managing your budget, discussed in the previous chapter, will hopefully allow you to put aside savings every month. Then you can start to invest that extra cash. Regardless of whether you trade your own stock portfolio or hire a manager to do it for you, know how the systems work.

You can own a business

Businesses take many different forms. You can open up a shop as a sole proprietor, deal with suppliers and customers, negotiate the rent, handle the management, accept personal liability for the business debts, and hopefully grow your enterprise and prosper. Alternatively, you can form a partnership with one or more associates and you can all share the long hours, responsibilities, and obligations and, with good luck, also succeed. But there is yet another way to gain from a thriving business without having to wipe the sweat from your brow: Look around for a well-run corporation and acquire partial ownership of it by buying its stock.

Why people buy stocks

When you acquire stock in a corporation you are, in fact, buying a piece of the company. You, just like Mark Zuckerberg, can possess a piece of Facebook (although, most probably, you would have a much smaller stake than he has), and in relation to the number of shares you own, you can cast your ballot on certain decisions, vote for members of the board of directors, and even publicly voice your opinion to the management and to your fellow shareowners if you choose to attend a shareholders' meeting. Some key advantages to buying equity in a publicly-traded company include:

- Not having any personal liability to creditors should the company fail, since the most you can lose is the amount you put in to purchase the shares,
- Knowing that if top managers leave, new leaders will replace them, and the company will continue to function (unlike what would happen with a small, private company that might go bust if the chief executives depart),

♟ Not having any management responsibilities as you would if it were your own company,

♟ Benefiting from the company's profits, either in the increase of stock price if/when you decide to sell or in the form of dividends (though this does not apply to share ownership in all companies),

♟ Being comfortable with the fact that when you wish to sell your shares, you can generally do so rapidly, and

♟ Benefiting from the oversight of bodies such as the Securities and Exchange Commission (SEC) and the Financial Industry Regulatory Authority, Inc. (FINRA).

Highest on the list of advantages, of course, is that your stock may go up in price because it moves in tandem with a strong market, because the business itself is doing particularly well, or because the market perceives that it will do well in the future.

On the other hand, while owning a portion of a company has its benefits, you have very little say in decision-making unless you hold a huge percentage of the outstanding shares. The board of directors determines policy, decides if, when, and how much you will receive in dividends, chooses the management, and decides how much shareholders will pay them from the company's coffers. To add to this, should the market falter, your company do poorly, or its products drop from public favor, the value of your holding will decrease.

Most investors buy a stock to benefit from the company's growth, not necessarily to have a voice and actively participate in the firm's management. Investors always can 'vote with their feet' and sell their shares of businesses that they believe are not well-run.

Is it worth the risk?

When you trade, the key concern is not always the value of the pieces being exchanged, but what's left on the board.
—Dan Heisman, American Chess Master and chess author

When chess masters sacrifice a piece, they intend to get a more valuable payback later on, and likewise with stocks. You sacrifice safety when you put money into the market since you might lose it... as sometimes happens. You hope that the short-term drops in the market, though upsetting, will eventually turn around and make your sacrifice pay off. If you look at the history of the stock market, investing in stocks has generally been a good bet, but as the standard Wall Street disclaimer says, "Past performance is no guarantee of future returns."

Over time, equities have delivered greater profits than most other investments. Just look at the long-term returns of the Standard & Poor's 500 and see that over the past twenty years or so, people who invested in stocks averaged about 9% per year (including dividends).[7] In order to have actually achieved this result, though, they had to have kept their money in the market the whole time, which is rare. Most folks, whether to pay for certain expenses or whether they got cold feet when the market tumbled, did not stay consistently invested throughout those decades. In fact, if they were unlucky, sold out their position for a short time, and missed the ten best days that the market performed over that twenty-year span, their average return dropped to about 5%. Since no one can predict market movements (in either direction), investors should not try to time when to enter and when to exit. Those who missed the thirty best days of the market during that period, instead of making about 9% per year, made less than 1%.

---

7   http://dqydj.net/sp-500-return-calculator/ as of February 2014. Past performance is no guarantee of future returns.

How to become a market grandmaster

If you take away nothing else from this book, remember this critical rule: grandmasters stick to their plans. And you should, too. Many Wall Street studies have demonstrated that when people invest in mutual funds, the funds themselves do fine, but the investors do much worse. How can that be? The individual investors, feeling the need to chase market performance, buy and sell the funds at inopportune moments. A Dalbar, Inc. study[8] showed that over a recent twenty-year period, when the S&P 500 Index averaged 9.14%, the average equity fund investor earned only 3.83%. People pouring money into the market during "bull" markets (when the market goes up) and pulling it out during "bear" markets (when the market drops) caused this huge discrepancy.

Many investors have a self-destructive tendency to overreact to news, whether good or bad. By the time they buy into a bull market, they've already missed much of the appreciation. And when they sell out, they often only do so after the drop. If you're going to get involved in stocks, train yourself to choose a strategy and stick with it. This, of course, does not mean buying a stock and thereafter ignoring it. Times change. Industries change. Sometimes it is necessary to update your portfolio. But act with caution. With your money on the line, before you do

---

8   2013 Quantitative Analysis of Investor Behavior, Dalbar, Inc., April 2013

anything, think of the three considerations that a chess professional employs prior to making a move:

- ♟ **Ignore the noise.** Don't allow *kibitzers* (the fans who watch chess matches and whisper their ideas to one another – sometimes loudly enough for the players to hear, too), family, friends, or your own nerves to second-guess you. Regularly confirm the soundness of your strategy, and then don't let yourself get distracted by anything else.
- ♟ **The system works.** Chess masters constantly follow the known, standard moves in the game for one reason: they work. Likewise, the model of buying quality stocks and funds and holding onto them for the long term has produced many millionaires. Will it work 100% of the time? Probably not. But buy-and-hold will most likely succeed much more often than trading stocks rapidly.
- ♟ **Stay cool.** Don't go for quick moves, and don't keep changing your strategy. Jot down this quote from Nobel Prize winning economist Gene Fama Jr., and the next time you want to follow the herd, read it: "Your money is like soap. The more you handle it, the less you'll have."

What types of stocks to buy

On the professional circuit, chess players participate in any one of a number of different tournament styles with names like "knockout," "round robin," or "Swiss." They may favor certain systems, but they must feel comfortable in all types of competitions. In the stock market, too, you might choose to buy individual stocks in sectors that you understand (it's no surprise that doctors frequently buy shares of pharmaceutical companies), but you also need exposure to other parts of the market in order to diversify properly. To get a listing of the "12 major market sectors" along with "Size matters: large, medium, or small-cap companies," go to www.RichAsAKing.com/bonus.

Common or preferred stocks

In considering stock ownership in a company, most people buy "common stock" with its potential for growth (or decline).

Investors buy preferred stocks, on the other hand, when they want to own shares in the firm and receive quarterly income, assume less risk, and don't mind not having voting rights. Companies issue preferred stocks with fixed dividends and pay this amount regularly out of earnings or other corporate sources. In contrast, with regard to common stock shares, the board of directors may choose to change or completely eliminate the dividends. If the company still has additional earnings available after fully paying the preferred shareholders, the board may then declare a dividend payout for common shareholders. Common shareholders will not receive any dividends until all the preferred shareholders have received their complete due.

In the event of bankruptcy, liquidators must pay bondholders and preferred stockholders completely before paying anything to the common shareholders. Regardless of the preference that preferred shares receive (over common shares) in the event of liquidation, they still have market risk, which means that depending on various circumstances in the market, they could go down in price.

Why you need overseas investments

Most countries offer investors the chance to participate in their nation's corporate growth through their stock markets. Since the United States represents only about half the world's market capitalization, it often pays to investigate foreign investment opportunities. For those worried about the perils of overseas investments, consider that in different countries growth rates, politics, currency values, and general economic conditions may differ, and because of this, the upturns in certain national markets can help mitigate the downturns in others. By incorporating geographic diversity into your portfolio, you distribute the risk factor over a wider investment landscape. Also, the United States stock market has never topped the "best performance" charts in any year, so investing beyond its shores opens up the potential for greater profits.

American Depository Receipts (ADRs)

If you want to participate in international investing, but do not wish to deal with foreign stock exchanges, consider purchasing American Depository Receipts (ADRs). An ADR is a negotiable certificate issued by an American bank that holds the underlying shares of a foreign corporation. ADRs represent indirect ownership of a given number of shares in foreign companies, such as Royal Dutch Shell Plc. (United Kingdom), TOTAL S.A. (France), Banco Santander, S.A. (Spain), Baidu (China), Magyar Telekom (Hungary), and Teva Pharmaceuticals (Israel). ADRs provide a convenient way to acquire global market exposure without the inconvenience and added expenses frequently associated with trading on foreign exchanges (e.g., foreign brokerage commissions, language differences, currency exchange fees, etc.). Because ADRs trade in dollars, and since they also pay dividends in dollars, currency changes between the dollar and the native currency of the underlying stock can create unexpected swings in the price of the ADR.

The easiest way to own lots of real estate

Many wish to enter the real estate market, but lack the time, money, or experience to oversee such an investment properly. If you are among this group, you may want to consider using Real Estate Investment Trusts (REITs). A REIT (pronounced *reet*) is a business that accumulates money through an Initial Public Offering (IPO), a secondary offering, or through the issuance of bonds. With the cash raised, professional real estate managers buy and develop specific properties. The company receives management fees and rental income from its assorted holdings, and over time it may sell the assets for a profit or loss. Some management groups have particular expertise in selecting and running niche property classifications, such as nursing homes, shopping malls, office buildings, warehouses, or residential complexes. Others focus on certain geographic areas that they believe have the greatest potential for gain. Hundreds of REITs trade on the American stock markets and represent hundreds of billions of dollars' worth of real estate.

Foreign countries have REITS, too. You can buy shares in a REIT in the same way that you would purchase any other stock – either as an IPO or as a purchase on an exchange. Whether you buy a domestic or foreign REIT, your profits, in the form of capital gains or dividends, will flow through to you from the income generated by renting, leasing, or selling properties.

With a traditional REIT, you essentially own a physical asset with rights to the income and profits that it produces. Regardless of whether you actually make any money, you can feel that the underlying physical assets provide a form of safety net.

Why not buy a property, rent it out, and collect rent?

One advantage of owning a REIT rather than holding one or two specific properties and renting them out yourself is that owning a REIT diversifies the real estate portion of your portfolio. Additionally, you don't need to start with the huge sums of money normally required to spread out the risk adequately over several properties. If you tried to mimic a professionally managed REIT, you would need to spend tremendous amounts of time and money to set up and maintain the program; and when you wanted to liquidate the portfolio or make new purchases, you would have to enter the challenging world of property agents, lawyers, banks, and competing real estate moguls. Buying or selling a REIT, on the other hand, simply entails calling your broker and placing the order. Moreover, consider whether you have the emotional endurance to manage a property as a landlord – collecting rent, fixing appliances, buying insurance, negotiating contracts, and possibly evicting tenants.

How do you choose a good REIT?

Though some mutual funds and money managers specialize in REIT portfolios, you may prefer to select the REITs yourself. If so, consider the following three points:

- ♟ **Management**: Confirm that the management team has experience in the type of real estate in their trust. Do they have a track record? How are they compensated? The long-term profitability of the investment relies on this team, so make sure they have the ability to excel.

- ♟ **Diversification**: Different sectors of the real estate market move at different times. Say the economy drops. Consumers will cut back on their mall walking, causing stores to shut down. As a result, shopping malls might suffer from less rental income. On the other hand, income from residential properties might prosper since those same consumers might need to rent homes if they can't afford to buy. If you purchase only one REIT, look for one with a diversified portfolio. However, if you put together a set of various REITs, you can select ones with different specializations.

- ♟ **Earnings**: Careful review of a REIT's balance sheet can protect you from falling into some common traps. For instance, when a property depreciates, that lower figure gets included in the regular income numbers; it could appear as if the company is losing money even though the monthly rental income remains steady. Examine the Funds From Operations (FFO) and Cash Available for Distribution (CAD) statistics that measure the amount of money available to the investors. When considering REITs, professionals usually look at the FFO in place of the EPS (Earnings Per Share) that they normally study for their other stock purchases. The FFO and CAD can generally give a better sense of cash flow from operations, which can ultimately translate into higher or more secure dividends.

Mortgage REITs

One type of REIT, called a "mortgage REIT," or "mREIT," does not actually own properties. Instead, this traditionally high-yielding entity trades real estate-secured loans. In essence, mREITs are finance companies, not real estate firms. As such, evaluating their books requires a different set of glasses. To make a straight real estate play, make sure you buy a traditional REIT, also known as an "equity REIT," and not a mortgage REIT.

Should you buy commodities?

Imagine trying to play a game of chess with no board, no pieces, no timer, no table, and no chair. Those five elements are the prerequisites to starting a game. In the financial world, too, without wheat, corn, iron, oil, and copper, what kind of economy would you expect to find? Commodities represent basic goods that the industrialized and also the non-industrialized world require. Years ago, trading commodities required specialized licenses, high-level training, and huge amounts of money. In today's market, though, using "exchange traded funds," (ETFs) which are types of mutual funds that trade on the stock exchange, you can buy and sell most major commodities as easily as you trade any stock, betting on either the upside or the downside. Though commodities engender substantial risks, since items like gold and oil can fluctuate wildly depending on political and economic influences, the potential for profit and diversification can make these investments a suitable part of a growth portfolio.

Growth or income?

Some corporations offer investors enhanced growth opportunities, while others provide their shareholders with streams of dividend income. Buyers can determine if they would like to focus on either of these two choices or opt for stocks that offer some of both.

Growth companies seek to expand their businesses through vigorous research, production, and marketing, and sometimes by merging with or acquiring other companies. Expect a growth company to use its earnings to further these goals. Growth investors forgo receiving current dividend income in the hope that the company's policy of investing in itself will pay off with greater future profits.

If you require current income from your stocks, you may want to consider a stable, less aggressive corporation – such as a utility company – that pays its shareholders quarterly dividends. You can find dividend payers in other sectors too, such as pharmaceuticals, telecommunications, or energy. Though companies do not guarantee to pay dividends, if they do well, you can reasonably expect their dividends to continue and perhaps even rise over time. A rising dividend can indicate a strong and optimistic management and a solid market share with consistent cash flow, so watch for a corresponding increase in the share price, too. As Peter Lynch, the former manager of Fidelity's Magellan Fund said, "The dividend is such an important factor in the success of many stocks that you could hardly go wrong by making an entire portfolio of companies that have raised their dividends for ten or twenty years in a row." Conversely, a company sometimes lacks the strength to maintain the dividend, and management cuts it. This generally causes the stock price to drop.

Those who want both growth and income often purchase older, well-established corporations that have steady earnings that they share with their stockholders. Shareholders of these companies anticipate slow and steady growth, combined with the distribution of revenue.

Limiting the volatility of your stocks

Don't fall for the myth of "safe stocks." No one can regularly identify risk-free investments, nor can they – or you – handpick on a consistent basis "conservative" equities that won't drop in price. The moment you sit down at a chess match, you will engage in some fighting, take some losses, and hopefully make some gains. If you invest money in stocks, don't expect a smooth ride either, no matter which market segments you choose, what dividends you anticipate, or how much preparation you have done. On the other hand, don't let the fear of unpredictability discourage you from investing. After all, whether you look at Warren Buffett or George Soros, John Paulson or Jim Rogers, all of whom made billions in the stock market, or whether you just consider the millions of people more like yourself who built up their retirement nest eggs by carefully buying and holding equities, you too can get into the game. You just need to maintain a long-term perspective, diversify your portfolio, set up and carefully guide your players, and then prepare yourself for a tough match.

CHAPTER VII

Strengthening Your Position with Bonds

Bonds often fit the bill for the less aggressive portion of a portfolio. Bonds derive their safety from the fact that their issuers (companies or governments) borrow money from investors and they must repay the loan on the "maturity date." While you keep your money in bonds, you receive a steady stream of interest payments, normally distributed every six months. When you hear people talk about "living off their investments," chances are they own a portfolio of bonds, also referred to as "fixed-income" or "debt" securities. Unlike stockholders, who actually own and participate in shareholder decisions, bond buyers simply lend a sum of money, receive a specified interest payment on a set schedule, and don't have a say in the way the company conducts its business.

How bonds are issued, traded, and priced

When corporations, municipalities, and national governments decide to raise money through the issuing of bonds, they generally begin by looking for suitable underwriters. An underwriter, often called an investment bank, agrees to purchase and then distribute the new issues to the public. Banking firms, anxious to get this business (and the large fees that go along with it), bid to determine who can assure the issuer that it will get the amount of money it requires at the lowest interest rate. The investment firm that wins the tender then sells the bonds to brokerage firms, other institutions, and individual investors.

Once the underwriters have sold the bonds, a secondary market develops. Some bond trades happen on an exchange like the New York Stock Exchange, and others occur in the over-the-counter markets. When investors call their broker to buy a bond, the broker searches bond inventories or goes into the market to get an offering that meets the required specifications at the best available price. Once bonds, or any security for that matter, trade in a "secondary market," the original issuer no longer benefits from the money that passes hands. For example, if ABC Company raises $100 million from a bond offering, it has that money and uses it. ABC no longer cares if one bond buyer sells some of those bonds to a different player in the market, since the price of that transaction will not affect ABC's financial situation.

Considerations in buying bonds

Do bond buyers lend their money in the hope of making a capital gain? Generally not. The majority of bond buyers, especially retirees or those nearing that stage, seek a steady, reliable source of income as a supplement to their pensions. They normally hold bonds until maturity. However, should they need to raise funds before then, they can sell their positions. The marketability of "debentures," as investors sometimes call corporate bonds, and the sense of security investors feel from knowing that companies must pay off bondholders' claims before giving anything to stockholders, add to the desirability of these investments. Bonds share many characteristics with pawns on the chess board; both are considered the slow, steady, and predictable parts of the portfolios.

But bonds aren't *always* stable. Some bond traders buy and sell fixed-income securities, focusing more on short-term profits than on long-term income. They consider interest rate movements and ongoing events that affect the debt instrument's current price as they make their choices. Some of these market participants, especially the more risk-oriented ones, also keep a trading eye on weak or failing companies whose stock and bond prices have plummeted. Along the same lines, they scrutinize troubled municipalities in the hope of picking up some good buys. In the aftermath of the economic turmoil in California, for example, several cities and towns declared bankruptcy. That created some interesting – if not risky – trading opportunities for Wall Street's bond desks. Similarly, even with the traditionally conservative pawns on a chessboard, expert players occasionally employ them as fighters.

U.S. government bonds: Why lend to Uncle Sam?

Backed by the full faith and credit of the government – and its power to tax its citizens to fulfill its debt obligations, U.S. government bonds offer buyers maximum security. Investors around the world buy these bonds since they feel that short of a global catastrophe, nothing could endanger their funds. Both institutional and private investors participate actively in the multi-trillion dollar "Treasury" market despite the fact that the yields compare unfavorably with the somewhat riskier corporate securities. Americans who own U.S. government debt not only benefit from the safety of the bonds, but also from certain tax benefits, since they don't have to pay state or local tax on the interest they earn.

The benefit of municipal bonds

U.S. states, cities, towns, villages, and various authorities (such as housing, transportation, or power supply) issue municipal bonds ("munis") when they need to raise money. They use the principal they collect to support ongoing state and local expenses and to help finance specific projects, such as establishing a hospital, building a school, constructing a new bridge, or erecting a barrier to hold back rising waters during a hurricane.

High-tax-bracket American bond buyers often choose municipal bond offerings because munis provide double, and often triple tax-free interest payments exempt from federal, state, and local taxes. You benefit from all three breaks if you live in the locale of the bond's issuance. For example, Manhattan residents might get a New York City municipal bond and pay no tax whatsoever on the interest payments they receive. (However, although you may not owe tax on the interest, you still must include the amount on your Form 1040 when filing income tax returns.) On the other hand, if you buy an out-of-state municipal bond, you will most likely pay your own state tax on the interest you receive because the states generally do not give a benefit when you buy a municipal bond issued elsewhere.

Traditionally municipal bonds offer a lower yield than comparable corporate bonds, since they have the "sweetener" of being tax-free. But if your tax situation is such that you don't get a chance to take advantage of the tax-free benefits, your portfolio might benefit from holding taxable, higher yielding bonds.

Three instances when munis can affect your tax bill

⚖ In some cases, you may have to pay the alternative minimum tax (AMT) on your municipal bond interest. Specifically, "private activity bonds," like those issued to fund the building of stadiums, hospitals, and the like, often don't enjoy the same status as traditional municipal bonds. If you own these bonds and must pay AMT, you could shell out 26% to 28% of the interest you earn... hardly tax free. When you buy munis, therefore, ask the broker to confirm whether your bonds fall into the category of private activity bonds. If so, simply choose different ones to buy.

⚖ A stealth tax can creep into your Form 1040 if you buy munis and collect Social Security. Though you don't pay tax on the actual interest from the bonds, the IRS considers that income part of your "modified adjusted gross income" (MAGI). They look at MAGI to determine how much tax to take from your Social Security payments. In fact, if you earn too much money... and we're not talking a lot, only about $25,000 and up for a single filer... you might owe tax on up to 85% of your Social Security benefits.

⚖ Though you generally pay no tax on the *interest payments* you receive, if you buy a muni and later sell it for a profit, or if you simply purchase the bond below face value and wait for maturity when you receive the full value, the IRS will consider that growth a *capital gain*, and you will have to pay tax on it just like on any other taxable investment. Along the same lines, you will owe capital gains tax on profits that your municipal bond mutual fund generates through its buying and selling.

Zero-coupon bonds

Do you ever look to the future and wonder how you will pay your toddlers' college bills, or how you will cover their distant wedding costs, or what will happen when your own retirement expenses begin? Perhaps you appreciate certain benefits of bonds, like their relative safety compared with stocks, but you don't need semiannual interest payments now to supplement your salary, nor do you even want to receive the interest payments because you know the temptation to spend them might beat out the good sense to reinvest them. The answer to these problems might just be zero-coupon bonds.

How do zero-coupon bonds work?

You purchase zeros at a deep discount to the face value, called "original issue discount" or "OID," and watch them grow based on a specified yield. For example, if you buy zero coupon Treasuries yielding about 3% and put down $5,500, you can look forward to getting back $10,000 in twenty years. Throughout the lifetime of the investment, you don't actually receive any income payments. Rather, the imputed interest automatically reinvests into the same bond, thus compounding your returns. Even though the issuer pays you zero every year (hence the name), they track the appreciation as if you had actually gotten the income and reinvested it immediately. Will you have to pay U.S. capital gains tax when you redeem your holding? No. Instead, you pay tax on a yearly basis on your "phantom income." Since your income remains in the bond yet you still must pay tax, you might choose to buy zeros in tax-deferred accounts such as IRAs (Individual Retirement Accounts). Otherwise, you'll find yourself in a negative cash flow position: no inflows from the bond, but outflows from your pocket on a yearly basis to cover the annual taxes.

What's the right price?

Most bonds have a par value (also called "face value") of $1,000, although some have denominations of $5,000 or $10,000. The interest rate, called the "coupon rate," refers to the yearly payment the issuer will make to the holder, so a $1,000 "4.5%" bond yields $45 interest to the bond owner every year.

Wall Street traders quote bond prices as a percentage of face value. Thus, a $1,000 face-value bond with a 5% coupon quoted at 94 means the price is 94% of $1,000, or $940. If you bought one bond, you would pay $940, receive $50 per year interest (that's 5% of $1,000), and on the maturity date, you would receive $1,000. Similarly, a bond quoted at 120 with a 10% coupon would cost $1,200 (which is 120% of $1,000) and pay a $100 coupon every year (10% of $1,000 = $100). The bond's issuer pays interest based on the coupon and the face value of the bond, not on the purchase or current market price.

Why would an investor pay $1,200 for a bond when he knows he will only get back $1,000 at maturity? Suppose that the seller bought this bond many years ago and got 10% interest. Each year, he received $100 in payments ($1,000 × 10%).

Now he needs money and wants to sell it. He looks around and sees that interest rates are down, and bonds such as his only pay 4%, which provides only $40 in annual payments to owners. He, of course, would want to get much more than par value for his higher-yielding bond and you, if you were the buyer and saw how large the yearly payments would be, might be willing to pay much more than the $1,000 face value.

Take the opposite scenario: You bought a 5% bond for $1,000 that paid $50 interest each year. Two years later, when the market rate on similar bonds has increased to 6%, you find it necessary to sell. If you tried to get back your $1,000, nobody would offer to buy it from you. Why should they, when they could buy other bonds paying 6%? Without some type of adjustment on your part, your bond would lack resale value. The only incentive someone would have to buy your lower-yielding bond would be if you agreed to sell it at a discount. Thus, you would need to lower your asking price from $1,000 in order to compete with the market.

Trading with interest (accrued interest)

What happens if you want to sell your bond before your next semiannual payment is due? Perhaps you've owned it for three months since your last payment. Are you entitled to three months' worth of the interest? Yes. The new buyer must compensate you, the seller, for the portion of the interest accrued while you owned the bond. Thus, at the time of purchase, the buyer will pay you the cost of the bond plus the appropriate amount of "accrued interest" owed. When the upcoming interest payment comes in, however, the new owner will see a credit for the entire six-month amount. (Normally, this sum is directly deposited into the brokerage account where the bond is held.)

Understanding bond yields

- ♟ **Coupon rate**. When a bond is issued, the interest that the bond will pay – the coupon rate – is clearly stated. For example, a $1,000 bond with a coupon rate of 6% will pay the owner $60 annually.
- ♟ **Current yield**. As long as the price of the bond remains at $1,000, the current yield will be the same as the coupon rate which, as in the above example, is 6%. However, if you buy a 6% coupon bond and pay $1,200, your current yield will be only 5% (which is the $60 coupon divided by the bond price of $1,200).

♟ **Yield to maturity (YTM).** If you buy bonds on the secondary market, find out the "yield to maturity" in order to understand your overall return. The YTM takes into account the amount paid for the bond (whether more or less than the face value), the coupon rate, and the number of years remaining until maturity, when you will get back the face value (par). Thus, if you paid $100 over par or $50 below par, for example, the YTM formula incorporates this information. Given the complexity of yield-to-maturity calculations, bond traders use bond calculators to get an accurate reading. Before making a bond purchase, check with your advisor, or use a bond calculator. If you wish to access a free bond calculator, go to www. RichAsAKing.com/tools.

♟ **Yield to call (YTC).** Many bond issuers include a "call provision" when offering new bonds. Callable bonds give the issuer the right to redeem the bond prior to its maturity date. Why would an issuer want to do that? Let's say a corporation needed $10 million. To get the necessary cash, the company issued 8% callable bonds. If interest rates stayed in the neighborhood of 8% or higher, the corporation would do nothing, except continue to pay semiannual interest. But what if interest rates in the marketplace dropped, and the issuer could refinance the debt and pay only 5%? At this point the corporation would probably call the bonds. They would pay the owners par (or sometimes more than par if that was in the original call stipulation), and reissue new bonds, swapping the 8% payments for 5% ones, similar to refinancing your home mortgage or swapping a pawn for a better piece. Including a call feature on a bond gives an issuer more flexibility, even though it generally must offer a slightly higher yield in order to entice investors to buy. Buyers get the enhanced yield for agreeing to accept the call risk – if interest rates drop they will receive their principal back prematurely. Then, if they wish to reinvest, they will have to buy a bond offering a lower yield.

Callable features vary, but most callable bonds include a condition that prohibits the issuer from calling the bond until a certain amount of time, such as a year or more, has elapsed. This period is known as "call protection." Whenever buying a callable bond, consider the very real possibility that you may only receive the attractive coupon for a short time. If that happens, and you reinvest at a lower rate, your overall return may be much less than if you had originally bought a non-callable bond that offered a slightly lower yield. You can calculate the yield to call in the same manner as the yield to maturity, but instead of using the maturity date as the end date of the investment, use the call date. Check it out and then decide if you would be satisfied with this yield if your bond were actually called.

Premium bonds: What makes them so valuable?

A premium bond is one that you buy on the secondary market for more than par value ($1,000). Why would you pay more than $1,000 if you know you're only going to get back $1,000? Find out at www.RichAsAKing.com/bonus.

Secure or not? Check the rating.

A common question you'll hear when two chess players first meet is, "What's your rating?" Using the Elo scale that measures the skill level of every player, you can get a pretty good sense of how a particular competitor will perform in a tournament. Is it always accurate? No. But it's pretty close – like bond ratings.

Some bonds offer outstanding security; others do not. All bond issuers run the risk of failing to make their periodic interest payments, or worse, defaulting on their debts and not paying some or all of the bond's principal upon maturity. Investigate the issuer's reputation, financial integrity, and future prospects for success before purchasing a bond. A high-yielding bond may cause you to sit up and take notice, but it could turn into a poor investment if the issuer runs out of money before it returns your principal to you.

How can you interpret a company's fiscal situation? Bond investors consult the ratings published by some of the major independent rating services such as Standard & Poor's and Moody's. These services measure the probability that an issuer will pay back the principal upon maturity and make timely interest payouts. They base their ratings on the issuer's existing debt, stability of cash flow, asset protection, management ability, and perceived capability to meet obligations. They also caution investors against using their ratings as a recommendation to buy, hold, or sell any specific security. Nonetheless, when the rating agencies change their opinion by upgrading or downgrading a bond issuer, the prices of the securities usually change accordingly.

Bonds with higher ratings normally offer lower interest rates, and issuers can generally borrow money relatively cheaply. Lower-rated bonds, sometimes called "junk bonds," pay richer yields, commensurate with their higher risk. Issuers of these bonds often require cash more desperately than their higher-rated peers, and they must offer higher yields in order to attract investors.

The table below outlines the grading system for bonds. In order to further clarify the ratings, Standard & Poor's sometimes adds a plus or minus sign to indicate that a bond falls at the top or bottom of its category. Likewise, Moody's sometimes adds a "1" after the grade to show that the bond is at the top of its category.

Junk bonds (a.k.a. high-yield bonds)

As you can see on the table, bonds get progressively more risky and more liable to default the farther down the scale they go. For this reason, the issuers of speculative-grade rated obligations know that they must offer unusually high returns in order to entice potential buyers. Similarly, the current owners of bonds issued by corporations that have fallen on hard times may find their ratings have dropped to B, C, or D. When this happens, these bondholders can keep their bonds and hope the issuers do not default or skip interest payments. Or, they can try to sell their bonds on the secondary market at a price well below par. At such a price, the daring new buyers will be getting very high yields as compensation for taking on these risks.

QUALITY	S&P	Moody's	Description
High grade	AAA	Aaa	Bonds judged to be of the highest quality. They carry the smallest degree of investment risk. Interest payments are protected by a large, stable margin. Extremely strong capacity to meet financial commitments.
Medium high grade	AA	Aa	Bonds that are judged to be of high quality by all standards. They are rated lower than the best bonds because margins of protection may not be as large. AAA and AA bonds are referred to as "high grade."
Medium grade	A	A	Bonds that have a strong capacity to meet financial commitments, but are somewhat susceptible to adverse economic conditions and changes in circumstances.

Lower medium grade	BBB	Baa	Bonds that are considered as medium-grade obligations – they are neither highly protected nor poorly secured.
Speculative grade	BB	Ba	Bonds that have speculative elements. Protection of principal and interest may be moderate. Less vulnerable in the near-term but face major ongoing uncertainties due to adverse business, financial, and economic conditions.
Highly speculative	B	B	Bonds that are vulnerable to adverse business, financial, and economic conditions but currently have the capacity to meet financial commitments.
Default	CCC	Caa	Bonds of poor standing. These issues may be in default or there may be elements of danger present with respect to principal and interest.
Default	CC	Ca	Bonds whose obligations are speculative to a high degree. These issues are often in default.
Default	C	C	Lowest rated class in Moody's list. S&P uses C to indicate currently highly vulnerable obligations.
Default	D		Bonds that defaulted on financial commitments.

What is junk worth?

Four main variables shape the motion of the junk bond market niche: default rates, economic strength, the direction of interest rates, and bank lending conditions. Bond players on the institutional level keep an eye both on the average default rate and on the average recovery rate. They know that unlike stocks, where you lose all your money if the company goes under, junk bonds can still repay after a default. In fact, on average, junk bonds have paid back approximately forty to fifty cents on the dollar after they've recovered from defaults.

Economic strength, the direction of interest rates, and bank lending conditions affect all bonds, but the junk bond market magnifies their impact. As the economy improves, buyers may race out to buy more junk bonds than other types of bonds because they believe the lower-rated companies can recover more strongly. Similarly, the up-and-down moves in interest rates and the ever-changing availability of credit from banks can also sway the sensitive and volatile junk bond market.

Retail investors should avoid holding large positions in individual junk bonds. Conveniently, though, many mutual funds and money managers specialize in this area. In selecting a specific fund, find one with enough assets under management to diversify broadly and whose managers have the experience to understand and navigate through this turbulent market.

Given the apparent risk of the junk bond market – they're called "junk" for a reason – should you seriously consider buying them for your portfolio? Sometimes taking an assertive stance in portfolio design fits well into your financial plan, and when you're looking for an asset class that can give you that extra push, junk bonds may fit the bill.

Susan: At times a player needs to play aggressively. Too passive an approach might mean sure defeat. For example, when I went head to head with Maia Chiburdanidze in the 2004 Olympiad, I came out of my corner fighting. In my fourth move, I already moved my queen into play, something you don't often see so early in the game. Then, in move fifteen, I sacrificed my queen so that by move twenty, I'd have a strong material advantage. Then I played carefully, watching my step with every move, until she finally resigned. Had I not started out the match with such a forceful position, I'm not sure the conclusion would have been so positive for me. It paid to take the risk.

"Put junk in the garbage. I want the safety of CDs!"

Grandmasters know that although bravery at the board may pay off, most of the time they'll look for more of a "sure thing." In fact, their moves will generally resemble high-quality bonds rather than junk. As an example, in a tight situation, they'll propose a draw rather than stretch for the win because the security of getting half a point in a tournament could help them more than the possibility of losing a whole point. Don't let anyone try to convince you that becoming a grandmaster of investing demands extremely aggressive tactics. It doesn't.

As such, if high-risk bonds don't sit well with your safety-oriented personality, or if your current financial position calls for a more conservative portfolio, consider buying bank certificates of deposit (CDs). Similar to corporate and government bonds, CDs pay a stipulated interest and they mature at a specified time. The U.S. government backs banks through the Federal Deposit Insurance Corporation (FDIC), giving you up to $250,000 of protection per institution where you have made deposits. You can check with the bank, or go to the FDIC's website (www. FDIC.gov) to confirm your bank's membership.

Investors have a choice of buying CDs directly at U.S. banks or through brokerage firms. In either case, buyers' main concerns most often center on the length of maturity and the interest rate. When brokerage firms handle CDs, they generally buy a large quantity and negotiate a favorable rate with the issuing bank. Then, they offer these CDs, usually in $1,000 units, to clients. Should you, as a client, want to sell part, or all, of your holding prior to maturity, you will not pay a penalty. Instead the broker will sell the CD units and depending on the going interest rate, you might get more (if current rates are lower than your CD is paying), or less (if rates have risen since the CD was issued) than you originally paid.

If you may need to cash out part of your CD investment before maturity, consider making the original purchase through your brokerage account instead of directly at the bank. Let's say you made a $25,000 brokerage investment in $1,000 units and soon thereafter needed $3,000 for a personal expense. You could sell off just $3,000 worth of CDs and still keep the remaining $22,000 until maturity. If you have an attractive rate on the CD compared to current interest rates, you can continue to enjoy the high rate on your remaining holdings.

If you buy your CD directly at a bank and wish to withdraw the money early, however, you will most likely pay an early withdrawal penalty, often amounting to the equivalent of three to six months of interest, and perhaps more for longer-term CDs. Also, banks often automatically renew CDs at maturity for a matching period at the new current rate unless you contact the bank and give them different orders. For example, if you buy a twelve-month 4.5% CD and a year later the rates drop to 3% for a one-year CD, you will get 3% on the rollover if you do nothing – even if the bank is featuring a 5% twenty-four-month CD at that time. Check with a bank salesperson before you buy, as the rules at different banks vary.

In recent years, banks have added new features to CDs. Now you can buy variable rate CDs, inflation-linked CDs, callable CDs, and even CDs that have a "death put" that allows an heir to cash it in at full value before maturity should the owner die. (You can purchase them directly in your brokerage account and still benefit from FDIC coverage (Federal Deposit Insurance Corporation) in the event the underlying bank defaults.)

Bond ladders

If you carefully design your bond portfolio, you can easily follow the classic "buy and hold" investment approach. Just as grandmasters don't have to reevaluate every piece on the board at every turn, if you set up a quality bond portfolio, you can relax a little bit, too.

Imagine your bonds as if they were a "locked-in pawn structure," wherein a series of pawns in the middle of the board each protects the other and none can move because the opponent has his pawns blocking the way. Though not necessarily a fighting stance, a chain of pawns is predictable (like bonds), not likely to change much (like bonds), and defensive (like bonds).

Why build a bond ladder?

Let's say you intend to invest $100,000 in a five-year bond paying 6%. You want to enjoy a steady stream of $6,000 yearly income, and in five years roll the bond over again for another five years. However, if interest rates are down in five years, for example to 4%, you would find your yearly income at that point dropping from $6,000 to $4,000.

By laddering your bond portfolio, instead of buying one large bond, select five $20,000 bonds with successive maturities of one, two, three, four, and five years. When the one-year $20,000 bond comes due, you can reinvest the principal in a five-year bond at the prevailing interest rate. Since at that point in time all of the bonds have advanced one year up the maturity ladder, the five-year position has been vacated and is ready to accept this new investment. Similarly, the following year you do the same with the original two-year bond, and so on. Generally, longer-term bonds pay higher yields than do shorter-term ones, and by following this rotating pattern, your replacement bonds can each be purchased on an attractive five-year yield basis. That's the first investment advantage.

The second advantage of this fixed-income strategy is that the ladder can potentially serve as a type of hedge against adverse moves in interest rates. For example, if you were to invest the whole $100,000 in a five-year bond and if interest rates were to drop around the time of maturity, you would have little alternative but to invest your entire sum at the lower rate. You could, however, mitigate this "reinvestment risk" by breaking up the original investment into smaller units and diversifying over time. In other words, if only one-fifth of your principal came due and you only needed to invest $20,000 at the new low rate, you would still benefit from owning some higher-yielding five-year bonds on your ladder. Conversely, if interest rates were to rise while you followed the bond laddering approach, you would get to invest at ever-increasing interest rates.

The parts of a ladder

In customizing your bond ladder, consider the three important sections:

- ♟ **Rungs**. Calculate the total amount of money you want to place in bonds and divide it over the number of years you wish to invest. That number tells you the total number of bonds, or rungs, on your ladder.
- ♟ **Height of the ladder**. Depending on your needs, you could have a short ladder, using fixed-income investments that mature every few months, to a very tall ladder, which reaches the longer-term bonds, hopefully giving you a strong cash flow and higher yields.
- ♟ **Materials**. Some people buy wooden ladders, and others go for aluminum. Your bond ladder can consist of corporate bonds, Treasuries, CDs,

municipal bonds, and other fixed-income securities, all of which have different strengths and weaknesses.

Chapter VIII

Mutual Funds: Let An Investment Grandmaster Manage Your Portfolio

A
s chess wizard and subject of the film *Searching for Bobby Fischer*, Josh Waitzkin noted in *The Art of Learning*, "the real challenge is to stay in range of [your] long-term perspective when you are under fire and hurting in the middle of the war." Whether playing chess, investing your money, or competing in world championship martial arts contests (as Waitzkin now does), the pressure can be intense. Can you always keep the big picture in mind when the daily grind constantly strikes at you? Since even black belts find it challenging to focus when under attack, think how much more difficult it is to focus with stress from work, volatile markets, and seemingly endless bills. Can you really concentrate on making daily investment decisions? Let mutual funds handle your money when you feel pressured by life and the markets.

What are mutual funds?
In a mutual fund, investors pool their money in order to gain ownership of a wide selection of stocks, bonds, or other securities. The fund itself operates as a single large account managed by a team of professionals. Investors, holding

shares of such a fund in regular brokerage accounts or in tax-deferred accounts (such as IRAs or variable annuities), own a proportional amount of every security in the portfolio.

Do you agree with this quote of ultra-wealthy industrialist Andrew Carnegie? "The way to become rich is to put all your eggs in one basket and then watch that basket." That approach worked for him. But what if you choose the wrong basket, forget to watch it one day, or if your eggs just never hatch? In fact, when dealing with your own hard-earned savings, spreading out the risk makes the most sense.

Why would you want to invest in a mutual fund and lose the ability to choose the holdings you like? Moreover, why would you willingly agree to take on the various management costs? What added value do you get from holding securities through the fund rather than on your own? Start to answer these questions by asking yourself: Do you have the time, experience, and knowledge to analyze and track a stock? Those who cannot confidently answer "yes" to all three parts of the question generally prefer to partake in the multi-trillion dollar mutual fund market. They choose to have a well-designed portfolio handled by an investment grandmaster from the moment they make their first move.

The openings of most high-level chess matches include a series of standard steps. The positions that appear on the board as a result of those moves usually set up the players with all of their basic strategic needs: controlling the center, castling, and developing their back pieces. Similarly, investing through a mutual fund will set up a logical opening for your financial purchases, as well as an ongoing monitoring of your holdings.

Seven reasons to buy mutual funds

Save time and lower your stress level. If you don't want to worry about which individual stocks to buy, when to buy them, and what criteria to use in deciding when to sell, consider the benefits of mutual funds:

1. **Diversification.** Although diversification helps to minimize risk, most people find it impractical to own hundreds – or even dozens – of individual issues. Notwithstanding the large outlay of cash necessary to get started, no one could reasonably handle the tremendous amount of research and paperwork involved in establishing and maintaining such a varied portfolio. A mutual fund, on the other hand, offers "turn-key" diversification.

2. **Easy to buy in small denominations**. Whether you wish to own many different funds, or if you just don't have a lot of spare cash with which to start, most funds let you begin with an amount as low as $250. Many savers use "dollar cost averaging" (buying a fixed dollar amount on a regular schedule, regardless of the share price). In so doing, they purchase more shares when the per-share price is low and fewer shares when the unit price is higher.

3. **Professional management**. An experienced team, led by a senior manager, researches potential companies that fit the criteria and meet the goals of the mutual fund. They analyze the key statistics, consider the fundamental value of the products or services the companies provide, and then purchase those securities that they feel will do well. The managers continue to monitor the holdings in their portfolio until a stock hits their target price, something changes in an investment's financial situation or in a particular sector of the economy, or until they identify an investment with greater potential – at which point they sell.

4. **Economies of scale**. Since the funds work with millions, and sometimes billions of dollars, they pay lower per-transaction fees than individual investors. Along the same lines, when bond fund managers invest, they make huge trades and normally get better pricing than "retail" investors get when they trade at the $10,000 or even $100,000 level.

5. **Specialization**. Mutual funds come in many varieties and have a wide array of themes, risk factors, and goals. For example, you can choose a conservative bond fund designed to provide moderate ongoing income and limited price risk, or a bond fund that will pay handsomely on a monthly basis but with many more ups and downs in price. You can delve into the world of computers by buying a high-tech fund that you hope will bring you big bucks, or buy into a package of more conservative blue-chip corporations that will distribute some income along with more modest appreciation. Some funds specialize in international markets, small companies, large companies, precious metals, health care, transportation, conservative securities, risky stocks – you name it. From the thousands of mutual funds available, you should have little trouble finding a fund that corresponds to your special interests.

6. **Transparency**. Mutual funds have a fully-disclosed, audited performance history. Having to report publicly about all of their results keeps the fund companies on their toes. Also, when trading your own account, can you really calculate your risk-adjusted performance? If not – and most people can't – how can you even know if you are any good at managing your money?

7. **Reduce anxiety of investing**. Many people realize that to manage their money well, they need certain strengths, including market knowledge, trading experience, self-discipline, emotional distance, patience, a set strategy – including a risk management plan, focus, commitment, interest, willingness to admit mistakes, an ability to cut through the hype, and of course, time. (This list sounds a lot like the characteristics of chess professionals.) People who lack even one of these qualities may start to sweat just when they need to pull the trigger on a decision. And just having that responsibility can burden many people with stress – not to mention the tension it can add to a couple's relationship. By handing over the day-to-day trading of a portfolio, though, they can eliminate all of the apprehension brought on by a deficiency in one or more of these attributes.

How mutual funds lower risk

Since mutual funds often own hundreds of different positions, they mitigate the risks inherent in owning individual stocks and bonds. Individual corporations can – and sometimes do – falter due to circumstances beyond their control. Politics, the economy, wars, fashion fads, advances in technology, and even the weather can all lead to corporate loss or failure. Of course, so can faulty decision-making and business practices. Remember Enron, WorldCom, Lehman Brothers, Bear Stearns, Borders Books, Global Crossing, JDS Uniphase, Syms, Nortel, Fortunoff, Washington Mutual, Wachovia…? They all went bust.

Can mutual funds avoid or lessen these market risks? Fund managers did own some of the failed firms, and they have no crystal balls. Nonetheless, by owning portions of many corporations, they limit exposure to the troubles of any one company.

Which fund suits you best?

Although you can find thousands of different mutual funds, it is neither necessary – nor practical – to consider them all. Grandmasters do not have to check every single possibility before making a move, since they categorize different scenarios. By seeing the big picture first, they can quickly decide where to focus their analysis. Similarly, start by reviewing the general classifications into which most funds fall and then begin honing in on specific selections.

♟ **Growth funds**. Buyers of these funds invest for long-term appreciation and expect to find names of familiar, established stocks in the portfolio. The managers of these funds look for increasing capital rather than high income from dividends.

♟ **Aggressive growth funds.** As the name implies, these funds seek to maximize their returns by investing in smaller, usually riskier companies with new products and new ideas. In addition to researching and selecting hopeful winners, managers of aggressive growth funds may also try to enhance the bottom line by using leverage and more aggressive trading strategies.

♟ **Growth and income funds.** The managers of these funds generally include dividend-paying stocks. Additionally, many funds in this class also include bonds and preferred stock that produce income and have moderate appreciation potential. Fund investors willing to forego some growth opportunities in return for income and a greater feeling of safety tend to choose funds from this category.

♟ **Balanced funds**. These funds usually contain a fixed proportion of stocks and bonds. The amount in bonds and cash equivalents in a balanced fund creates a steady flow of income, while the equity component should provide some growth. Be wary if you have developed your own personal asset allocation model (e.g., what percentage of your money should be in stocks, how much in bonds, and what amount in cash). A balanced fund could make it difficult to adhere to your personal asset allocation model, since the fund management may adjust their allocation from time to time or you may have trouble determining exactly how the fund has allocated its investments, and this could knock your own model off-kilter.

♟ **"Global" and "international" funds.** Similar, but not identical, these two classes provide an opportunity to invest on a worldwide scale and take advantage of the fact that more than half of the world's business takes place outside the United States. By including overseas investments in your portfolio, you can participate in the growth potential of foreign economies, which often do not rise and fall in conjunction with each other. "Global" funds include investments in U.S. and non-U.S. companies, while "international" funds do not contain American companies. Managers of these funds research and track prospective corporations, handle foreign currency conversions, and follow the various political and economic scenes in both developed and non-developed countries.

♟ **Sector funds**. These funds generally focus on a specific aspect of the economy or on a particular geographic region. They can encompass areas such as healthcare, energy, transportation, communications, biotechnology, banking, gold, and more. There are Australian funds, emerging nation funds, metals funds, utility funds, real estate funds, and the list goes on. Although sector funds may include a large number of stocks, you miss out on the "diversity protection" you have with non-sector funds. During the late 1990s, when technology stocks were all the rage, tech funds soared. When the market crashed in 2000, though, the tech funds took a beating. In 2002, U.S. small-cap stocks dropped over 20%, only to fly up by almost 50% the following year. Then commodities topped the sector race, returning over 21% in 2005, until they lost their vigor in 2006, returning almost nothing. Soon thereafter, real estate funds became hot... until they imploded in 2008. Then people celebrated 30% to 40% growth of foreign stocks in 2009 and 2010, only to watch their profits begin to slip away in 2011 with a 12% loss. The year 2012 ended with fixed income returning about 4%, half of what it had done the previous year, and in 2013 the category dropped 2%. The winner for 2013 was the small-cap stock index with a 39% increase, a significantly better showing than it had done two years earlier when it lost over 4%. And the list goes on....

♟ **Bond funds**. The term "bond funds" includes various subgroups of funds focusing on: maturity (long, intermediate, short, and ultra-short term), taxable government issues, tax-free municipals, corporate bonds, high yield, convertible, international, and more.

♟ **Risk level**: Bond funds, unlike equity funds, serve as a source of continuous income for buyers with lower risk tolerance. "Lower risk," however, does not mean "no risk." The underlying companies (and

sometimes municipalities) inside the fund can fall on hard times and default, or partially default, on their periodic interest payments or final repayments of principal. Also, market sentiment, interest rate moves, and changes in credit ratings all influence bond pricing. Negative trends in any of these can lower the share price of the fund that owns the affected bonds. Of course, just as in stock funds, if one holding goes sour, the entire fund may lose some value, but will probably still retain much of its strength. When buying shares of a bond fund, review its portfolio and see if its bond selections match your personal tolerance for risk.

♞ **Economies of scale**: One of the key benefits to bond funds lies in the economies of scale. Bond managers normally trade in large pieces, anywhere from $100,000 to $1 million or more. They get better pricing than individual bond buyers (think: wholesale vs. retail). That's why, even though you pay added fees by buying a mutual fund, you may still get a better overall deal than if you buy the bonds yourself.

♞ **Interest rate risk**: If interest rates begin to rise, previously issued bonds – which looked perfectly acceptable when they were originally purchased – will go down in price. Conversely, in a falling interest rate scenario, bond prices will rise and so will the value of your fund. Compare this with owning bonds directly. If interest rate changes cause the value of your bond to vacillate, you can choose to hold it to maturity to receive the full face value. Bond funds have no maturity date; if rates move against you, you can't just "wait it out" until the end.

Mutual funds come in many formats. Go to www.RichAsAKing.com/bonus to learn about:

♟ The difference between a mutual fund and an index fund.
♟ Open-end mutual funds vs. Closed-end mutual funds.
♟ Factors that create a discount or premium in fund pricing.
♟ Tax exposure with closed-end funds.

Seven reasons for selling mutual funds

If you sell your funds, or any investment for that matter, without making a large profit, you may feel as though you have made a mistake. People often have a lot of emotional baggage tied to their sell decisions, and they frequently maintain positions for too long. It's important to realize that selling is the logical conclusion to buying. Moreover, disposing of a fund at the right time will improve your overall position. But how will you know when it's the right time? Here are some guidelines:

1. **Changes in management.** If the advisory team of your fund changes, look for signs of a new investment philosophy or simply a weakening of returns. If the new manager's approach or results no longer meshes with your goals, sell!

2. **Style drift.** A noticeable change in the management's choice of investments may indicate a potential style-drift problem. If your large-cap fund wanders into the small-cap field, even if it continues to perform well, this move might adversely affect the diversification within your portfolio as a whole. Although the management team has leeway in choosing appropriate investments, watch out for marked deviations from the stated goals. For instance, a fund designed to represent conservative long-term holdings may, according to the prospectus, purchase up to 45% in small cap stocks. If you bought into this fund because, in the past, it focused on blue-chip holdings and now it has changed its character to include the maximum allowed percentage of more risky small caps, you might determine that this fund no longer meets your needs. Interestingly, only about half of domestic mutual funds remained style consistent, meaning they stayed in the same market areas, according to Standard & Poor's data.[9]

3. **Drop in performance.** When returns diminish, or when share prices drop, many investors rush to sell. However, counterintuitive as it may seem, poor results do not always lead to further poor performance. In fact, one study that examined mutual funds over a ten-year period found that the top performers in the first five years had about a 50/50 chance of maintaining their glory in the second half of the period. Similarly, the poorest performers at the beginning also had about a 50/50 chance of becoming top performers toward the end. So believe the phrase, "past performance is no guarantee of future returns." When investigating a fund's drop in performance, look to see if the fund itself is experiencing intrinsic problems, if there has been a change in management, if this particular market sector is suffering economic woes, or if the entire market is losing

---

ground. Try to determine why your fund is dropping. Benchmark your holding against a relevant index or against other funds with similar aims. If your fund is below par within its own class, then reconsider whether this investment is worth holding.

4. **Changes in your personal goals**. Life events, such as switching jobs, moves, and family happenings, all affect financial decision-making and influence mutual fund buyers to favor one type of investment over another. For example, young investors can normally afford the risks associated with aggressive funds as they have many years ahead to recoup if losses should occur. As they grow older, however, their needs and obligations may change… and so should their investments.

5. **Tax issues**. For some people, the tax efficiency of a fund may represent an important factor in considering whether to sell or continue holding. Those in high tax brackets should look for funds that trade in the most tax-efficient manner. In addition, if you plan to sell a fund with a large capital gain, you might want to select one of your "loser" funds to sell at the same time. Balancing your losses against your gains can serve to lower your overall tax bite.

6. **Too big**. Sometimes a fund does well and attracts a lot of attention. Whereas the managers may have handled $50 million efficiently, they may not have the infrastructure to quickly accommodate large additional inflows of cash. They may end up holding a lot of money in reserve, making rash decisions in an attempt to put all the money to use, being unable to increase existing positions due to the possibility of exceeding legal limitations, or lacking enough staff to research new ideas. Furthermore, if the fund focuses on a specific market sector, that field may not have enough liquidity to absorb additional significant sums of money. Imagine this: If you were the manager of the American Funds "Growth Fund of America," one of the world's largest mutual funds, with assets in excess of $100 billion (as of 2014), and if you wanted to put 1% of your fund's money into a new holding, you would face a considerable hurdle trying to find a large enough corporation whose shares you could buy. Over 5,000 traded companies have capitalizations of under $1 billion. So if you put a mere 1% of your cash into one of them, you would own the whole company. Fund managers want to invest in companies, not to buy

and run them. As a mutual fund shareholder, closely examine your supersized funds.

7. **Too many**. Some people collect mutual funds like others try to collect Facebook friends. If you have too many funds to track and analyze, maintaining your investments becomes a full-time job. Moreover, you could easily end up with a large concentration in one stock if several of your mutual funds own it in their portfolios. Frequently, people who hold twenty or thirty different funds could achieve all their goals with five to ten well-chosen positions. Additionally, consolidating mutual funds can help save on fees and simplify your administration.

Avoid 5 common mutual fund mistakes

Watch out for the common mistakes that people make when buying funds, which include:

- **Chasing returns**. When funds' prospectuses say, "Past performance is no guarantee of future returns," they mean it. With new funds, in particular, be wary. When they start small, a few lucky picks in the portfolio could give them stupendous returns. But as they grow and increase the number of holdings, each individual position will have less of an effect on the total return. With any fund that you examine, no matter how long a track record it touts, make sure that you not only look at the average annual return but at the year-to-year returns, too. A fund that averaged 10% over the past five years might sound great. But what if it made 50% five years ago and 0% every subsequent year? True, that averages to 10% per year, but is that the type of investment strategy and potential volatility you want?

- **Misunderstanding the fund's objective**. If you want safety, don't buy a growth fund; but if you want to try to make a lot of money, a money market mutual fund won't help much.

- **Not understanding how your tolerance for risk matches – or doesn't match – the risk level of the fund**. Look at the historical volatility of the fund to get a sense of the types of ups and downs it has experienced in different market environments. If the fund doesn't have a long enough history to show you both a bull and a bear market, don't buy it.

- **Not diversifying your own funds**. Owning three different technology funds that likely move in tandem does not constitute diversification.

Spread your money among different sectors, countries, and themes. If you don't feel qualified to make these choices, have a money manager do it for you.

♟ **Not knowing when to sell** (see the seven reasons to sell a mutual fund, discussed previously).

To help you avoid the errors that trap people, consider using one of the comprehensive research companies like Morningstar. They provide details on return rates going back many years, along with income, dividends, capital gains distributions, sales loads, expense ratios, management fees, portfolio turnover, and performance data. You can get information on equity fund style and the size of the companies contained in the portfolios. And if you want bond funds, the research firm lets you know the quality, length of maturities, and yields of the holdings in the fund. In addition, Morningstar uses a rating system going from one star (lowest) to five stars (highest) that buyers, as well as financial professionals, often deem very useful. While Morningstar clearly states that such ratings only indicate past results, and do not predict future outcomes, many people still count on these stars to screen and choose investments.

Whether you use Morningstar as your reference source or *The Wall Street Journal, Financial World, Barron's, Forbes,* Lipper, S&P, or any other respectable journal or service, be aware that a sizable number of mutual funds that are given top ratings one year often drop way down on the scale the following year, and a glowing report in no way guarantees your principal.

The best place to look for fund information

Before a big match, a chess grandmaster will study the games of her opponent. What better way to find out what to expect than to closely examine the original source? Likewise, you can get detailed information about funds by going straight to their defining documents. Contact each fund company (or your advisor) and ask for a copy of the prospectus. This detailed legal document conforms strictly to SEC requirements and provides in-depth information. Each prospectus includes sections on investment policy and objectives, administrative procedures (how to buy, sell, and exchange shares), a review of risks, historical background about the fund, net assets, investment income, realized and unrealized gains and losses, total returns going back ten years (or fewer for newer funds), turnover ratio, expenses and fees (including sales loads, contingent deferred sales charges, 12b-1 fees, and management fees), and other important data.

Should you pay for a mutual fund?

Funds' prospectuses detail sales charges, fees, and general expenses. As for-profit businesses, mutual fund companies – even "no-load" funds – do not work for free. Normally, a no-load fund doesn't charge an entrance or exit fee, but simply takes its management fees and overhead expenses from the fund's asset base. A fund with a load, on the other hand, assesses the sales charge to pay the cost of the financial advisor or intermediary. Whether you should choose a load or a no-load fund depends on how much effort and oversight you plan to give to your portfolio. Do-it-yourselfers can benefit from lower fees because more of their money stays invested and compounds in the fund. However, they must invest extra time to research, select, and manage their funds… and time is money. Those who don't feel comfortable making investment decisions, who lack the time or expertise, or who want their money managed by a professional to whom they can turn in difficult times, will likely benefit from a load fund offered by a full-service advisor.

All funds have to cover their own expenses for operational and administrative costs, and they do this through an expense ratio that gets assessed periodically. Many mutual funds offer multiple classes of shares, with the only difference between them being how they assess charges (not the security selection within). For a complete discussion of the costs involved in mutual funds, go to "Fund Expenses and Tax Example" at www.RichAsAKing.com/bonus.

How you pay tax on mutual funds' profits

For tax purposes, the IRS does not treat mutual funds in the same way as regular corporations. Rather, the tax authority sees the funds as a conduit for money. As such, the fund does not pay taxes on the interest, dividends, and capital gains earned on the securities in the portfolio. Rather, it passes these obligations directly on to its shareholders. (Mutual funds do pay taxes on other forms of fund income, such as fees and sales charges.)

Certain funds with a high turnover ratio generate a great number of tax events for their shareholders. Consider the turnover rate of a portfolio to see what level of taxes to expect. Though some funds change 80% to 100% or more of their positions during the year, others have more of a buy-and-hold philosophy. Look for information about a fund's turnover ratio in its prospectus.

Don't pay tax on someone else's gains

Sometimes, timing can save you money. Most funds make their capital gains and dividend distributions around the end of the calendar year. If you plan to buy into a fund, consider doing so after it has made these distributions. If you buy the fund right before it pays out, you will appear on record as the owner of the fund and have to pay tax on the profits (which may have come into the fund months before you bought your shares). To see an example of how you might get stuck paying more taxes, go to www.RichAsAKing.com/bonus and click on "Fund Expenses and Tax Example."

PART D

Getting Rich Using Chess Strategies

CHAPTER IX

64 Strategies to Make You Rich as a King

The Game of Chess is not merely an idle amusement; several very valuable qualities of the mind, useful in the course of human life, are to be acquired and strengthened by it, so as to become habits ready on all occasions.

—Benjamin Franklin

For hundreds of years, chess coaches around the world have taught their students the following sixty-four lessons. At various times in your life, some or all of them will probably apply to your personal financial decision making, too. By adhering to the chess principles below when handling your money, you can develop skills, practical knowledge, and the motivation needed in your quest to become as "rich as a king."

1. Every move must have a purpose

Excellent chess players make sure that every move they perform brings them one step closer to achieving their goal. Conversely, amateur players, incapable of developing and executing a strategy, frequently reposition a piece randomly on the board when they have no idea of what to do. Different personalities may err in this way for a variety of reasons. As Nobel Prize winning economist Daniel Kahneman points out, "Individuals who invest for themselves by and large lose money... because they are overconfident." Investors (and male ones in particular) want to appear like shrewd traders, so they often buy or sell some stock just to look good. Their overconfidence fools them into believing in their own aptitude. Ultimately, though, their moves frequently have no purpose.

2. Don't feel money is burning a hole in your pocket

Everyone suffers from the "grass is greener on the other side of the fence" syndrome, and when folks park their cash in money markets and bank deposits, regardless of the yield they receive, they feel they should be earning higher rates on those funds. The urge to find greater returns often drives them to place their money in inappropriately higher-risk securities. But you don't have to make an investment just because it's there. Sometimes you should do a "waiting move" in chess if you have no better tactic available. Likewise, you can hold cash as a "strategic asset," waiting until you find a truly preferable alternative.

3. Develop purposefully, and not just for development's sake

When you make an investment choice, make sure that your move will actively advance your overall goal. For instance, chess players "develop their pieces" early in the game. This expression refers to activating the bishops and knights so that they can enter the fray on the board instead of remaining tied to their own back row. However, developing pieces does not mean simply shifting them from one sector of the board to another. Coordinate the motion of the bishops and knights in the same way that you would coordinate your stocks and bonds. Think of each move not only as a solitary investment, but as part of the bigger plan.

Take a look at the illustration of these two chessboards. Both of them show a game near the end of its opening phase. In the amateur game on the left, White has developed its pieces but has no particular strategy. Black, on the other hand, has coordinated its knights and bishops, creating a powerful force in the center of the board. Compare that to the grandmaster game (Polgar vs. Computer, 1995, Israel) where, by move #9, both sides had developed and placed their pieces purposefully so that each one was working with the other to attack the opposition's ranks. (In the professional game, both sides played aggressively throughout the long 93-move match. In the end, the computer resigned when it realized it had no chance of saving the game.)

Amateur game

Polgar vs. Computer

To develop your stock portfolio purposefully, ask yourself the following eight questions before making any purchase:

- ♟ How will this stock complement the others in my portfolio?
- ♟ Do I understand the business?
- ♟ Why will this stock go up in value?
- ♟ Which events would hurt the stock price?
- ♟ Can the company easily handle its debts?
- ♟ How will changes in the overall economy affect this company?
- ♟ If I buy it now, at what price will I consider selling it?
- ♟ How does the company perform relative to its competitors?

4. Accumulate small advantages

Whoever sees no other aim in the game than that of giving checkmate to one's opponent will never become a good chess player.
—Grandmaster Max Euwe, World Chess Champion (1935-1937)

Many chess books have been written about the concept of accumulating small advantages until you win. But look no further than one of the most basic lessons of chess tactics to see this lesson come to life. New chess students often start with an exercise in which they have a king and queen and their opponent has only a king. The board might look like this:

Inexperienced players might never find a way to force the black king against a wall in order to reach checkmate. Checkmate could look something like this situation below (where the black king is in check and has no place to run):

Frequently, amateurs will mess up, causing a stalemate. You cannot lose if your opponent only has a king left because one king cannot checkmate another. However, if White forces the black king into a situation as seen below that is *not* check, but where the black king cannot make any legal moves (meaning a move where it won't put itself in check), this situation is known as a "stalemate," and in tournaments both sides earn half a point. Look at the board below. It's Black's turn, but the king cannot make any legal move. White has squandered its winning position and, instead of checkmating Black and winning a full point, has ended up with only half a point for a stalemate.

Black to move. Stalemate since Black is both not in check and cannot move.

Those who haven't studied the tactics of using the combined effort of a king and queen to beat an opponent who has only a king might end up chasing the enemy king around the board, never making mate. However, those who know the process will win every time. White must slowly compel Black towards the side. Every white move pushes the black king a bit closer to the wall, and with the white king and queen cooperating, they can reduce the squares available to Black by creating a checkmate net. White will succeed in this technique by accumulating many small advances. After having taken enough small steps, White will claim victory in the game.

Grandmaster-level games rarely contain blatant blunders, but a professional player won't wait until her opponent gives the game away with a bad move. Rather, she'll build her defensive and offensive fortress slowly, accumulating small advantages wherever possible. Similarly, since you can't bet your future on the lottery, you also need to accrue money in reasonable, steady amounts. Over time, a collection of seemingly trivial sums can help you score high in the financial game. Try the following tools to accrue a modest, and then hopefully large, fortune:

- ♟ **Regular savings**. Squirrel away $5 per day and monthly or quarterly put it into a stock mutual fund for twenty years. If you net 6% per year on that pool of money, you'll end up with over $67,000.

- ♟ **Lower fees and expenses**. Look for ways to reduce pesky, small, recurring cash outlays. Let's say you stop buying lottery tickets (and save $20 per week), transfer your banking relationship to a lower-priced firm (saving $400 per year), pay off your credit card every month (or better yet, switch to a debit card) and save $2,000 per year in interest payments, and renegotiate your cable and cell phone bills (save $30 per month). Examine your budget to find other possible savings routes. Just implementing these alone would allow you to sock away $3,800 every year. Try investing that money for the next twenty years along with your "regular savings" above and you'll add another $140,000 to your hoard.

- ♟ **Better salary or a second income**. Could you find a job with a better salary, or perhaps work part-time in something you enjoy? If you currently earn $100,000 and could manage to make an extra 10% through switching jobs, working overtime/part-time, or a combination of both, or if your spouse could bring in that extra money, you'd have $10,000 more in your pocket. Invest it, rather than spend it, and over twenty years it could grow to $368,000 (if the money grows at 6% per year).

- ♟ **Reduce your lifestyle … *a bit***. Could you manage if you spent 2.5% less? Most people could find a way to cut back 2.5% of their cash outflow. If you spend $100,000 each year and can drop that by just $2,500, and if you then invest that money at the 6% mentioned previously, you could rack up an extra $92,000 twenty years down the line.

- ♟ **Tax savings**. Though we all need to pay our fair share of taxes, try to use many simple tax-economizing techniques to build your nest egg. How can you save on taxes?

♞ **Contribute to a 401(k).** Only about a third of young workers contribute to employer-sponsored retirement plans. Many don't realize that employers usually match a portion of their contribution to 401(k) plans. If you allot 15% of your income to your 401(k) and your company matches a part of it, such as 5% of your income, that's like getting an extra thirty-three cents for every dollar you put in, giving you an immediate return of 33%. Imagine that you save $17,000 each year. You will get a current tax deduction on the money that you contribute, and all the gains that you make over the years will be tax deferred. Assuming the same returns as the above "regular savings" model (6% compounded for twenty years), you'll have $625,000. If you manage that savings and return rate for forty years, you'll top $2.6 million.

♞ **Maximize IRA contributions**. If you can't participate in a 401(k), at least put the maximum allowable into an Individual Retirement Account (IRA). If you add $5,500 to a tax-deferred account each year, assuming again the 6% rate of return, it could grow to $202,000 in two decades.

♞ **Save your tax refund**. Because of payroll withholding, average salaried workers receive a refund from the government of about $2,500. Since you didn't use that money in the first place, why not save it with the money mentioned above? With compound interest, that yearly savings could grow to $92,000 in twenty years.

Ready to start with these savings? Add it all together, from the $5 daily savings and the lower fees all the way to the 401(k) retirement plan savings or IRA. If you keep that up for twenty years, you could end up with an impressive $1.4 million. And even if you only make half of these accumulation moves, you'll have about $700,000. Not bad. By building up your savings in small increments, you can checkmate a lot of financial opponents.

5. Make the most of your time

In the same way that small changes in your savings and spending habits can help you to gather quite a fortune over time, not making the right moves now can cause you to suffer from the opposite outcome. A chess game where Player A makes two moves for every one move by Player B would quickly end with a devastating loss for Player B. Likewise, you will experience a similar effect if you save your money in low-yield bank deposits and then stand by and watch inflation eat away at its value. If you keep putting off starting a savings program until tomorrow, you'll be like a chess player who says to her opponent, "You can make the first five moves in the game, and then I'll start to play."

Imagine if the twin sisters Ann Landers ("Ask Ann Landers") and Abigail ("Dear Abby") had both decided, at age 25, to save $5,000 annually for retirement... except Abby forgot to start mailing in her checks until she was 30. If they retired at 65, and if they both averaged 6% return on their investments, Ann would have accumulated $820,000 while her twin sister would only have amassed $591,000. Simply missing those five years of savings at the beginning would have cost Dear Abby nearly a quarter of a million dollars.

"Act now" is certainly an important lesson, though it doesn't necessarily mean to always invest money. Take the time to review all of your options, including the possibility of keeping money in the bank. However, don't equate procrastination with a strategic delay. The clock continues to tick, taking time away from both chess players and investors, so make sure that you advance your strategy every step of the way.

6. If you can't explain your choice, don't do it

Stock brokers call some companies "story stocks," meaning they've got an interesting angle that attracts buyers. Too often, though, investors pick up a stock because they heard a single compelling bit of news, and they think they have done enough research. These stock enthusiasts remind skeptics of the legend of renowned money manager Peter Lynch who ran the Fidelity Magellan Fund from 1977 to 1990. Lynch's wife one day bought some hosiery called "L'eggs." When she told her husband that the product was fabulous, he bought shares of Hanes, the manufacturer of L'eggs, for the fund. After that, Consolidated Foods, later called Sara Lee, bought Hanes out, and the fund made thirty times its money from the stock... all because Mrs. Lynch found some stockings she liked.

The L'eggs myth leaves out a critical detail. Peter Lynch said that when his wife told him about the product, he "did a little research." For Lynch and his team of analysts, that meant that they studied everything, from the price-to-earnings ratios and earnings growth, to the operations, management style, and experience. He didn't just hear from his wife about the product and call in an order to buy a million shares of Hanes. Dan Simons, co-author of *The Invisible Gorilla*, summed up the idea well: "If you decide to invest in an individual stock because you feel you know a little bit about it, you are probably overestimating your knowledge of that stock and that company because by investing in that individual stock you are essentially saying that you know more about that stock than the market does as a whole, and it's pretty rare that that's the case unless you're an insider, or really an expert, or Warren Buffett."

7. Know the purpose of every piece on your board

 *Doug: When I sit with new clients, I often ask them, "Why do you own this stock or fund?" Though a few people can explain their rationale, more often than not they say, "My friend told me to buy it a few years ago," or, "There was some good news about it when I bought it, though I don't remember what it was," or, "My husband owned these stocks before he died twenty-two years ago and he really knew the markets well," or one of the scariest replies: "Do I really own that?"*

When you start a chess game, task each of your pieces properly. The pawns act to shield the other pieces. The knights and bishops, along with the deadly rooks, serve as the core of the army. The queen, though the most powerful piece on the board, mustn't engage in battle too early in the game because she may get captured. And finally the king, which represents the whole purpose of the game, starts the game with one mission: Don't get into trouble.

Determine the purpose for buying a new position before actually purchasing it, and constantly reevaluate what you already own by asking yourself, "If I had any spare cash today, would I buy that investment now?" If you answer *no*, then it's time to consider selling it.

8. Fix a bad investment

> *In positions of strategic maneuvering (where time is not of decisive importance) seek the worst-placed piece. Activating that piece is often the most reliable way of improving your position as a whole.*
> **—Mark Dvoretsky** and **Artur Yusupov**, *Positional Play.*

When making most investment picks, you have plenty of time to analyze the situation. In fact, if you feel pressured to make a quick decision, remember what Warren Buffett said: "In investments, there's no such thing as a called strike." In other words, if you let a good pitch go by... that is, a good investment... and you don't go for it, you can always wait for another one. Unlike in baseball, in the investment game you won't get called out on strikes for not swinging. If you feel pressure from someone to invest, just walk away. That's often a sure sign that the seller is more interested in making a commission than in helping you.

When considering what to sell, look for the worst investment you have. Is it a low-yielding bank deposit or money market fund? Do you have a stock whose fundamentals no longer look as positive as when you bought it? Has a specific mutual fund been lagging the index for a long time? By improving the individual pieces of your account, starting with the worst ones, you will create a grandmaster portfolio step by step.

9. Time is on your side

If you feel you don't have the time to organize your financial affairs before you begin investing, do you honestly expect you'll have more time later to fix them? Amateur chess players often start their games by trying to grab as much territory as they can with their pawns. They don't want to waste time – "lose a tempo" (a "tempo" in chess refers to a single move or turn) – by bringing out their knights and bishops early on because they prefer to get the instant gratification of building a solid pawn presence in the middle of the board. Soon their opponent will start picking off those pawns, though, since they don't have a solid support structure. Take the time to move each of your pieces into the correct slot, even if it seems as if you don't have enough moves to do that. Your opponent has the same number of moves as you, so don't think you need to rush.

Here are eight money moves to make now. True, they'll take some time. But it's time well invested.

♟ Learn the basics of investing. Even if your goal is not to become a financial expert, at least understand the tools available to you. Professional advisors can help you to a much greater extent if you already have a core education.

♟ Compile a list of your assets. This document is called a "Net Worth Statement." Use the free RAAK worksheet at www.RichAsAKing.com/tools.

♟ Confirm that you have adequate life, disability, and health insurance.

♟ Start an emergency fund with about three-to-nine months' worth of expenses in it… in cash. Don't try to invest the money in anything other than money markets or short-term CDs. When trouble comes, that spare money could make the difference between stability and bankruptcy.

♟ Keep track of your income and spending, always making sure that your lifestyle costs lag behind your income.

♟ Fund your retirement savings plans to benefit from the advantages of tax savings and compound interest. Meet with the human resources department representative at work to enroll in the 401(k), or ask your broker to set up an IRA.

♟ Rebalance all of your investment accounts. Make the necessary buy and sell decisions to get your actual investments as close as possible to your desired asset allocation. Review your position either quarterly or semiannually.

♟ Write a will. If you die intestate (without a will), the state will determine how to divvy up your assets. Get your estate in order.

10. Avoid traps

Susan: What I dislike about playing against computers is that they don't blunder and you can't trick them. But when I play against people, I can set traps. Once I have even a little material advantage, I can whittle away at their position until I win the game.

While you may not get trapped by the market itself, watch out for common errors and for unscrupulous market players who try to ensnare you. Rather than learning from your mistakes, try to learn from other people's slip-ups. Here are four common traps:

♟ **Believing in higher-than-market returns with lower risk**. Bernard Madoff managed to convince his victims that he had found a way to ace the markets every year, regardless of the economic situation. But Madoff wasn't the only one, and to this day, Ponzi scheme operators of one type or another con many investors. No matter how well salesmen present themselves with impressive titles, fancy watches, or smart vocabulary, don't believe that they have found the magic formula to outperform the rest of Wall Street. The "secret to success" snake oils offer neither real secrets nor success. Bobby Fischer once pointed out, "My opponents make good moves too. Sometimes I don't take these things into consideration." Respect the competition out there. With all the transparency in the marketplace today, it's almost impossible to find a perfect investment that no one else has discovered. Just as you shouldn't leap to capture your opponent's queen if it looks like it's offered for free, you should second guess an investment program that proffers to give high, riskless returns. You might just find out that your opponent placed the queen on the sacrificial square in order to checkmate you on the next move.

♟ **Rolling over short-term CDs for years**.

> *A nickel ain't worth a dime anymore.*
> **—Yogi Berra**

Literally speaking, certificates of deposit are as safe as "money in the bank." But take a moment to reexamine that money-in-the-bank feeling of safety. For short-term needs, bank deposits make sense. But over a longer term of three, five, or ten-plus years, inflation turns this safe money into a potential trap. Don't allow the bank to automatically roll over your CDs every time they mature. Look at all the available options with each liquidity event so you don't fall into the trap of always investing your money at the lowest possible yield.

♟ **Buying on credit**. An occasional "buy it now, pay for it later" moment may seem innocuous. However, American consumers have become addicted to debt, with nearly a trillion dollars of credit card debt alone! Buying on credit has become the new norm. People have lost their homes, gone bankrupt, and destroyed their families because of too much debt. Avoid that trap by refusing to buy on credit, and certainly don't apply for new credit cards that allow you to borrow more and more. If you don't have the cash to pay for something now, just wait.

♟ **Assuming that money buys happiness**. The pursuit of happiness does not end with the accumulation of wealth. In the old world of chess, sacrificing everything for the game was acceptable, if not encouraged. But unlike the chess players of a hundred years ago, who were often known for their strange social habits, today's chess professionals have found a balance between their careers and their personal lives. Follow that example in handling your finances. Don't let any money ideas overwhelm your life to the point where you're miserable, or where you damage family relationships. Being happy with your lot in life is far more important than the number of dollars on your net worth statement. After all, consider all the celebrities who had millions upon millions, but were miserable and self-destructive. Robin Williams summed up their situation clearly: "Cocaine is God's way of saying you're making too much money."

11. Take care, even with the small moves

Very few experienced chess players would consider starting a game by moving their far-right pawn up two spaces like this (h4):

Though a player might make an argument that White could win by starting with h4 (moving the pawn in "h" up to the fourth row as his first turn), most people would find it hard to advance from this opening move all the way to checkmate. A French player, Marcel Desprez, employed this strategy and for that he got an opening named after him. But aside from that moment in the spotlight, Desprez hardly ranks among the chess world's top tier players. Beginner chess players might make careless pawn moves, perhaps moving a pawn up one square (when you're allowed to move it up two), and then for the next turn moving it up another square. But if the player had initially launched his pawn two spaces ahead, that second move could have been avoided and that turn used for something more productive. Similarly, in the Desprez Opening, the uninspiring move on the side of the board neglects the center and only gives a very small chance of a future payoff. One benefit of Desprez's strategy is that it can illuminate an important mistake that investors make.

As an investor, what would happen if instead of investing $50,000 in an exchange traded fund (ETF), you buy one share per day at $50? In about four years, assuming 250 trading days per annum, you will have accumulated the position you had originally wanted. However, this inefficient method of buying would significantly outweigh the defensive benefits of dollar cost averaging. Each purchase would cost a commission, take time, and increase bookkeeping and accounting charges when you eventually sell.

This example of breaking your purchases down into numerous tiny buys might seem extreme, but investors frequently find inefficient ways of handling their money. Perhaps they'll buy a stock and then sell it a month later. Or, they will transfer money back and forth between banks in order to get a fraction of a percent higher interest, racking up transfer fees and wasting time. And some people just make weak moves, like buying additional shares of a low-quality mutual fund simply because they already own some shares in it.

If you were educating yourself about the market and wanted to test the waters with real money, you might want to research a few companies, choose one or two you believe show promise, and then make a few small stock trades. In so doing, view the added cost of commissions as the tuition required to attend the "School of Experience." However, as a general rule, make careful and efficient investing the hallmarks of your money decisions. Spend more time thinking about the choice than acting on it. Even small decisions, like opening pawn moves, need concentration since you must make many of them, and together they will affect a substantial part of your financial health. Carpenters have a wise expression that applies to finance and chess as well: "Measure twice. Cut once."

12. Sometimes you just need to sell

> *Every block of stone has a statue inside it*
> *and it is the task of the sculptor to discover it.*
> **—Michelangelo**

To build a solid framework for your pieces on the board, like designing a structurally sound portfolio, first chip away the parts that don't belong. Chess players often decide to give up a piece that doesn't fit into their overall plan in order to ultimately prevail. And in effect, portfolio managers do the same thing.

Though, "it is always better to sacrifice your opponents' men" than your own (Grandmaster Savielly Tartakower 1887-1956), there comes a time when a sacrifice of your own could propel you to victory. For example, if you were playing white in this game, would you capture the black knight with your queen (a8xb8)? After all, that black horse has its own queen as protection, and most players wouldn't consider trading their queen for a knight.

Amazingly, White went ahead and executed that attack (Susan Polgar vs. Peter Hardicsay 1985), and predictably, Black's queen captured the white queen (Qxb8). Was White now losing, without its queen, or simply removing superfluous pieces in order to gain a strategic advantage? The deathblow came on the next move, when White's knight moved from c3 to e4. Black promptly resigned, realizing that even though its side had a material advantage (more pieces), White's pieces were so well-organized that Black didn't stand a chance.

Regardless of where Black might move in this situation, White would place the knight on f6#, wrapping up the game with checkmate. (In chess parlance, putting "#" after a move indicates "checkmate.")

Anyone managing a portfolio must look for opportunities to sell underperforming positions, even if those assets are wearing a queen's crown. By selling a security, you release cash that you can deploy elsewhere. If you own ABC Stock, for instance, but you would do better with XYZ, then by maintaining your position in ABC stock you've lost in terms of opportunity cost.

Practically, it's impossible for individuals to reevaluate every position in their portfolios constantly. However, during periodic account reviews (on a quarterly or at least semiannual basis), ask yourself how you can make your money work harder. Do you have an investment that you consider to be the "queen" of your account? What would happen if you sold it? Could you do any better with the proceeds?

Unfortunately, if you feel too confident in one of your positions, you may not even consider the alternatives. Garry Kasparov noted the parallel problem with chess players: "I've seen – both in myself and my competitors – how satisfaction can lead to a lack of vigilance, then to mistakes and missed opportunities."

13. How to maximize profits from weak pieces

Every pawn is a potential queen.
—**James Mason** (Chess writer, 1849-1905)

The metaphor of promoting pawns to queens applies to many areas of finance: Save your pennies, since each one can grow over time; reinvest dividends to benefit from compound interest; or even troll through your attic in case your grandmother's old iron might have antique value. However, the metamorphosis from one piece to another has another interesting parallel in the world of investing. You've got a pawn that, compared with the other pieces on the board, lacks power. If treated right, though, and watched over on its journey, this meager piece can become a queen. Think of this path when choosing sectors in which to invest. Look at the relatively anemic parts of the market, find stocks with potential, buy them, and then stick with them as they slowly make it to their ultimate success.

All too often, people invest in sectors that recently performed well. But how much further up can they rise? Just as you can't elevate a queen to become a king, stocks that have peaked may have only one way left to go: down. However, if you buy into the areas that are out of favor and have underperformed competing segments, you may have a great deal of upside potential. Consider the folks who invested in the high-tech sector in the 1980s. They owned companies that made "operating systems" before anyone knew what that meant. Yet over the years, these firms advanced step by step until they became the Microsofts and Apples of Wall Street. Did they crash during the internet bubble of 2000? Indeed. But that was after they were already queens. In other words, the time to have bought these stocks wasn't in the late 1990s after they had already made their switch from pawns to queens. The time to have acquired them was years before.

No one can accurately judge every cycle in the market. Think how many people started buying real estate in 2006 and 2007, only to get crushed a short time later. The take-away from this concept is to avoid the crowds, since once they start buying into a sector you've probably missed the boat. Rather, follow the Wall Street saying and "buy when there's blood in the streets." Watch over these investments like a chess player watches over a pawn and perhaps one day you'll see your least valuable piece promoted to the strongest one in your portfolio.

14. Make money by waiting

When people have trouble selecting an investment, they frequently adhere to the "first come, first served" theory. They go with whichever broker called them first or whichever ad initially caught their eye. Though studies have shown that men make quicker (and worse) investment decisions than women, both sexes spend too little time considering their options. Amateur chess players suffer from similar impulsive decision making, often making the first move that comes to mind. Chess coaches, on the other hand, guide their players – even their grandmaster-level clients – to reject spur-of-the-moment moves when the only way they can explain their rationale is to say, "I thought of that idea first."

Having professional management, whether in the form of a mutual fund, a money manager, or a financial coach, can separate you from your emotional drive to act quickly. But if you nonetheless choose to trade on your own, take these steps *after* you find an investment you like but *before* you call in the order:

- Remind yourself that the investment will still be there tomorrow. So wait a day.
- Look for other, similar investments and compare and contrast. Can you explain the material benefits of your first choice over the others?
- Set definitive buy and sell criteria, specifically the price at which you would sell.
- Divide a page in half. In the first column, write a list of why you believe this idea will outperform others. On the other half of the page, jot down the possible risks. Are your points emotional or logical? Cross out the emotional ones, leaving just the bottom-line facts, and then evaluate whether you have sufficient reason to purchase the position.
- Imagine presenting the idea to a professional investment committee. Would you have a solid argument for directing funds towards this particular idea as opposed to another? Then, imagine presenting the idea to your spouse. Make sure you can explain it in terms that anyone can understand. If you find this difficult, reconsider writing the check. Remember, overly complex investments in the hands of amateur investors usually lead to poor results.

♟ Remove the stress by going for a walk, sleeping on it, or just putting the decision aside for a few days. Under pressure, people tend to anticipate positive outcomes for no particular reason. If you feel the tension building up inside, you might rationalize that the investment will probably be okay ("After all, lots of other people are buying it.") so that you feel better. Letting your emotions guide your investments may well take you down the wrong paths.

15. Respond promptly to danger

If your king is under attack, you don't worry
about losing a pawn on the queen's side.
—**Garry Kasparov** (World Champion, 1985-2000)

In many sports, coaches tell their athletes, "A strong defense is the best offense." Investors, however, frequently ignore this wisdom. For example, when indications of the housing crisis began to surface in 2006, people still kept drawing cash from their home equity lines of credit. They spent money that they didn't have on depreciating luxuries and used their residences as collateral to buy highly leveraged, overpriced real estate. Rather than playing defensively, stockpiling cash, and cutting spending, many people went on the offensive, burning through funds at unprecedented rates. When the banks called for the repayment of these loans, millions of Americans lost their homes. About half of these folks were older than fifty. In the oldest and most vulnerable age range, those over seventy-five, the foreclosure rate grew more than eightfold from 2007 to 2011. Rather than defending their castles, these individuals spent too much time worrying about how much money they could borrow. When they couldn't make their house payments anymore, they finally had to resign from the homeowner game.

You could derive many lessons from the events surrounding the housing crisis, and there is plenty of blame to spread over who caused and perpetuated the calamity. But ultimately, *you* move your pieces. You can play defensively, not spending more on your house than you can afford, not borrowing money to buy consumer products, and not signing up for one credit card after the next. Or you can play offensively, hoping – and praying – that you'll have enough cash flow to pay next month's bills. For every decision you make, double check that you are not putting your core assets at risk. Don't "bet the farm," which is literally what people did. Never put your house, your retirement, your emergency funds, or your family's safety at financial risk. And if you find yourself in a situation where you've already gone too far, stop! Fix the problem before you take any new steps. It's much better to sell your house now, even at a loss, than to have the bank force you to sell it later.

16. Be aggressive, but play soundly

> *Attack! Always attack!*
> **—Adolf Anderssen** (1818-1879)

 A discussion about protecting yourself against foreclosure by your bank alongside a lesson about attacking might appear to be contrary points of view. However, a closer look at "Always Attack" Anderssen's games shows the sagacity of his comment. In the 1850s and 1860s, Anderssen was considered the top player in the world. One hundred and fifty years later, in fact, David Shenk wrote *The Immortal Game* about the history of chess. Shenk gave his book the title based on the phrase that chess commentators use to describe Anderssen's 1851 game against Lionel Kieseritzky. Analysts of the game point out that almost every one of Anderssen's moves either directly struck his opponent or prepared him for a later attack. His audacious sacrifices of his rooks, a bishop, and eventually his queen, set him up to checkmate Kieseritzky with three minor pieces, a feat deserving the title of the "immortal game."

But how far can you take this aggressive "attacking" approach? Not as far as you might like. Chess enthusiasts love to look at the games of Mikhail Tal, who was known for his fascinating combinations, daring sacrifices, and tactical improvisations. In one of the last games of his life, he left the hospital where he was dying of kidney failure to play in a blitz competition where he defeated Garry Kasparov. Tal, known as the "magician from Riga," held the title of world champion for only one year. He was clearly a master of forceful play, besting most of the top grandmasters at various points in his career. But with all of his hard-hitting style, he could not occupy the top slot for long.

In chess, you need to strike at your opponent. If you keep accepting or offering draws, you will never win. On the one hand, if you fight, taking risks like Anderssen and Tal did, you will create the potential for success. Following their lead, it certainly pays to focus on winning and to ignore the negative influences around you. On the other hand, however, in both the worlds of chess and investments, look for a balance. Just as in today's defensive realm of grandmaster chess it's not clear that Tal's approach would work well, so too in investments. Someone may tell you about a hot deal that made him millions, but that already happened in the past and now the markets have changed. Don't "just do it" because you like the action. Rather, play like an aggressive grandmaster, which means fighting hard *and* thinking clearly at the same time.

Combine aggressive play, which can help advance both financial and chess players to the top of their fields, with more positional and defensive maneuvers. Temper your thinking in both areas with the words of the fourth World Chess Champion, Alexander Alekhine (1892-1946): "During a chess tournament, a master must envisage himself as a cross between an ascetic monk and a beast of prey." As an investor, you will have times when you must abstain from an extreme lifestyle (hopefully not to the extent of living like a monk), and other times when you can push hard. In finding the balance that works for you, follow these rules:

- ♟ Just because you're young, don't make too many high-risk bets on one-in-a-million penny stocks. Focusing on those chancy plays will inhibit your overall investment development.
- ♟ You only have a limited amount of money, so use tools like mutual funds and index funds to spread out the risk.
- ♟ Remember the opening goals of chess: get hold of the center, develop your fighting pieces, and castle. Same with your investments: set up your basic portfolio and retirement plans, choose some aggressive stocks or mutual funds, and protect your core assets with an emergency fund and proper insurance.

17. Risky playing will tire you out

Though chess grandmasters may appear to always play fiercely, the fact is that they are frequently much more conservative than you might think.

Susan: A lot of people misunderstand Bobby Fischer's games. He played uncompromising chess, with a very conservative style and a sound basis before starting an attack or sacrificing a piece. Though some thought he was a killer at the board, it wasn't because he took huge risks. In fact, Bobby and I spent quite a lot of time analyzing games. I saw that he was always looking for ways to layer attack upon attack against his

opponents, suffocating them. He never just tried something crazy. I tried to copy both his style and Karpov's in my games, building a rock-solid foundation before commencing my attacks.

Though the active world of day trading, penny stocks, and commodity markets attracts a number of ambitious investors, many of these people end up quitting soon after they get involved. Either they go broke, or they just can't stand the stress. Attempting to build your nest egg through vigorous investment schemes will, statistically, fail – so why get started in the first place? Most likely, if you position yourself like Bobby Fischer, you'll build a large foundation from which you can continue to grow. On the other hand, if the temptation of high-octane investing gets the better of you, use this list of "techniques to lower the stress of trading" and read it when you get bowled over by the tension of the transactions:

- ♟ **Reduce the volume of your trading**. Every order you enter requires time and energy (not to mention commissions and fees). Slowing down allows you to focus more on each buy and sell.
- ♟ **Use limit orders and stop-loss orders**. Let the order-entry systems execute your trades when they reach your price targets, and let the "stop limit" orders protect you from adverse moves in the prices of whatever you're trading.
- ♟ **Stick to your trading plan**. If you've chosen a buy or sell price, stick to it. Don't start second-guessing yourself.
- ♟ **Keep an eye on the volatility of the market**. For example, while trading futures or currencies, when the news heats up and causes great market turbulence, reconsider your entry and exit points and, more fundamentally, whether you want to continue trading in that market segment at all.
- ♟ **Avoid bouncing from one market to the next**. One person simply can't follow too many world situations simultaneously.

18. Don't attack a well-protected area

If your opponent has castled and set up a defensive wall around his king, don't charge right in. Instead, target the periphery. Go for small wins on the battlefield, gaining material advantages in increments. Design an attack on a pawn, or try to limit some of his pieces from advancing. But don't start a kamikaze charge towards his king or queen. (These World War II suicide air attacks only managed to hit a ship about 14% of the time. The odds of success were weak then and similarly, on the chessboard, a long-shot attack will probably work even less often.) And in the stock market, if you try to make big money in a sector that already achieved great strength, you may find that you've missed your target, too.

Very often investors look at an area in the economy and make comments like, "The housing market has made a great recovery," or "Internet stocks have really proven themselves." Then they start throwing money at these already-appreciated securities. Before you join the herd, look outside the box. Search for value in the stock market in areas that have taken a beating, that no one particularly likes and, of greatest importance, that may have a turnaround in the future. Though it's natural to want to join the winning team, remember your chess game and don't attack a well-protected piece. Seek out a more vulnerable area, a piece (or business) that has not yet made its important move.

19. Never play a risky move

Susan: When I prepare for chess games, I cannot count on my opponents making a mistake; but I must recognize when they err. I look for small strategic mistakes since they don't usually make big ones.

Though you may hear an extraordinary story of someone cashing in on a hot stock tip, realize that the transparency and efficiency of the markets makes finding such a deal rather unlikely. By the time you read about an undervalued stock in the paper or in an unsolicited e-mail, the whole of Wall Street has already heard about it. Here are some of the lures that drag people into losing trades:

- ♟ Hot tips from friends or pump-and-dump brokers,
- ♟ Unsolicited cold calls,
- ♟ Spam e-mails touting a great deal (and listing all the company's previous winners),
- ♟ Frequent press releases from the company, even though they have no revenue,
- ♟ Reverse stock splits (which give the stock a higher price per share so they have more *perceived* value, but no more *actual* value).

The temptation to buy a risky stock, or any potentially ultra-high yielding investment such as a lucrative offer involving gold, foreign exchange trading, oil and gas partnerships, real estate, and more, can draw even the brightest investors into the depths of bankruptcy. Don't presume that the market will overlook some information that you, with a modicum of good luck, managed to find, and leave a diamond sitting on the table for you to grab. When you spot an inefficiency that you think you can exploit, make sure you fully investigate it so you're not making a brave and risky move (read: irresponsible), but rather an informed investment choice.

20. Don't accept a draw right away

In traditional chess tournaments, the winner of a game gains one point and the loser gets zero. If the game ends in a draw, where neither side can achieve checkmate or where the two players mutually agree to a tie, they each walk away with half a point. When your opponent offers a draw, however, don't jump to accept. Sometimes the stress of the game or the fear that you might not find a winning solution may lead you to agree to the proposal. But before you do so, stop for a moment and analyze. Understand why your opponent believes he *cannot* win. Obviously, if he thought he had a winning combination at his fingertips, he would continue playing until he could beat you. If, however, he has spotted the strategy that would lead to your victory, which is why he would prefer a draw, then you need to try to find it, too.

Sometimes the stock market also offers you a draw. For example, let's say you carefully research a company and then buy its shares. A year later, the stock price has hardly moved, so you sell. By doing so, you may have made the mistake of accepting a tie. Before selling the stock, reevaluate its underlying characteristics. If the reason you bought the stock still applies, then even though you might have gotten the timing off, the investment can still stand on its fundamental value. It's nearly impossible to time the purchase and sale of stocks to correspond to the low and high of the share price.

Too often, investors buy a portfolio, watch it drop and then recover, and then sell. Just like accepting a draw, they're not giving their investment enough time to grow. Before you write that check to the brokerage firm to start investing, make sure you will be able to stomach the ups and downs and not just sell out the moment you break even.

21. Castle early because it's a proven technique, but...

Why risk your core assets trying some new idea that may fail? Though innovation may lead to success, even the greatest investors follow the basic rules, which include vigorously protecting their money. In most of the highest-level games, grandmasters strive to set up their pieces in accordance with the traditional protocol of castling because they know that if they don't, they may be setting themselves up for failure.

 Take a look at Polgar vs. Vanheste 1985. Jeroen Vanheste, playing black, waited until the game was almost half done before castling. By that time, White had not only castled, but had also set up a multifaceted assault, eventually leading to Black's resignation.

22. ...there are times when you should not castle

Formulaic approaches lead to success in most areas of life, from chess and investing to performing surgery and drafting legal contracts. However, exceptions may arise, so evaluate every situation on its own merits. Grandmasters won't castle (or will delay the move) if:

- ♟ Castling would expose the king to more danger than if it stays put.
- ♟ They have something more urgent to do like capturing an enemy piece or protecting their queen.
- ♟ They have a weakness in their position, such as having lost the "g" pawn, which would otherwise serve to protect the king after it castles, or maybe they lost control of the center of the board. In those cases, expert players would likely choose not to castle, or would castle to the other side of the board.

Since castling parallels the concept of buying insurance (because both of them protect your core assets), think about when you should and shouldn't buy insurance. Though in most situations you need basic coverage (life, health, disability, home, car), the following facts should make you reexamine the standard formula:

♟ "I do not provide any source of income or monetary value for my family." If your death would not have a monetary effect on your household, then you probably don't need life insurance. However, if you choose not to get it today, it may be harder to get coverage in the future (if you develop some illness, for example).

♟ If you've examined the healthcare policies that you have from work or the government, and if you believe they are permanent and will always cover your needs, then you may not need to buy supplemental health insurance.

♟ People with enough savings can sometimes skip over disability insurance. Depending on the amount you earn and the size of your emergency fund, a short-term disability might not checkmate you. But what would happen if you were to suffer from a severe physical trauma like an accident (on average, Americans will be in three to four car accidents during their lifetimes) or a sickness (about 800,000 Americans suffer a stroke each year, a quarter of whom are *under* the age of sixty-five), and you ended up bedridden for years? You can lower the premiums you will pay on disability insurance policies by agreeing to a larger deductible or to a longer period before the company starts paying. Make sure the policy you have reflects your financial reality.

♟ Homes rarely burn down and cars generally don't get totaled. If you have enough resources to absorb the burden of replacing real estate or automobiles out of pocket, without damaging your long-term chances of stability, then you can probably raise the deductibles (thus lowering the premiums) or possibly eliminate certain policies. But don't abandon third-party insurance, which pays if you injure someone else. Replacing a car or a house has a maximum price. Paying the cost of damaging someone else physically, though, has almost no ceiling. As such, everyone must have third-party coverage.

23. Prepare to attack long before you fire the first shot

Grandmasters often allot many moves to setting up for future attacks. In fact, they seldom spar at the opening of a game. Rather, they guide their pieces from one place to the next, scheming to launch an assault sometime later. Like snipers, these experts wait for the critical moment to act and only then pull the trigger to either slay an enemy or protect a friend.

You can see this prepare-your-support-pieces-to-protect-your-attack model in action by looking at most traditional chess openings. For example, in several of the games between Garry Kasparov and Mikhail Tal in 1987, the players used the "Nimzo-Indian Defense" so that by White's third move, the board looked like this:

 Count all the pieces targeting square d5. Both sides have a pawn and a knight raring to attack that central square. That's four pieces targeting one location before the end of the third move of the game! In one specific game, when Black (Tal) later moved the d7 pawn to d5, that's when the battle began. Because both players had defending pieces already in place, they had an equal exchange. If one of them had failed to prepare in advance, though, he would have lost material.

There's a stock trading concept that adheres to this idea of getting ready long before you make your big move. Let's say you want to buy a stock at a certain price, but you don't have the money available now. Perhaps you're selling your house, won't get the money until closing in six months, and you're concerned that the price of the stock you want will go up in the meantime. In other words, you want to defend today's price so that it's available to you tomorrow. The tool you could use today is known as a "call option." Though options trading has many risks, and you should only consider it after you've studied the system well and found a professional who can advise you, take a look at one way to use call options at www.RichAsAKing.com/bonus.

24. Defend your pawns. Like convertible bonds, they have a great future.

Chess players love getting a pawn to the last row of the board and promoting it to a queen. Grandmasters defending against this transformation will naturally struggle to restrict their opponent's access to that Holy Grail. But you can get your pawn there; it just requires help. In order to make it all the way to the other side of the board, you will need backup from some of your strongest pieces.

On the board below, look how Black's rook shepherds over the pawn on c2 as it prepares to go to the final row and convert to a queen. This 1984 game, Istvan Szecsenyi vs. Susan Polgar, ended at this point when White (Szecsenyi) resigned. Even though his rook on c7 controlled the promotion square c1, he saw that after he would move his king to e1 (or almost any other move instead) in order to threaten Black's d2 rook, Black would simply move the rook to d1+, checking the white king (the plus sign after "d1" denotes "check"). The rook not only attacks the king, it also creates a defense in the first row for the pawn to move to c1 and change to a queen. White would then have to exchange its rook for the newly created queen, ultimately losing that rook. With such a material advantage at that point, Black would quickly win.

White's turn: Istvan Szecsenyi vs. Susan Polgar

> Though the pawn might have been considered a second-class citizen throughout much of the game, once it threatened to go that final step, it represented Black's decisive, game-winning asset.

Just as pawns may transform into queens, "convertible bonds" are sophisticated assets that can change, too. They can convert from bonds into stocks. These specialized corporate bonds normally have lower yields than other comparable bonds, as the convertibles offer a different sweetener. Since owners of convertible bonds can elect to convert their holdings into common shares of the issuing company, these investors have the potential to promote this otherwise low-yielding bond into a queen of an investment. For example, assume the convertible bond pays a coupon of 3%, and has a conversion ratio of 20:1 (meaning that the bond holder can exchange one bond for twenty shares of stock, each share being worth $50 at the time of the offering). Like most bonds, the convertible is issued at $1,000 per unit. The investor, collecting 3% of $1,000 every year, keeps an eye on the price of the stock. If the value of the stock pops up to $60 per share, for example, he could then convert the bond into 20 shares of stock. With those shares now trading at $60, the value of the investment would jump from $1,000 (the original cost of the bond) to $1,200 (20 shares of stock multiplied by $60). Regular corporate bond holders in the same company would continue to collect their usual interest payments, but they would not benefit from the upside move of the shares.

The convertible bond also has a defensive characteristic. If the underlying stock does not go up in price, convertible bond holders still continue to receive their regular yearly interest payments, albeit lower than what other bond holders get, and they will get their $1,000 per bond principal back at maturity (presuming the company doesn't default).

If you're thinking of owning convertible bonds, look at them in the same way that a grandmaster views pawns. They're an asset that's not as powerful as others on the board, but if they're well-tended, they might end up becoming top-performing pieces. Also, just as unseen risks can threaten pawns, so too with convertible bonds. Specifically, watch out for:

♟ **Callable bonds**. To protect their interests, many companies issue callable bonds. When an issuer calls a bond, it returns the face value of the bond to you *before* the actual maturity date and the deal is over. Though you do get your principal back, including the interest due to you, you miss out on the possibility of converting to equity.

♟ **Low returns**. Since convertible bonds generally pay lower interest than other corporate debt, unless you actually make money from converting the debt into equity, you will likely end up with disappointing gains.

♟ **High risk**. Frequently, smaller, less stable firms that cannot raise money via a stock or regular bond offering instead issue convertible debt. Look closely at the issuing company to determine why it's using the convertible bond model instead of either straight equity or debt.

25. Double your power

While one chess piece can present a threat, two together can create an impenetrable force. Frequently, chess experts will line up two pieces that have a similar pattern of moving in order to deliver a "one-two" punch.

For example, how do you think Black felt in this game (Polgar vs. Karpov 1992), when a pair of white rooks confronted its king? Each rook was protecting the other while at the same time presenting the threat of checkmate.

Indeed, two moves later, White delivered the final blow, adding the queen's mighty power to an already strong location. White pulled the rook on g6 back one square to g5 so that the queen could slide through the opening to h7 and checkmate Black.

Investors, often not satisfied with their lot, sometimes forgo this important chess lesson of consolidating their forces. Instead of strengthening their more powerful positions, they regularly scatter small bits of money here and there, hoping to find something better than what they have. Even worse, they'll frequently sell a good investment in order to free up cash to try an unknown possibility. Rather than follow this course, look at your own positions, find the more successful ones, and add to them. This concept of pairing up your strong pieces, that is, putting more money into your strong investments, can certainly strengthen your current asset pool.

26. Playing flexibly vs. sticking to a strategy

People miss the point when they say that playing flexibly causes you to veer off your strategic course. Strategy games require constant adjustment to changing circumstances unlike, for example, building a model airplane, where you must follow every step in a specific order. If you tried to assemble a model airplane from a kit, skipping or changing steps along the way, you would end up with a mess of plastic and glue. Rather, chess resembles the constructing of a skyscraper, which includes the architect's plans alongside the on-the-ground builder's techniques. An architect starts with a plain sheet of paper, an understanding of his tools and assets, and a review of his constraints, such as time, regulations, and money. He then creates a blueprint for the structure, which is the strategy document. When the construction begins, that's when the builder's tactical skills come into play. As surprises unfold due to unexpected variations on the ground, supply-chain or worker problems, legal questions, or even complaining neighbors, the contractor must remain flexible to deal with each of these issues. That doesn't mean he changes the overall strategy. Instead, he makes minor adjustments to the plans in order to resolve the obstruction while staying on track. So for builders, chess players and, of course, investors, advancing flexibly and sticking to a strategy are not opposing concepts.

27. Tactics make you win

Though the Wall Street community preaches the importance of financial planning, and this book is no exception, without proper tactical execution of your plan, you will likely fail. In fact, someone adept at handling money tactics could succeed even without an overall plan, despite the lack of strategy. If you've ever played chess against a street chess gambler, you've likely lost a few dollars. These players cannot compete on the professional circuit, however, because they lack the depth of strategy. In terms of tactics, though, they've got a huge advantage over most beginner and intermediate players.

Too many people assemble financial plans, often paying thousands of dollars to advisors to guide them, but when it comes time to actually make a move, they put it off. It's like the way certain people prepare their wills. They think about it, they know it's important, and sometimes they even write the wills, but they never get around to signing them. Amazingly, over half of Americans don't have wills, though 100% of them will die. Don't allow yourself to be a perpetual planner who neglects to make a move. Just as planning to diet *tomorrow* won't help you lose weight, thinking and thinking and thinking about your finances won't make you rich unless you actually start with the tactical side of saving and investing.

28. Profit from trading pieces

Country singer Kenny Rogers famously noted, "You got to know when to hold 'em, know when to fold 'em." Perhaps a lot of chess players hum this tune when contemplating an exchange of pieces. How can you decide whether to swap chessmen or just hold what you have? Generally, if you've got more material than your opponent, it pays to make the trade. In terms of percentages, the logic goes as follows: If both participants have their original 16 pieces, each individual one equals about 6% of the arsenal (though obviously some pieces are more powerful than others). If you find yourself ahead by one, and then swap most of the rest of the pieces, you might arrive at the endgame with five pieces against your opponent's four. That's 25% more ammunition in your lockbox. Don't oversimplify this theory. Even with a numerical advantage, if you have poorly placed assets relative to the other side, the extra piece won't make a difference. All else being equal, though, go for the exchange if you have more pieces on the board.

Investors can follow a similar model of swapping pieces of their portfolio in order to come out ahead. As in chess, you may not feel the benefits of the exchange until later, but when you do reap the reward, you'll be happy that you engaged in the tactic known as "tax-loss harvesting." Many investors use this method of liquidating their losing positions and then using those "realized" losses to offset realized gains when filing their tax returns. For example, if you bought stock ABC at $100 and you sold it at $120, you would owe tax on the $20 profit. However, during the same year, if you dumped the loser XYZ stock that you had bought for $60 and that had dropped to $40, you would recognize a loss of $20. On your tax return, you would declare a gain of $20 on ABC and a loss of $20 on XYZ for a net gain of zero – no tax due. But watch out for the two-fold catch: (a) what if you believe XYZ will recover and you don't want to sell, and (b) what if you sell XYZ to realize the loss and then buy it back a few days later because you change your mind and believe it has great potential?

The IRS disallows the use of a loss if you sell a security and then buy it back within a 30-day period. Known as the "30-day wash-sale rule," this directive stops people from selling stocks (or any investments) just to actualize the loss and then turning around and buying them back right away. By forcing the month-long waiting period, the tax authorities figure that if you expose yourself to enough risk (that the price of the stock will go up and you have to pay a higher price to buy back in) you won't be so quick to sell just to save on taxes.

Some investors, after they sell, begin to experience seller's remorse. They begin to worry that being out of XYZ for even a few weeks could cause them to miss out if the stock pops up. They might then make the mistake of selling the stock for a loss and simultaneously buying "call options," which would allow them to purchase the stock at a certain price for a specified period of time. That way, if the stock price rises, they can exercise their option to buy the stock and still benefit from the upside. Wise to this clever approach, the IRS disallows using the loss on the prior sale. They claim that the call option is a "significantly similar" security to the stock because it moves in tandem with it. As such, selling the stock and buying the call here continues to be an economic "wash," not eligible for claiming a tax loss.

So how can you use your losses and still benefit from the upside potential? Here's where the chess analogy can help. When you exchange pieces with your opponent, you should get something very similar to what you lose: a bishop for a bishop, a queen for a queen, or perhaps a knight for a bishop. Try that same idea with your investments. Let's say you own a bond from the EFG Company, which matures in four years and has an "A" rating from Standard & Poor's. On top of that, this bond currently shows a $5,000 loss. In the multi-trillion dollar bond market, you won't have a hard time finding a similar bond, perhaps from the LMN Company, which also comes due in around four years and has a similar rating from the rating agencies. Sell the first bond and buy the second and you will get to use the loss against other gains and, at the same time, still have a very similar investment in your portfolio. Because different companies have issued the bonds, that is, you sold the EFG and bought LMN, the IRS will not consider the securities significantly similar and will allow you to use the $5,000 loss to offset other gains you may have.

Tax-loss swaps don't offer you this "best-of-both-worlds opportunity" only in stocks and bonds. If you own ETFs (exchange traded funds), you can unload a losing position and buy a similar fund at the same time and possibly make use of the tax-loss. Find out more by reading "Benefiting from losses in ETFs" at www.RichAsAKing.com/bonus.

29. Develop during exchanges

If a grandmaster chooses to swap pieces with her opponent, and she has a choice as to which piece she can use to make the capture, she'll usually select a piece that could benefit from further development. Early on in a game, for example, she will try to make each move not only challenge the opposition, but also try to take over space in the center of the board. At the end of a game, too, she will look to accumulate extra benefits from each move.

At the end of this 1980 game, take a look at how White sacrificed the bishop for a pawn (Bb6), not normally considered an equal trade.

Polgar vs. Kiss, Budapest (move 35)

Black accepted the trade, capturing the white bishop on b6 with the c7 pawn. White then followed up by taking that pawn with the knight so the board looked like this:

Now, at this point, the white knight simultaneously threatened both the rook and queen (which had no escape route), so Black resigned. Thus, White not only swapped pieces, giving up a bishop in exchange for a pawn, but dramatically improved the position of the fighters to the point where Black no longer had any possibility of success.

When you sell an investment, whether to gain the tax benefit or to strengthen your portfolio, plan to take the money and develop it, making it more productive by transferring it to a new and even better investment. All too often, investors feel the need to do something, anything at all, which leads them to make lateral exchanges. For example, they'll sell one mutual fund and buy another, even though the newer one doesn't offer any additional benefits compared with the older one.

Insurance policy swaps can, at times, also help you develop your assets. Many people use a "1035 exchange" to transfer assets from one variable annuity to another without exposing themselves to taxation. The benefit of these types of switches could include lower insurance cost (for example, if your health has improved), working with a better company (if the original one develops solvency problems), or simply taking advantage of better features. However, beware of some of the reasons why replacing an existing policy could harm you:

- ♟ Exiting an existing annuity or insurance policy might entail surrender charges.
- ♟ Even if terminating one policy won't cost you any fees, the new policy might lock you into a new surrender charge period. Being locked into the new policy might mean you won't have immediate access to the money (even though you may have qualified under your old policy if the surrender period had ended).
- ♟ The new policy might have various hidden fees that cost more than those found in the original policy. Compare the fees for administration, M&E (mortality and expense), maintenance, surrender charges, and fund expenses.
- ♟ Will you have a greater investment selection in the new policy? Check that the new policy not only has a wide variety of fund choices, but also see to it that the funds represent all the basic asset classes (stocks, bonds, money markets, real estate, commodities, etc.).
- ♟ Does the new policy lock you into buying funds only from their company? Getting stuck in their proprietary investment choices could limit your returns.

30. Trade off bad pieces immediately

Just like chess players, investors must also consider when to let go of an asset. An underperforming position can often wreak havoc on your overall situation, so try to dispose of it as soon as possible.

If you're in the middle of a chess game that looks like this, how can you improve your position? Get rid of a "bad" piece.

White has a miserably positioned bishop on g3. If it were Black's turn now, his knight should ideally move to g6 to make sure that White's bishop will not have the chance to trade for the knight. Then, the white bishop on g3 would have little future for the rest of the game, due to the white pawn on f2 and the solid chain of black pawns on e5, f6, and g5 blocking its mobility. On the other hand, if it is White's turn, the only correct move is to exchange the practically useless bishop on g3 by capturing the knight on f4.

Though you must expect, and even ride through, volatility in the stock market, when fundamental adjustments occur to the detriment of a company, don't wait around for some messianic solution. Follow the wisdom of the Steve Miller Band: "Take the money and run." Don't spend weeks mulling over a decision to sell a stock. If the original reasons for owning it no longer apply, just get out, even if it means you will lose money. Consider cutting your losses now in order to avoid an even greater potential loss in the future. Think how investors in Washington Mutual, Inc. looked at its rating downgrade on September 15, 2008. They had placed their trust in the 119-year-old institution and all of a sudden the venerable stalwart became shaky. Those who sold immediately got some of their money out. However, those who waited ten days woke up to the headline that the U.S. government seized the Washington Mutual Bank and placed it into the receivership of the Federal Deposit Insurance Corporation (FDIC). It was the largest bank failure in American history in terms of assets under management. With FDIC backing, *depositors* in the bank had almost no risk and did not lose anything. *Shareholders*, however, had no government backstop to protect them. Many companies have suffered a similar fate, from airlines to banks, car manufacturers to energy companies, and the list could go on. In most cases, there were some indications of fundamental changes in the firms. But it's impossible to spot all of the developments and make correct decisions every time about whether to sell a stock. However, if you want to own a portfolio of equities, you need to watch them on a very regular basis, not just once a month. Determine if short-term issues like earnings reports or bad weather caused changes in a stock's price, in which case you may want to hold on and ride through the instability, or whether more serious problems have arisen that should trigger a sell order, such as downgrades, negative developments in the industry, deteriorating fundamentals, changes in management, a share price that way outpaces valuation, illegal activities, or government initiatives that will crush the industry.

31. How time will make you wealthy

In the drive to control as much of the board as possible, grandmasters know that they can't do it all in one stroke. Just to lay the foundation of their strategy, they use openings that can range from ten to twenty moves deep. With the average high-level game taking about forty to fifty moves per side, champions know that ultimate triumph comes from long-term strategies. Like everyone, they would love instant victory. But in reality, they prepare to play for many, many moves.

To build wealth, plan to invest for the long term. Like Warren Buffett said, "Only buy something that you'd be perfectly happy to hold if the market shut down for 10 years." Short-term investors are gamblers; some will win and some will lose. But those people who maintain their portfolios over a span of ten or more years give themselves many benefits:

♟ **Delay the paying of taxes**. Since you only pay capital gains tax when you sell, put off paying the taxman by holding onto a position. Warren Buffet, who says his time frame for keeping a stock is "forever," unless something fundamentally changes in the company, has owned some stocks for decades, never paying a penny of capital gains tax (though he does pay tax on a yearly basis on the dividends that the stocks yield).

♟ **Limit commissions**. Even if you trade with a discount broker, every transaction fee nibbles away at your profits. Holding instead of trading means that you keep more in your pocket.

♟ **Simplify portfolio upkeep**. Short-term players constantly check the news, watch the charts, borrow on margin, and look for ways to improve their models by buying newsletters, attending seminars, and testing various strategies. With all of that, do they make more money than their long-term counterparts? No.

♟ **Ignore the news**. Though serious investors keep abreast of the happenings on Wall Street and around the world, they don't alter their portfolios in response to CNN or Fox News headlines; they stick with their financial plans. They've witnessed events that have shaken the markets, but through wars, inflation, and Republican and Democratic presidencies, recovery and profits were right around the corner. In fact, think about explosive historical news occurrences and their effects on the markets. Whether you look back at the attack on Pearl Harbor (1941), the Kennedy Assassination (1963), Black Monday (1987), the Asian economic crisis (1997), the terrorist attacks of 9/11/2001, or the credit crisis of 2007, you will see that long-term growth quickly followed short-term market drops. Naturally, what happened in the past does not guarantee anything about future events. But if you really think that the current world you live in has no parallel to the past, read *This Time Is Different: Eight Centuries of Financial Folly* by Harvard professors Carmen Reinhart and Kenneth Rogoff. In their exhaustive study of 800 years of economic development in over 66 countries, they point out that economic history just keeps repeating itself. Interestingly, the authors are not only policy-shaping powerhouses, but Rogoff also happens to be a chess grandmaster who recently impressed the chess world by achieving a draw in a 2012 blitz game against the world's highest-rated chess player ever, Magnus Carlsen.

♟ **Benefit from compound interest**. Whether you count on Albert Einstein's recognition that compound interest is "the most powerful force in the universe," or whether you just do the math on a spreadsheet, you'll see that nothing beats reinvesting your earnings so that they can earn money for you, too. Let's say that you're fifty-five years old and you want to accumulate a million dollars by your retirement at age sixty-five. Assuming you could make 6% per year on your investments, you'd have to sock away over $5,400 per month to reach that goal. If your twenty-five-year-old son asks you for advice on how he could accumulate the same million dollars by the time he turns sixty-five, you could tell him some good news. If he put away $500 per month, just one tenth of the amount that you needed to save, he would arrive at that million dollar mark. Long-term investing and reinvesting the income and profits certainly makes wealth accumulation more achievable.

♟ **Minimize impact of mistakes**. No matter how diligently you study *Rich As A King*, work hard and earn an MBA, or even a PhD in economics, you will surely make at least a few mistakes along the way. Even if *you* don't err, but just suffer because of a market shake-up, you can ride through the bad times. Compare the leeway afforded to a long-term investor with that of a short-term investor who may, for example, intend to buy a home next year. If he saves his down payment in an equity mutual fund and then the market collapses, he might have to make a pretty tough phone call: "Hi Ma! Is my old bedroom still available?" On the other hand, if his investments take a hit and he has no plans to use them for a couple of decades, he can just hang on.

♟ **Mitigate risk**. About a third of one-month intervals of the S&P 500 have been negative. But if you look at one-year spans, you'll see that only about a quarter were negative. Expand your frame of reference to five years, and you'll find that fewer than 10% of these periods were down. And as you begin to look over even lengthier blocks of time, such as fifteen or twenty years, you won't find a single negative period. Does this mean that if you just park your funds in the market and wait twenty years, you definitely won't lose any money? Sorry, no guarantees here. However, this study illustrates that people who stayed in the market for longer stretches of time lowered their overall risk.

♟ **Collect more dividends**. Depending on the types of companies you own and the market environment, dividends paid will normally range anywhere from a fraction of a percent to a high in the teens. For the fifty years ending in December, 2013, the S&P 500 average annual price return was about

6.6%. Had you reinvested the dividends during that period, your return would have been nearly 10%.[10]

32. Don't always exchange a pawn for a queen

 Think about the joy a chess player feels when he sees his pawn about to move onto the eighth rank. He'll promote that pawn to a queen and then crush his opponent. Take a close look at this board. Should White switch his pawn for a queen?

What would happen if White's pawn moved to f8 and became a queen? The black king would have no place to move. The game would end in a stalemate.

---

10   Source: http://dqydj.net/sp-500-return-calculator (as of February 2014). Past performance is not indicative of future results. This example does not take into account taxes and fees.

In a case like this, White's winning move would have been an "under-promotion," making the pawn into a rook instead of a queen. Black's king would have only one option, moving to h6. And then White would move the newly-minted rook to h8 on the next move... checkmate! Though everyone recognizes the awesome power of queens, sometimes they're not the right piece in your situation.

White should under-promote
and make a rook

Black has only one place to go...
Checkmate!

Exchanging cash for an investment, much like trading a pawn for a more powerful piece, requires that you carefully consider exactly which piece would help you to win the game, not which one is the strongest. How often do people hear of a great stock, buy it, and then discover that it radically alters their intended asset allocation model? Or someone may feel that one of his mutual funds has done so well over the years that he loads up heavily on that position... only to find that now it does him more harm than good. Before you convert your cash to any specific type of security, start by asking yourself which asset class you need. Don't start by asking, "Should I buy a six-month CD or a healthcare mutual fund?" Rather, begin by exploring whether you need more growth or income. Then drill down in that asset class to choose the right investment for your current situation.

33. How to hit your target by missing the bull's-eye

Though focusing and goal-setting will certainly help you hit a target, sometimes it's impractical to go straight for your main objective. When a grandmaster sees that her opponent has built a mighty blockade around his king, she doesn't keep launching attacks against the royal leader. Neither does she resign saying, "his defenses were too strong." Rather, the skilled chess player will slightly reset her sights, perhaps building up pressure on a location near the king or even provoking a weakness on the other side of the board. Then, after gaining control of the secondary objective, she will craftily create a path to strike the fatal blow against the king.

Don't always try to steamroll straight towards your goals. Many common impasses will arise along your road to financial freedom, such as losing a job, bad investment results, divorce, sickness and, of course, procrastination. Let's say you intend to save $1,000 per month, but find that you never seem to do it. Rather than abandoning the idea, reset your goal. Save $500 instead. At least you're getting close to your target. Likewise, if the market drops, don't give up on investing, saying that you could never achieve your return objectives. Rather, use the opportunity to add more money to your portfolio, buying stocks at a cheaper price. If you lose your job, spend extra time figuring out how to trim your budget. If you had intended on building up a million-dollar nest egg, but now you don't think you can hit that goal, don't abandon it. Just adjust it. Try accumulating $850,000 instead. When you improve your situation, go back to the million dollar mark.

One of the most famous search engines, Yahoo!, can be seen as an acronym: You Always Have Other Options. Remember this when playing chess and when managing your money. If one arrow misses your target, try hitting it from a slightly different angle. You can always approach from another side. Any options you choose, though, must point you in the right direction.

34. If you blunder, don't give up fighting

Susan: In 1991, in Munich, I sat across the table from Grandmaster Boris Gelfand. Playing with the white pieces, he used a standard "English Opening," with which I was very familiar. (In this standard opening, White starts by moving the "c" pawn up two squares from c2 to c4.) But in the 12th move, he placed his knight on d1, a move I hadn't anticipated. I remember

thinking to myself, "Whoops, I missed this one!" I was likely to lose a fighting piece or, at the very least, a pawn. It was a big disappointment and, in fact, I did end up losing a piece and was clearly in a bad position. Later on, I was down a rook for a couple of pawns and I think some people would have resigned. But I didn't. I kept battling and gained some ground. Eventually I managed to come back and save the game, which ended in a draw, a far better result than losing.

Some players say to never resign, no matter how bad your position may seem. "You never know," they joke. "Perhaps your opponent will die." And it's true. Anything can happen.

The psychological benefits of positive thinking often outweigh the advantages of technical skill in many sports and, sometimes, in finance as well. So when money issues disappoint you now and then, think of some of the inspirational and very determined folks you've read about. Remember J.K. Rowling who was surviving on welfare while she wrote *Harry Potter*? Today she's worth over a billion dollars. Or do you like examples of regular folks who decided to dig themselves out of debt by following pundits such as Dave Ramsey, who advocate cutting spending to the point of eating rice and beans? As Dave quips, "If you'll live today like no one else, later you can live like no one else."

Will you make mistakes along your path to success? Certainly. Everyone does. Don't think that you need to be smarter or luckier, or that you need to wait for the government to fix everything and find you a job. Rather, when facing setbacks, recalibrate your plan and then stick to it. Paste this Calvin Coolidge quote on your refrigerator to help you persevere in achieving your goals:

Nothing in this world can take the place of persistence. Talent will not; nothing is more common than unsuccessful people with talent. Genius will not; unrewarded genius is almost a proverb. Education will not; the world is full of educated derelicts. Persistence and determination alone are omnipotent. The slogan "press on" has solved and always will solve the problems of the human race.

35. Identify threats

To differentiate between real and perceived financial threats, follow an orderly system to identify authentic danger. Chess players sometimes have a mental checklist of considerations that they review before every move, and top on that list is, "What are the threats against my pieces?" A grandmaster may not have to go through an actual series of "what ifs," but until you've achieved that rank in chess as well as in finance, it never hurts to question yourself. On the chessboard, you only have a maximum of sixteen pieces, so scan each one to ascertain if it is in danger. With your money, use the same approach. Examine your accounts and ask yourself, "Is this investment at risk? To what degree?" If you feel that you have too many different positions or portfolios to effectively identify trouble, either consolidate your accounts, use money managers to handle the day-to-day oversight, or do a combination of both.

36. Answer all <u>real</u> threats

Chess great Aron Nimzowitsch (1886-1935) once complained to the arbiter of a game that his opponent was smoking. The judge replied that the challenger had merely placed his unlit cigar on the table. To that, Nimzowitsch countered, "Yes, but he is threatening to smoke, and any fool knows that the threat is more powerful than the execution."

Just as chess players classify threats as either perceived or genuine, you should also distinguish between real hazards and merely potential distractions. A Home Depot moving into town creates a real threat for a mom-and-pop hardware store proprietor, for example, and the owners would need to take defensive action. On the other hand, if you owned a small rental apartment and your tenant balked when you mentioned raising the monthly payments, you might worry that he wouldn't renew his lease. But just because you can imagine a possible threat does not mean that it's real. Moreover, you can usually resolve minor threats or made-up concerns rather quickly, disarming them by simply looking at the situation more closely.

In your stock portfolio, focus on real threats, not minor blips in the market. If a company's quarterly earnings report comes in a few cents below analysts' expectations, the stock price will likely decrease… no big deal. If you own a typewriter manufacturing enterprise, encyclopedia publishing firm, answering service company, pay phone booth franchise, or other such doomed industry, however, you've got a real problem on your hands. Though the vanishing of an industry may not be as obvious as the replacement of Bible-copying monks by the printing press, keep your eye on the trends. Will consumers continue to go to video rental stores to pick up DVDs? Can the print-a-newspaper-every-day-and-throw-it-on-a-guy's-driveway model really survive the invention of iPads and e-readers?

Can U.S. textile mills and clothing manufacturers compete against foreign labor markets? What's going to happen to the wired phone companies? How about coal mining and all the related transport industries like trains and trucking? Do you think the future will include mail delivery? Will robots and driverless cars quash industries like fishing, mining, transportation, and garbage collection?

Think about the threats that you face every day. Are they fundamental market-moving possibilities, or just normal turbulence? Deal with the big things, but follow the Napoleon paradigm for the small ones: When Napoleon was serving as a general in Italy at the end of the 18th century, he was overwhelmed by mail (much like what we find in our email inboxes today). According to Ralph Waldo Emerson, the French leader instructed his secretary to "leave all letters unopened for three weeks. [Napoleon]… then observed with satisfaction how large a part of the correspondence had thus disposed of itself and no longer required an answer." Don't let yourself get overwhelmed believing that everything is a menace. Let the small things go.

37. Don't move your protection

The foundation of many chess tactics lies in setting up a defensive piece, and then moving another piece into the established safe zone. As long as Piece A protects Piece B, the second piece can remain on its square. But what happens if the defender moves away? All of a sudden, Piece B becomes vulnerable.

See how the white knight on c3 protects the pawn on e4 against an attack by the black knight?

If White's knight moved from c3 to e2 now, it would abandon its responsibility for the pawn, and Black would surely take it.

In chess, if you've placed a piece onto a guarded square (one that is protected by another one of your pieces), always make sure that your defense remains steadfast. To see this concept in terms of your money, think of your fiftieth birthday. Imagine that you took to heart the lessons of compound interest, and you had deposited $5,000 per year into an Individual Retirement Account (IRA) from age forty onwards. If you averaged 6% per year on your investments, you'd have around $70,000. To commemorate your half-century landmark, you decide to remove the money from your IRA and buy a small cottage by Oregon's Rogue River where you like to go rafting. This move would possibly be a big financial mistake.

Withdrawing the money from your retirement account is like moving that knight away from its position defending the pawn. The IRA account-styling defends your money against taxes since, on a yearly basis, you don't need to give the government any part of the dividends, interest, and capital gains that you earn within the account. The IRS takes its due only when you actually withdraw the money. If you partially or totally cash out funds from the account before you turn 59½, you'll cancel that tax delay mechanism *and* subject yourself to paying full taxes on the amount you receive, as well as a 10% early-withdrawal penalty imposed on people taking a distribution before age 59½. If you are in the 35% tax bracket, you'll start by writing a check for $24,500 to the United States Treasury, and then kicking in another $7,000 to their coffers for the early withdrawal penalty. Instead of having $70,000 to fund your vacation house, you'll have $38,500. When you have any sort of shield in place for your assets, whether a retirement account, annuity, trust, corporate structure, options strategy, or other protective plan, carefully review the repercussions of removing the defense *before* you take any action.

38. Get a free piece

Even in the highest level games, a situation might arise where a grandmaster can grab an opponent's piece without giving up one of her own. Though rare, these opportunities can completely change the outcome of a match.

Susan: Finding myself in a rather poor position in a 1988 game against the Soviet-born, Israeli grandmaster Jacob Murey, I was considering resigning. We were playing on stage, and after I made my fortieth move, I decided to step away from the board for a few minutes. I walked through the audience and out the back door of the theater. A few minutes later, as I returned to the board, I saw Murey's move: a mistake! I made a final killer response, putting him in check and threatening his queen at the same time. He might have followed other paths, but instead he inadvertently allowed me a free piece. His mistake! It couldn't have happened at a better time for me, because I made my first grandmaster norm[11] at that tournament, which I needed to get on the path to obtaining my grandmaster title.

Though behavioral finance experts caution against accepting free offers (see Chapter I about "Why you should walk away from free offers"), this does not mean that you shouldn't grab hold of a good opportunity when one comes along. Understanding that no one on Wall Street will give you something for nothing, you can still try to find advantages that cost little or nothing. Consider some of the great, free investment tools available to you (you can find links to these and more at www.RichAsAKing.com/tools):

- ♟ **Research, stock quotes** (Yahoo! finance, fund analysis, etc.). In years gone by, stock brokers were the gatekeepers of the most critical information needed to make investment choices. You couldn't even get a live stock

---

11   In order to qualify for certain titles, including "grandmaster," players must pass certain "norms" in which they demonstrate a high level of performance at several tournaments.

quote without calling them. Yet today, those very professionals often use the same free services that are accessible to retail investors to mine the data available on the web. You can find facts like the ratings of mutual funds, revenues of companies, track records of managers, and hundreds of intricate details of publicly traded securities.

♟ **Free fantasy stock market games**. Before you begin trading on your own, practice with mock money using a free online stock trading simulation. Though people's real-life results often differ greatly from their make-believe models, online virtual reproductions of the Wall Street markets can provide an invaluable education. Much like chess students can practice thousands of sample chess puzzles to sharpen their skills, you can try out stock exchange challenges without risking a penny.

♟ **Financial calculators**. Many websites, including www.RichAsAKing.com, encourage visitors to keep returning by posting free online calculators that can help the users make wise decisions. You can find free online systems that will help you with the following calculations:

♞ **Debt planning** – how long will it take you to pay off your debts?

♞ **Social Security pension** – figure out how much you could collect, and at what age you should apply for benefits.

♞ **Computing net worth** – reconcile your assets and debts to understand how much you've actually got.

♞ **Converting your traditional IRA to a Roth IRA** – which type of retirement account will give you the most money in your golden years?

♞ **Deciding on a mortgage payment option** – wouldn't it help if you could test various possibilities to choose the best one for you?

♞ **Saving in a 401(k)** – enjoy the benefits of both tax-deferral and employer matching. Find out how valuable a 401(k) plan is to you.

♞ **Budgeting** – though you can purchase programs that do cash flow analysis, help you pay your bills, and synchronize with your bank and brokerage account, sometimes all you need is a basic tool that allows you to enter your income and expenses and view how they balance (or don't).

39. Fork your opponent

When you fork another player, you use one of your pieces to attack two or more of his so that no matter what he does in defense, he will lose at least one of them.

Here's a clever forking opportunity that arose during the 1984 Polgar vs. Boguszlavszkij game.

Susan: First I captured his rook on e8 with my rook from e1, knowing that he would then capture my rook with his knight (f6xe8).

 I then moved my queen to f8 (a square that was protected by my bishop on d6), which not only threatened that knight, but also put the black king in check. Boguszlavszkij had no other choice but to run away to h7 with his king, leaving me to capture the knight. By threatening both of them with my queen, I was guaranteed to get one of them. At that point, realizing he had no chance of saving the game, my opponent resigned.

In financial terms, creating a "fork" means enhancing an asset that you have, making it fulfill two or more goals. When looking at cash in the bank, you might find some forking opportunities. How can you move that liquid asset in such a way as to make it more potent? Check out this four-pronged fork that could make that money more powerful:

1. **Tax benefit**. Make a contribution to an Individual Retirement Account (IRA) and enjoy tax savings.
2. **Increase your wealth**. Invest the money that you placed in the IRA in stocks to benefit from the potential growth.
3. **Lower your risk**. Instead of buying individual stocks, instantly diversify your money using mutual funds.
4. **Benefit from compound interest**. Set up the funds on dividend reinvestment to plow your earnings back into the growth investment.

By thinking like a grandmaster, you can change a slow-moving savings account into a four-pronged tactic that could put you on the path to becoming as "rich as a king."

40. Don't get forked

The corollary to forking your opponent, of course, is: don't get forked yourself. In other words, don't let a single financial problem tear through the multiple foundations of your money world. Let's say, for example, you don't pay a credit card bill in a timely fashion. You reason that millions of other people have delayed or defaulted on payments, so it's no big deal. But that one default, or very late payment, can soon set you up for a massive fork. Here's what might happen:

- ♟ Debt collectors will hound you day and night at home, work, or school. Take heed of the old folk wisdom, "The only man who sticks closer to you in adversity than a friend is a creditor."
- ♟ Your credit score will plummet. Don't think that a low credit score only means that you'll have trouble getting loans, which is bad enough. Some landlords, employers, and insurers check credit scores, too, and they discriminate against people with low numbers.
- ♟ Creditors will attempt to garnish your salary. Could you really survive on a smaller salary while you pay off the debt?

The debt won't go away. The longer you wait to pay what you owe, the more you'll have to pay. There's an old Yiddish proverb that describes this very well: "Interest on debt grows without rain."

41. Don't get pinned

Beware of lining up one piece in front of another, allowing your opponent to pin you. Here's an example of a painful pin:

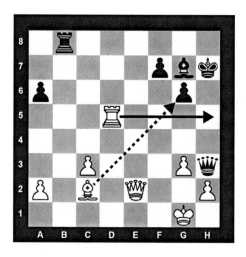

White's rook can fork Black by moving over to h5 and threatening to capture *both* the black king and black queen. Though you might think that the black pawn on g6 could capture the malevolent rook once it moves to h5, that can't happen – the pawn is pinned by the white bishop on c2. If that g6 pawn moves away from its spot, the white bishop would capture the black king. The pawn therefore simply cannot make that illegal move, as that would open its king up to check. And if Black captured the rook with its queen, White would use its queen to capture the black queen. Again, Black's pawn could not capture the white queen because the pawn is pinned. Ultimately, Black's king must flee to g8 because of the pinned pawn, and it will lose its queen.

If you are in a family-owned business, you probably recognize the feeling of being pinned. You cannot move away since you might lose a valuable piece on your financial board, like your income, pension, or health insurance. And could you get another similar-paying job and the prestige associated with it? If you resign, will your family feel as though you've abandoned the ancestral dream? Owners of family businesses often have a hard time hiring talented workers. On the one hand, if they choose to employ someone from within the family, the relative might lack skills, experience, or drive. On the other hand, if they look outside the family, not only might they offend their kin, but their candidate pool will be limited. After all, would you want to join a company where the only upside is that instead of answering to the patron, you can look forward to answering to his son one day? Watch out for any investment or business situation where you may become pinned, unable to maneuver to a better spot, because the consequences of your move could be dire. As chess master and prolific writer Fred Reinfeld (1910-1964) noted, "The pin is mightier than the sword."

42. Death traps

The ultimate trap in chess is, of course, checkmate. Under attack, the king either cannot escape, or he can only flee to another unsafe square. In fact, any piece – and any investment – can fall into the snare of a cunning opponent (at the chess board or out in the economic field).

What move could White make to trap one of Black's pieces?

Black has left its bishop (d6) exposed to an ambush, and all White needs to do is set it up. By edging its pawn up to c5, White leaves no escape route for the black bishop. Look at every possible square available to the bishop and you'll find that wherever it lands, it will get captured by White.

In much the same way, many people get trapped by illiquid investments. They look at their portfolio and suddenly realize that some piece is effectively lost.

Doug: An elderly woman once stopped by my office and told me how she had just found the greatest investment. A nice gentleman had told her that he was part of a group buying cheap agricultural land that was soon going to be rezoned to become a city. He helped the woman to buy a piece of land and guided her to take a mortgage against her home to buy a second parcel. "When they start building high-rises," she smiled, "I will make back five times the amount I invested." After researching the arrangement, I explained to her that the odds of success in the venture were slim. Moreover, she had committed herself to monthly mortgage payments on the loan while she hardly had enough income to cover her current monthly expenses. When she asked the salesman to give her money back, or to at least sell her land to someone else, he said that was impossible. There was no secondary market for this deal and the only time they would consider buying back shares was after the entire project was sold to investors. Talk about trapped! She had moved a valuable piece of her net worth into an investment that was doomed and she couldn't even sell.

Non-liquid or semi-liquid investments come in many forms, from stamp and coin collections to hedge funds and real estate deals. Liquidity restrictions in and of themselves do not necessarily classify something as a bad deal. However, be aware of falling into the trap of being unable to access your money. In most cases, with stocks, if you see them tumbling, you can put in an order to sell. But how quickly could you sell artwork, antiques, or apartments, if you needed the money? Unlike listed securities, more obscure speculations are difficult to value, tricky to store, and expensive to sell.

43. An insurance trap

As an investor, you constantly confront a ruthless adversary known as uncertainty. When you don't know what to expect from the future, how can you make decisions now? Wouldn't you like to trap the fiend of doubt so that no matter what happens in the market, it will always lose? If you're trying to plan for retirement, for example, wouldn't you want to eliminate uncertainty and know how much income you'll have coming in each month? For many, the solution to this puzzling question is an insurance product called an "annuity." Though annuities have pros and cons as all investments do, they can help people gain a sense of predictability about their future.

In general terms, when you buy a "fixed" annuity, you give the insurance company a chunk of money and they promise to pay you a monthly sum for the rest of your life, regardless of market conditions. For many people, this idea works very well, at least for a piece of their portfolio. But before you get started with annuities, make sure you understand all the ins and outs so you don't get outwitted and trapped, especially when you think that you are the one doing the trapping. Consider how the following features of fixed annuities can help you ensnare the "uncertainty opponent":

- **Safe**. Since the State (not the Federal Government) often covers you if the insurance company holding your assets becomes insolvent, you can sleep well at night. Pretty well, anyway. It's not an absolute guarantee, and there are limits, much as there are limits on how the FDIC will back your bank deposits.
- **Predictable**. Because, as their name suggests, fixed annuities pay a fixed monthly amount, you know what to expect.
- **Tax efficient**. If you buy a "deferred" fixed annuity, you give the insurance company money today and, at some point in the future, they will begin to give some money back. During the accumulation phase when they hold your funds, earnings accrue to you tax free. However, the party ends when you start to get withdrawals, either as a lump sum or as monthly payments. At that point, you must pay tax on the earnings, and here's the catch: You'll have to pay the government based on your *ordinary income tax rate*, which may be significantly higher than your *capital gains tax rate*. Though fixed annuity investors certainly enjoy a tax benefit, it's not necessarily a panacea.

♟ **Linked to inflation – for a fee**. Getting a predetermined monthly payment may sound great, but the buying power of that money will decrease over time. A $1,000 monthly check when you're sixty will buy you only half as much stuff when you're eighty if inflation averages 3.5% per year. You can ask the insurance company to link your payments to the "COLA" (cost of living adjustment), which they will happily do, as long as you pay a little extra.

Though fixed annuities have clear benefits, weigh them against the disadvantages as well:

♟ **Expenses**. Compared with similar, non-annuity products, fixed annuities tend to have higher internal fees and selling commissions.
♟ **Penalty for early withdrawal**. If you need to take out money before you hit 59½, the IRS will hit you with a 10% penalty for premature withdrawal.
♟ **Low rate of return compared with other choices**. When shopping for annuities, you'll probably find that the yield they offer falls below what other investments provide. This makes sense given the higher costs of the annuity, but may not make sense for you to buy one.
♟ **Illiquid**. Given the back-end fees for selling, the high upfront costs, and the taxes (and/or tax penalties) for getting out of annuities early, you may find accessing your money simply costs too much.

Setting a trap for uncertainty can help to give you peace of mind. As you prepare your portfolio, keep in mind that it's best to purchase a fixed annuity during a high interest-rate period since you lock in the prevailing rate on the day you purchase it. Depending on your life situation, net worth, and needs, annuities can either solve many of your problems, or cause more trouble. Given their complexity, take time to carefully review the small print before investing.

44. The dangerous discovery for bond buyers

The last thing a chess player wants is to get caught in a "discovered check," when an opponent reveals an attack by moving a blocking piece out of the way of an attacking piece. Similarly, a retiree dreads the possibility that a hidden attack will ambush his "safe" bond portfolio. Both situations occur when the relied upon protection slips away.

While examining a chessboard, a grandmaster confirms that no threats loom against her pieces. In particular, she verifies that her king is not in check. On this board, Black might feel secure since the two pieces that the white knight currently can attack are both protected, meaning that if White launches an assault against either pawn (d7 or f7), Black could capture the knight.

But that feeling of safety will disappear when White, instead of going after one of the pawns, makes a much better move: knight to c6.

By moving the white knight away from its current square, White opens up a check against Black. See White's queen on e2 checking the king? The king has no place to run, so Black is forced to move a blocking piece onto square e7. Only two candidates can move there, the black queen or the black bishop. In either case, the white knight will capture the black queen. Whether the queen remains on d8 or moves to e7, it lands within the knight's target zone. (You might note that Black could also block by moving its knight to e4, but White's queen would simply capture it and put Black into the same dilemma as before.)

In the same way that the one effective move of White's knight hopping over to c6 changed the black king's status from "safe" to "risk," bond investors, too, can find themselves exposed to a discovered check called "reinvestment risk." In the financial scenario, bondholders fear a drop in interest rates. If their high-yielding bonds mature after rates have tumbled, the newly released cash creates a weakness in their portfolio. For example, let's say that you retired in 2000, sold your $500,000 stock portfolio, and bought ten-year bonds with an average interest rate of 8%. Your income would have been $40,000 each year. Not bad. Assuming none of your bonds defaulted, you established a "golden-years" budget based on the income you received from your bonds. Ten years later, though, you got hit with a "discovered check." All of your bonds matured. Through no fault of your own, the Federal Reserve Bank had been lowering interest rates, and your core asset, the "king" of your portfolio, your bonds, were now at risk – reinvestment risk. When you went to buy more, you discovered that you simply couldn't buy similar bonds and earn 8%. In fact, you could only get about 3%. So instead of looking forward to $40,000 each year, you were now going to bring in only $15,000. To make up the difference, you'd either have to start eating into principal or else drastically lowering your standard of living. Either way, it would be like losing your queen in order to protect your king. Not only did you get hit with a discovered check against your king (your bonds), but the economy simultaneously attacked your queen (your principal and/or standard of living).

Though no perfect solution exists to protect you against reinvestment risk, the bond ladder could help. As described in Chapter VII, to set up a ladder, you buy bonds with different maturity dates, say two, four, six, eight, and ten years. Instead of putting all of your money in a specific issue, you diversify by time. This way, you mitigate some of the abovementioned risk of waking up one day and finding that you can only get a fraction of the income you were expecting.

45. How to react against a killer attack

Some situations are so deadly that there just is no defense at all.

White is about to embark on "double check," leaving Black no escape.

By moving its bishop to g7, White inflicts the most dangerous type of discovered check – the "double check." Both the bishop and the rook (h1) are attacking the black king. Black has no pieces to block, and even if it did, it couldn't intervene in two places. In fact, Black only has one place to go, which is to move his king to g8.

Unfortunately for Black, the escape route to g8 only delays the inevitable for a moment, since White will now move its rook to h8... checkmate!

What could Black have done in this case? Nothing. Though there may have been many steps earlier in the game when Black could have made better decisions, at this point it's over.

So what do you do after suffering a miserable defeat? Learn from your mistakes and move on. Here's the lesson that applies to every aspect of life: Win with grace; lose with dignity. Runners lose races; lawyers lose cases; world chess champions lose games; and investors lose money. Sometimes.

Sometimes you will end up in a situation where a stock you own drops, bonds default, or a divorce devastates your savings. Sometimes you'll lose your job, get ripped off by a tenant, or need to support your family members who never bothered to save. Sometimes you'll pay a deposit to a builder for an addition to your house and then he'll vanish. And sometimes a hacker will steal your identity, ruin your credit score, and sell your credit card numbers to thieves. In these and similar situations you would lose. So... then what?

Either you can sit around and bemoan your losses, or you can look at what happened, study your good and bad moves, and then get ready for the next match. Chess players (like pathologists examining a corpse to determine the cause of death) call this a "postmortem." If everyone who flunked threw in the towel, you'd never have heard of these famous folks who failed... but kept on trying:

♟ Here's a company you've never heard of because it went bust: Traf-O-Data. This was the first (failed) venture of the man who went on to found Microsoft, Bill Gates.

♟ Look out of your window and you won't see any cars manufactured by the Detroit Automobile Company. It closed its doors in 1901. But its captain went on to create a new eponymously named car company, Ford.

♟ The most popular vacation spot in the world was started by a man who was fired from a newspaper job because, "he lacked imagination." That same fellow bankrupted another business before he eventually came up with an idea for a magical kingdom… Disney World.

From Thomas Edison and Albert Einstein to Isaac Newton and the Wright Brothers, and from Oprah Winfrey and Jerry Seinfeld to Bobby Fischer and the Beatles, all successful people have had bad days, months, and even years. Yet despite setbacks, they moved on to the next tournament and started again. Don't let your failures stop you. Let them launch you towards even greater successes.

46. What to do when there's nothing to do

When amateur chess players have the opportunity to take on a pro, they usually report that they could not find a single move to make. The less-skilled competitors inventory their pieces and comment to themselves, "I can't go here. Or there. Nope, that doesn't work either! Drats! There's no place I can go."

Investors often have the same sense of dread. Concerned about where to place their money, some of them figure, "I can't go into the stock market now. It's just hit the top. And I can't buy bonds because interest rates are too low." Then, rather than spending more time analyzing, they take a chance on one or more of the riskier ideas that they've come across, with the hope that Lady Luck will guide them to riches. Unfortunately, though, many of the junk bonds, commodities, and structured products that they try end up making their situations worse. When confronted with a circumstance where you don't know what to do, don't let a new idea that you've never heard of become your first step… and this applies both to investing and chess. If you're concerned that you don't have a good move to make, or a good investment to select, follow these steps:

♟ **Do nothing**. Start by just waiting a day or two. "Sleeping on it" as a method to improve decision making has proven to help people learn more effectively, manage stress better, and reach more logical conclusions. Let your mind rest and you will likely find that you have more options than you had originally thought. If you're a chess player listening to your seconds tick away on the clock, you can't wait too long. But you can close your eyes very briefly to clear your mind and then look at the board with renewed insight.

♟ **Put your prejudices aside**. Don't eliminate any routes at the outset. If you tell yourself, "I'm not going to buy stocks because I lost so much money last time," it's like a chess player saying, "No matter what I do, I won't move my bishop since it got pinned in the last game I played." Consider all of your options for the current situation, and only then start to eliminate the ones that won't work.

♟ **Look for a move that will give you a small advantage**. Just as you probably won't find a way to checkmate your opponent in the next couple of turns, you also won't find a prophetic investment that will turn you into a millionaire. However, you might find a higher-yielding bond or CD. Perhaps you can locate a well-run mutual fund and start by putting a few thousand dollars into it. In the same way that a good chess move may only slightly advance a piece, a solid investment decision could entail only a minor improvement at this point – but it keeps you moving in the right direction.

♟ **Once you have identified some possibilities, speak with your advisors**. Whether you work with a professional financial/chess coach, or rely on advice from other experienced mentors, turn to them for guidance before deciding on a course of action.

♟ **Go for the safer choice**. At some point, you need to act. Don't fall victim to decision paralysis as a result of over-analysis. Recognize that not doing anything is a choice in and of itself, and it may be a poor selection at that. But if after careful consideration you still find yourself at a crossroads, choose the more conservative option. You're much more likely to regret and sell an investment that goes down soon after you purchase it, in which case you will lock in your loss. But if you've chosen to purchase a bank certificate of deposit, for example, even though it may not provide you with capital gains in the long term, at least you will have stopped yourself from buying and soon selling something else at a loss. And in the meantime, you're collecting some interest.

47. Block your opponent

Look at things from more than one perspective and attempt to play the game from the other side of the board. Try setting up your pieces so that your opponent feels that he has no way to attack you. Make him feel that no matter where he chooses to move, your pieces will still control more turf.

Likewise, with your money decisions, consider all the obstacles that might creep up on you in the future, and set up your pieces to stop them in their tracks. Worried about paying college tuitions? Move some money into a 529 plan. Think that you might get sick and become unable to support your family? Move money into a disability insurance policy. Anxious about funding a family vacation? Move a monthly sum into a "holiday account." In Chapter III on financial planning, you saw the six steps for putting together a plan. The third one on that list was, "Identify barriers to achieving your goals." Grandmasters contemplate what moves their opponents may make in the future and then they set up their pieces in order to stop them dead in their tracks. Do the same thing with your money. Look at what's coming down the pike, both in the near term and the long term, and set up your investments to deal with each event. That way, when the problems or goals arrive one day, you'll have the available cash to meet them.

48. Undermine your opponent's plan

Doug: When Susan and I were working on this book we took a break for a quick game of chess. Knowing that I couldn't outwit her with some new idea, I followed the classic strategy of controlling the center of the board, developing my pieces, and castling early. Just at the conclusion of the opening, I couldn't believe it. I spotted a way that I could checkmate her! I moved my knight into position, and then waited for her to make the only reasonable move. Without even blinking, though, she did something completely different from what I expected. Before I knew it, I lost my knight, then my rook, and then the game. So much for my beating a world champion!

Susan: Come on, Doug. Did you really think I didn't see what you were planning?

In chess, you cannot hide any secrets on the board since both sides can see everything. Though the stock market might seem to harbor some level of secrecy, government regulations keep it rather transparent. Many of the other stock players out there, your opponents, are grandmasters of the game of investing, so don't think that you're going to spot some obvious flaw in market pricing that they won't see.

Once you realize that you won't find a magic money maker, you can shift your attitude from being a trader to being an investor. *Traders* count on finding inefficiencies in the market that other people haven't discovered and then they make short-term transactions to profit from them. Since there are an abundant number of players in this trading game who can spot the same ideas, act on them faster than you can, and dilute or eliminate your advantage, your trade stands a slim chance of coming out profitable. On the other hand, *investors* hope to ride along with the expansion of a sector, or the economy as a whole. Over the past decades, more companies have created more goods that more people buy. That's growth. Historically, if you owned a broad piece of the stock market and just held on, you made money.

Doug: Don't bother trying to beat a world champion. Believe me, I tried. It's embarrassing. But you can hire one to manage your money in the form of a mutual fund or money manager. Better to join them than to fight them.

49. Gain the initiative

Chess players always want to dictate the pace of the game. Since White starts, it has the initiative at the outset, but it can easily lose that advantage. For individuals in the money world, sinking into debt causes them to lose the initiative since they must make choices in response to what the lender requires, rather than making decisions for themselves. When you consider the magnitude of debt that burdens Americans, you can see why so few can ever gain the financial initiative. Almost half of all Americans carry a credit card balance from month to month, owe an average of around $16,000, and pay about 15% interest. On top of this, about 70% of all car purchases involve an auto loan. And the borrowing doesn't stop there. Add in mortgages, medical debt, and student loans and you're talking about trillions of dollars of commitments that keep people from getting ahead.

Want to gain the initiative in your financial game? Start by paying off what you owe, cutting up your credit cards… or at the very least limiting your use of them, and promising yourself to never again become a slave to debt. Wilhelm Steinitz, the first undisputed world chess champion from 1886 to 1894, noted, "Only the player with the initiative has the right to attack." If you want to earn the right to become as "rich as a king," start by eliminating debt. Then you'll gain back the initiative so you can attack the markets, that is, invest for the long term, in order to build your wealth.

50. Take your money out of the bank

If you keep each of your chess pieces neatly protected in your back row, you'll lose rather quickly. Instead, activate your team by positioning each member where it can have a hold over the most turf.

The tactical wisdom to bring your pawns to the center of the board and get your knights and bishops into the game early on stems from the principle that players should take control over as many squares as possible. A knight in the starting position, for example, can move to only two squares. But, as the diagram shows, move the white knight to f3 and now it has five possible destinations:

Likewise, if you only keep your money in low-yielding checking accounts, money market funds, or short-term CDs, you will miss the opportunities for it to become more powerful. It's true that now that the knight in the above example has left its perch of safety, a black piece can come and threaten it – but what are the alternatives? Leave it on g1 doing nothing, eventually to become the target of an attack? That's like believing money in the bank will always maintain its value. Eventually, inflation will clobber it. Keep your cash working for you by engaging in this three-step review:

♟ Is my emergency fund (three-to-nine months' worth of expenses) fully funded? This account will earn very little interest and, in fact, lose real value when you calculate the effects of inflation. That's the cost of liquidity.

♟ Do I have enough money in the bank to cover current expenses? Going into debt costs more in the long term, so make sure to keep your current account balances topped up.

♟ Where can I invest any other money I have in order to make it more active?

Don't keep large chunks of money in the bank for decades. Once you have fully funded your current and short-term cash needs, use the rest to build up your portfolio.

51. Don't look for the most creative way to win the game

It's tempting to look for imaginative ideas both on the chessboard and in the world of finance. But follow the advice of Irving Chernev, one of the most prolific chess authors ever, who advised, "Play the move that forces the win in the simplest way. Leave the brilliancies to Alekhine, Keres, and Tal."

Though you can always find anecdotes about people who made millions on a penny stock, unusual overseas real estate deal, or day-trading strategy, realize they are the exception, not the rule. The most reliable approach to wealth building, employed by Certified Financial Planner™ practitioners around the world, entails the six-step formula which, if followed carefully and repeated over and over, will give you the best chance of success.

♟ **Step I**. Gather your information
♟ **Step II**. Define your goals
♟ **Step III**. Identify barriers to achieving your goals
♟ **Step IV**. Choose an asset allocation model

♟ **Step V**. Choose your investments

♟ **Step VI**. Monitor your progress

Notice that not one of the steps in the planning process is called, "Find some really hot, new, creative investment that will make you millions." Go with what works.

52. Maintain your concentration

Most successful people have an outstanding ability to focus. Everyone can concentrate for a while, though many cannot sustain a high level of attentiveness for an extended period of time. David Shenk, author of *The Genius in All of Us*, gave a great example of the importance of focus in an article he wrote for *The Wall Street Journal*: "Baseball legend Ted Williams was widely considered the most gifted hitter of his time, endowed with spectacular eye-hand coordination, exquisite muscular grace and uncanny instincts. 'Ted just had that natural ability,' said Hall of Fame second baseman Bobby Doerr. But to Williams himself, all that innate miracle-man stuff was just 'a lot of bull.' He insisted his great achievements were simply the sum of what he had put into the game. 'Nothing except practice, practice, practice will bring out that ability,' he explained. 'The reason I saw things was that I was so intense... It was discipline, not super eyesight.'"

 *Susan: Following an educational philosophy that my father had developed over the years, my sisters and I were homeschooled. Among other things, our regimen included math, foreign languages, literature, and of course, chess. The difference between our studying and that of our peers was that when we touched on a subject, we didn't just study it for two forty-five-minute periods a week. We spent hours and hours, never letting up until we knew the topic. As chess was our #1 interest, we each spent thousands and thousands of hours focused on the game from a very young age. We didn't become "The Polgar Sisters" because of some heavenly gift. Instead, we discovered that the recipe for success starts with desire, grows with determination, and is topped off with hard work. Without our daily focus on becoming chess champions, we would have been lost.*

Chess players often remark that the hardest game to win is a "won" game. Time and again, when a player has a significant enough material advantage, he loses his focus. Rather than thinking about the board, he thinks about the tournament, his last game, or the snack stand outside. Investors regularly have difficulty sustaining concentration on their money board, too. They may make a good investment and then, satisfied with their profits, wander off to their next interest. If you tend to occasionally veer off course, that's normal; however, understand the potential consequences. The wealthy people who have "won" the game often lose money when their focus gets blurred. "Riches-to-rags" stories abound about rock stars, bankers, entrepreneurs, boxers, football players, and others who had it all and then lost it. When you read their stories, you often find that they lost their focus. How can you prevent this from happening to you? Think of what the inventor of the telephone, Alexander Graham Bell, said: "Concentrate all your thoughts upon the work at hand. The sun's rays do not burn until brought to a focus."

53. How to avoid weak pawns in your finances

Anxious to develop their stronger pieces, amateur chess enthusiasts sometimes neglect their more trivial troops. By leaving a pawn unprotected, or by putting one pawn directly in front of another so the back one cannot advance, they create a "weak pawn." These players reason that they shouldn't waste time on their relatively scrawny pieces since that would take resources away from the mightier ones. Or they don't even have a rationale. Rather, they just overlook certain areas of the board. Regardless of the excuse, those who create weak pawns will ultimately suffer.

Though any investment that you overlook, or any sum of money that you place into a weak idea, may drag you down, beware of a common money-loser that people often don't even consider as part of their financial picture: cosigning on loans. Stopping by the bank for a few minutes to put your signature on some forms may seem as innocuous as a pawn on the chessboard. You want to help out a friend or family member, and you presume that you'll never hear about this issue again since, for example, your cousin assures you that he'll make his car payments every month. But by signing that agreement to step up and make the payments if your cousin can't – or doesn't – you create a potential weakness in your money map that might trap you later. Similarly, student loans sometimes extend over twenty years. Do you still want to be on the hook to pay off your niece's loan when she's forty-one?

Banks and lending agencies require a guarantor because they know that statistically many borrowers will default, and they need protection. In fact, they want you to jeopardize yourself so that they, the professional lender, won't have to. The Federal Trade Commission describes the danger of cosigning very clearly in the notice that it requires creditors to give cosigners: "You are being asked to guarantee this debt. Think carefully before you do. If the borrower does not pay the debt, you will have to. Be sure you can afford to pay if you have to, and that you want to accept this responsibility. You may have to pay up to the full amount of the debt if the borrower does not pay. You may also have to pay late fees or collection costs, which increase this amount. The creditor can collect this debt from you without first trying to collect from the borrower [depending on the State, this may not apply]. The creditor can use the same collection methods against you that can be used against the borrower, such as suing you, garnishing your wages, etc. If this debt is ever in default, that fact may become a part of your credit record."[12]

Many people draw a red line for themselves against ever cosigning on a loan. If you want to make sure that you never have this weak pawn in your finances, refuse to backstop someone else's debt for these four reasons:

♟ People need cosigners when they lack sufficient financial strength to get a loan on their own. By definition, you're exposing yourself to a real hazard.

♟ Do you really want to risk your financial future on your friend, distant relative, girlfriend, or boyfriend?

♟ Cosigning a debt isn't a bureaucratic procedure to help someone get a loan. It is a legal document filled with small print that makes the cosigned debt 100% yours. If, for any reason, the primary borrower stops paying, you have no recourse but to start shelling out the money. Can you afford to pay the loan? What about in five years? Are you sure that you will continue to be financially stable at that point? If not, prepare yourself for the attacks of the lender who will hound you with collection agents and drag you into court. If you pledged collateral such as your house or car to back the loan, get ready to have those items taken away in legal proceedings (which you'll probably have to pay for – both your legal fees and the creditor's).

♟ Cosigning on someone else's debt can lower your own credit score. Lenders may count that contingent liability against you when deciding whether to approve loans for you.

54. Tools to lower fees and limit trading

Have you ever ridden in a car with someone whose foot jumps back and forth between the gas and brake pedals? Other than making you carsick and wasting fuel, he also generates needless friction on the brakes. Extraneous activity on the chessboard, such as moving a bishop one square and then moving it one more on the next turn (rather than thinking ahead and then shifting it to its ultimate destination in one round), creates a similar effect. Instead of using the energy from all of the pieces working together to advance a strategy, inefficient movements simply waste resources. Much like the heat from the brakes dissipates into the air, the player's time, effort, and initiative vanish as well.

Overtrading a brokerage account engenders similar losses. Whether through lost opportunities, wasted time, or poor results, investors often create needless friction in the form of commissions, fees, and spreads. If you decide to sell one stock and buy another, make sure that the trading tactic represents a real material advantage to you. If yes, it's worth the cost of the commissions. But if the trade seems more like a lateral move between two companies (or two bonds, two mutual funds, two annuities, etc.), then reconsider the transaction and investigate further.

Rich As A King Action Point:

Do you find yourself constantly tempted to trade? Try this RAAK Action Point: Pretend you are a king, a real king. Will you sit around all day watching CNBC, MSNBC, or browsing the multitude of investment internet sites out there? Surely not. It's those alarmist media outlets that constantly present breaking news that make you think you need to act immediately. Instead, guide your empire with carefully planned wisdom. Have your princes, knights, lords, and ladies handle the day-to-day dealings of the kingdom. In other words, use investment advisors, mutual funds, and money managers to oversee daily market volatility while you do monthly and quarterly reviews. By separating yourself from the moment-to-moment excitement of the stock market battlefield, you won't swing your sword too much (that is, trade excessively), and you will thereby limit investment expenses.

55. Make sure all your pieces work together

In the same way that grandmasters determine how each piece affects the others, and just as you synchronize your various holdings so no sectors or asset classes unbalance your overall allocation, you also need coordination among your professional consultants. Open communication between your investment advisors, lawyers, accountants, and insurance agents helps to make sure that everyone understands and is working together to help you achieve your goals.

 *Doug: A couple from a wealthy family once presented me with copies of a $1.2 million dollar brokerage statement. "We're not happy with the performance of our broker, Doug. We'd like to transfer the account to your care," they said. Before making any changes, though, I suggested that we consult with the tax lawyer who had set up the extended family's trusts. "We'll talk to him, Doug. No need for you to get involved," the client replied. At the next meeting, I asked if they had gotten the go-ahead from their tax consultant. They answered that they hadn't been able to get in touch with him, but they couldn't see why there would be any problem. I persisted, saying that the account was complex and could have many potential problems if they simply liquidated it. Still uninterested in having me speak directly to their tax man, they promised to call him themselves. The next day, the clients called me to tell me the summary of their discussion: "Our tax lawyer told us that by changing the structure of that account, which had been carefully designed to avoid estate taxes, we might have ruined our family's estate planning strategy, which could have exposed us to huge death taxes. Thanks for encouraging us to speak with him, Doug."*

In the same way as you orchestrate your chess pieces so they can support and defend each other, bring your advisors together, whether face-to-face or on the phone. They all want to assist you, but it's up to you to help them help you.

56. The surprise attack that will wipe you out

One chess tactic called the "skewer" can annihilate an opponent. Similar to a "pin," a skewer targets two of your opponent's pieces that are lined up. Usually, the more valuable of the two pieces must flee, allowing the capture of the other one. Investors must watch out for this, too.

The classic skewer example looks like this, where both sides have equivalent material in the endgame:

You might think this game should end up a draw. But White needs only to move its king to one side, for example to e3, to put Black into check.

The black king, now staring down the barrel of the white rook's rifle, must step aside to avoid capture. And following that dodge, White can pounce on the black rook.

After losing the game, Black should spend some time evaluating how he let himself get skewered. Did White really plan a surprise attack, or did Black simply line up his king in front of his own rook, creating the liability? In blitz games, played with a clock that gives both sides no more than five minutes to make all their moves, skewers – and the similar tactic, "pins" – frequently show up on the board. But in longer, more thoughtful games, especially at the grandmaster level, you'll find fewer of these types of plays. Why? Because the most skilled players always keep their eyes out for such surprise attacks. Do they stop them every time? No. But by being able to see all sixty-four squares, they can generally spot them coming.

As an investor, you lack the same vantage point that allows chess players to observe every piece on the board. However, you can see a lot, and in many – though not all – cases you can often stop yourself from falling victim to a surprise attack. Here are a few common mistakes that you might easily avoid if you just take a moment to think about them:

- ♟ Instead of writing a check made out to the financial institution where they want to invest their money, some investors make the check payable to the agent or broker. The recipient can then simply cash the check and run away with the funds.

♟ Some people believe that if they invest a lot of money in a low-priced stock, they only need the share price to go up by a couple of dollars and they'll reap a huge profit. They fail to notice that this "couple of dollars" might represent a growth in the price of the stock of hundreds of percent. What are the odds of that happening? Put another way, if a person buys 100,000 shares of a twenty-five cent stock for a total gamble of $25,000, he may calculate that his investment would grow to a quarter of a million dollars if the price per share rises to $2.50 – but that's usually not the result. Rather than improving his financial situation with this deal, he soon discovers that there was a very good reason why the stock was trading for only twenty-five cents: it was on its way to three cents!

♟ Looking for a great opportunity, investors frequently chase returns. They hunt for the mutual fund that performed the best over the last couple of years and then buy it. Unfortunately for them, it doesn't always work. These funds may suffer from the statistical reality called "reversion to the mean." In other words, successful funds will often become poor performers and, over the long term, their returns will revert to the average.

♟ If someone offers you free money, take it. Your 401(k) represents one of the very rare times when you can actually get free money. Employers frequently match a certain percentage of the amount that you put into your retirement account. For example, if the company offers a "dollar-for-dollar match up to 5% of your salary" then each dollar you contribute will do double duty. If you put in a dollar, they will, too. Some firms offer lower than a 100% match, but regardless, when people who have the chance to get such a great deal decide against it, they're opening themselves up to a surprise attack one day when they don't get a large enough pension.

♟ Here's another 401(k) easy-to-avoid error. In plans where employees can buy shares of their own company's stock, about a third of them choose to do so. Didn't their grandmothers ever teach them not to put all of their eggs in one basket? If the company goes bankrupt, these unlucky folks will not only lose their jobs, but their savings, too. (Remember Enron or Bear Stearns? Many of those workers lost not only their employment when the companies went bust, but also their pensions.) Don't line up your job (a.k.a. your king) with your savings (a.k.a. your rook). If one gets pushed to the side, you don't want to lose the other one, too.

Before making any money decision, start by asking yourself what new risks that move will create. If you don't, prepare to be skewered.

57. How **not** to be broke

It's funny how people complain about not having money, yet they've got new cars, TVs, and iPhones. Sadly, they're really broke, or worse. Buried in debt, they actually have a negative net worth. How did they end up that way? They got caught by a "decoy." Grandmasters use decoys to lure their opponents into unfavorable positions. Similarly, credit card companies and other lenders use marketing gurus to fashion decoys that ensnare consumers.

On the chessboard, you might see a decoy that looks like this:

If White threatens the black king by moving the pawn from b4 to b5+ (the "+" sign in chess notation means "check"), what choice does Black have? The only possibility is to capture that pawn. Momentarily, in fact, Black might feel pretty good because it seems as if he's getting a free piece. In fact, if he inventories his own arsenal, he'll see that along with his king, he has a queen, knight, and two pawns. White (after the loss of the pawn on b5) would have only a king, queen, and pawn.

However, with White's next move, Black will realize that he's just been the victim of a decoy. He captured a piece, thinking he had a solid position, only to discover that he's being checkmated with White moving the queen to c4. Checkmate!

Certainly, when you're out in the shopping mall and a sale appears before your eyes, don't assume you're getting something for nothing. Rather, view it as a decoy. The store owners try to make you feel like a winner, but really they are luring you to put yourself further into debt. In your investment portfolio, too, you can also accumulate debt. Brokerage firms lend money to clients "on margin." The company holds your stocks and bonds as collateral and happily extends credit to you. With the extra liquidity, you can either go shopping on Main Street or on Wall Street. The debit card that most brokerage firms offer often permits you to take out more money from your account than the actual cash position. In addition, let's say that you want to buy $50,000 of a stock but only have $30,000 available in cash. Don't worry. They'll lend you the extra $20,000. However, beware of this multifaceted decoy. Though you think you're innocently borrowing money, here are some of the pitfalls:

- ♟ **You have to pay interest.** Will the investment you make with the borrowed funds go up faster than the rate of interest you're paying? Are you positive your choice will increase in price? If it doesn't, not only will you lose on the investment, but you'll compound this loss by still having to pay interest.
- ♟ **You will pay a larger fee.** Normally, bigger trades entail higher commissions. Had you only invested your own money in the above example, you would have paid the brokerage firm based on a $30,000 trade; however, with the extra $20,000 of borrowed money going into the investment, you will pay more for the transaction costs.
- ♟ **You might get a "margin call."** Any person who has ever invested on margin fears the dreaded margin call. In the above example, what would happen if the $50,000 stock plummeted in value? Once the brokerage firm realizes you don't have enough collateral on hand to guarantee the loan they extended to you, they would call you to deposit more money immediately, or else they will sell out some or all of your position to protect themselves. They're careful not to lose on the loan. You need to be careful too, and not get distracted by the allure of borrowing money.

58. Ruined by your own team

When castling, players sometimes create such a solid, static fortification around the king that they make it more susceptible to a deadly attack since it cannot move itself out of harm's way. Too much protection of a valuable piece can actually stifle its movements.

In a common opening, after castling, you might find a phalanx of pawns surrounding each king like this:

Those three pawns in front, though, could eventually lead to a "back-rank problem," where the pawns block their own king's escape route. In the following situation which could happen at the end of a game, can you see how White can checkmate Black in two moves (or at least win a rook)?

Sacrificing the queen, White captures the rook on d5. Black's bishop then captures the white queen.

By moving the bishop from c4, however, Black opens up the "c" row, allowing White to move its rook to c8 and... checkmate! The black king, once considered safe behind those three pawns, is now trapped behind them.

Back-rank attacks teach an important financial lesson: Sometimes overprotecting a valuable asset leads to its ultimate downfall. You can witness this problem in the case of parents who give too much protective support to their children.

Consider those folks who hover over every aspect of their children's lives, buying their young sons and daughters iPhones and iPads and anything else they want. As the kids get older, they receive expensive sneakers, shiny bikes, and eventually a new car. All of their tuitions and extracurricular activities, no matter how expensive, get delivered to them, along with credit cards to use without needing to pay the bills. Finally after grad school, an internship or two, and paid-for rent, the children – now in their late twenties or thirties – must face the world. They feel like kings, since their parents treated them that way. But like the kings who were forever protected in the back rank, many have been so sheltered that they cannot parry against any threats and they do not know how to navigate through the basics of handling money on their own.

At the board, to avoid getting stuck in a back-rank check, all you need to do is move one of those pawns up a square at some point in the game. By doing so, the king can slip out if under attack. Likewise, any kid who had to earn his allowance, get a part-time job, and become involved in handling his money from a young age will later understand the concept of budgeting and of setting up an emergency fund. Then, if financially attacked, he'll have an escape route, too.

When preparing your children for becoming responsible adults, sit them down at a chessboard and show them how they don't want to be like the king who grew up with so many bodyguards around him that he didn't even know how to handle his own sword.

59. The backup plan you need now

Standard chess strategy calls for castling so that the pawns, and other pieces as well, will guard the king. However, an adroit opponent looks to cut down those defensive pieces, ultimately exposing the king.

Here's an illustration of White destroying Black's castled-king's defenses.

Early on in this game, Black castled, and its pawn on a7 is the remnant of the original shield. After White moves its rook to d7, Black has no defense against White's next checkmate move, which would be rook to a7 – checkmate! Take a look:

First this...

...then this...

At the beginning of the game with a team of defenders in front of the king as a result of castling, Black wrongly presumed that everything would be okay. However, throughout the game, White chiseled away at Black's defenses until there was nothing left at all.

Do you presume your retirement income is secure, just as the black king assumed he was safe? Prepare for the potential retirement disaster if your main source of cash flow, usually your pension and/or social security, defaults. "Can't happen!" you say? Don't be as naïve as the black king in the above example. Simply read the report that the Social Security Administration sends you, listing your benefits (order it at www.ssa.gov/myaccount). On the cover page of that document, they admit that in the not-too-distant future, they will collect less income than they have to pay out and that over time they may have to cut benefits. Can you feel them chipping away at your defenses?

If you have a pension on which you rely, think how you would feel if you read one of these actual headlines about your retirement fund sponsor:

- ♟ Cries of Betrayal as Detroit Plans to Cut Pensions (*New York Times*, 7/21/2013),
- ♟ AMR [American Airlines] offers to freeze, not terminate, pensions (*Reuters*, 3/7/2012),

♟ Alabama Town Stops Paying Retirees' Pensions, Some Residents Destitute (*Huffington Post*, 12/23/2010),

♟ United Air Wins Right to Default on Its Employee Pension Plans (*New York Times*, 5/11/2005).

Even if your pension doesn't default, it could change. See what appeared in the news about these economic stalwarts:

♟ Boeing will freeze pensions for 68,000 nonunion employees – including managers and executives, all the way to the top – just as it did with the 33,000-member machinists union two months ago (3/6/2014).

♟ U.S. Postal Service has defaulted on a $5.6 billion payment for retiree health benefits (10/3/2013). The Postal Service also defaulted on these payments in 2012.

♟ GM Announces U.S. Salaried Pension Plan Actions (6/1/2012): Expected $26 billion reduction in U.S. pension obligation; 118,000 salaried retirees overall impacted; 42,000 offered lump-sum payment.

♟ Bank of America reported in note 19 on page 241 of its 10-K (2/23/12): "In connection with a redesign of the Corporation's retirement plans, after the end of 2011, the Corporation announced that it will freeze the benefits earned in the Qualified Pension Plans effective June 30, 2012." How do the workers feel about their frozen benefits? It's a lot of small print to go through, and most Bank of America workers probably didn't manage to plow through the hundreds of pages of the report. In any case, though, they may find a substantial difference between what they had expected from their pension and what they will actually get.

♟ Caterpillar switches from a "defined benefit" to a "defined contribution" plan. "Most current employees will have their pensions frozen when the change takes effect," Caterpillar spokeswoman Bridget Young said in a statement recorded in the *Peoria Journal Star* (8/26/2010).

♟ "Washington Redskins will stop participating in the NFL pension plan for non-football employees" (*The Washington Post*, 4/24/2010). It wasn't a problem for the athletes, but for all the people in the Redskins support group, which include many more folks than the players themselves. These individuals now have to rethink their retirement strategy.

Grandmasters constantly monitor the defense around their indispensable pieces, especially the king, and prepare backup plans in case the enemy gets too close. Though you may have a pension plan, prepare for the possibility that it might make some changes along the way or perhaps the entire program may default. Bolster your personal savings account in order to have an alternate source of retirement income in the event that your pensions disappoint you.

60. Buying at the best price

Market professionals debate whether to buy stocks "at the market" or at a limit price. When you place a market order, you'll get the current best price on the security. But with a limit order, you'll get filled only if the stock trades at your stated price or better. For most long-term investors, whether they pay a few cents more or less for their purchase probably won't make a significant difference. If you want to own the position, in most cases just go ahead and buy it without setting a limit, lest you set your limit too low and never get an execution on the trade.

On the other hand, more active traders will tell you that limit orders play a critical role in their tactics. Just as grandmasters will pursue an enemy's king until they finally get it, traders will carefully plot each order they make, sometimes gently increasing the level of their limit, until they get the stock at the price they want. In both cases, though, there is the risk of chasing the target so much that it slips away completely.

A well-thought-out king chase could look like this:

White can set a limit for the black king by moving its rook to f8+ (check). With no alternative, the black king escapes to g7.

The next move for White would be another attack, moving the rook from f1 to f7+, again putting the king in check, and forcing it to h6.

White's final move mates Black: rook to h7#.

By carefully setting limits on the black king, White escorted the piece to its demise.

When you go after a chess piece, or a stock for that matter, don't focus exclusively on the target to the point that you neglect the bigger picture. For example, if you have determined that your portfolio should have 5% in a certain index fund, go ahead and buy it at the market. On the other hand, if you want to buy a low-volume stock (not too many shares trade daily), use a limit order to ensure that as you purchase the position the price doesn't shoot up, making it cost much more than you had anticipated.

61. Don't be a chased king

Like a chased king, investors often scramble from one investment to the next, always feeling under huge pressure to evacuate one position and commit to another... and then to another, and another. Some folks buy a stock, hear some bad news, and then swap out for a different company. In more extreme cases, investors trade in and out of mutual funds, bonds, or sometimes even real estate. Though they would argue that they *must* make the trade before they lose their original investment, it behooves them to examine what got them to this uncomfortable position in the first place. Either they *are* wrong that they need to make the trade – the first investment is fine, or they *were* wrong when they bought the first investment. In either case, poor research and lack of commitment led them to become a chased king. Therefore, when you invest, especially when dealing with larger sums, consider all of the squares around you before you move. That way, when bad news arises, as it inevitably will, you will have already considered the risks and will have the wherewithal to stick with your original decision.

62. Go for a stalemate with the IRS

> *We'll try to cooperate fully with the IRS, because, as citizens,*
> *we feel a strong patriotic duty not to go to jail.*
> **—Dave Barry**

What happens if you make a mistake in preparing your taxes? Sometimes you could make an innocent miscalculation, or your brokerage firm, or your boss might send you an amended 1099 or W-2 after you have already filed your return. Other folks might have more nefarious inaccuracies on their returns. These could include anything from claiming ineligible dependents (like the millions of people who claimed their pets as dependents) and failing to report domestic workers, to not reporting income ("I had to pay tax on the money I earned when I painted that guy's house?" or "Gambling winnings are really taxable?") and not including offshore bank accounts or mutual funds. No matter the situation, if you owe tax to the government, they're going to checkmate you, and they'll probably hit you with penalties, interest charges, and the threat of jail if you've played a particularly bad game.

Grandmasters recognize when they've got an unsolvable problem, too. Whether they've made an obvious mistake or their opponent has just been particularly shrewd, experienced players can spot an impending checkmate. Rather than losing the game, which would normally mean getting zero points in a tournament, they try to salvage at least some credit and go for a stalemate, which would mean earning half a point.

A stalemate position in chess requires two conditions:

- A player is *not* in check, and
- There is no legal move the player can make.

Here, White put Black in a stalemate position. It's Black's turn, and there is no place for the king to move that would be safe, yet the black king is not in check either.

Look at this concept in terms of any of the tax reporting points listed previously. Let's say you had made a mistake and, if the IRS figures it out, they will win. What can you do to create a stalemate so at least you walk away with half a point rather than zero?

A good chess player who has made a mistake will try to force a stalemate. Take a look at the next board and see how much extra material Black has on this board. Both sides have their kings and queens, but Black also has a bishop and two more pawns than White. Imagine that's the amount of evidence the IRS has against you!

It looks like a clear loss for White, whose troubles include bad positioning compounded by a smaller army. But there's hope to retain some credit by moving the white queen to f3+. Black's obvious response would then be to simply capture the white queen.

Now it's White's turn again. Look closely at the board. The white pawn on a3 cannot move because it is blocked by the black pawn. Only the white king has some wiggle room. But does it? There is not a single square to which it can move where it wouldn't put itself into check. Stalemate! By making a smart move, sacrificing the queen, White turned the loss into a stalemate.

Can you also turn losing tax problems into a stalemate so at least you don't lose everything?

Tax professionals advise their clients to use certain methods when they need to clean up a mess with the IRS. First of all, don't try to hide the problem. It will only get worse. The simplest tool you can use is the 1040x, which is an IRS form that allows you to amend a previously filed return. You can correct your filing status (single, married, head of household, etc.), dependents, income, deductions, exemptions, or tax credits. Though you may have to pay some tax and interest, you'll likely avoid penalties. Instead of losing the game big time (i.e., with fines or jail time), you'll come out even – or at least better off than losing.

For more complex reporting problems, you will need the help of an accountant and a tax lawyer. From time to time, the IRS offers tax amnesty periods. These programs create limited-time opportunities for folks to report and pay in exchange for forgiveness for criminal liability. Depending on the terms of the amnesty, the IRS may also forgive some or all interest and penalties. But if they target you for a tax investigation of past-due taxes, you will no longer have the chance to enter the amnesty program. If you find yourself in a situation where you forgot or neglected to pay money you owe, rectify the situation as soon as possible. Walking away from the tax game with a stalemate is always better than losing.

63. How perpetual check can save your life… and your money

Low interest rate environments are a nightmare for retirees. Since their bonds and bank deposits yield lower returns than what they had expected they would receive, they feel a looming financial checkmate. Unfortunately, in this vulnerable state, some people place their money in highly speculative investments, rationalizing that since they need the income, it's worth the risk. But it's not, and they can learn this from the chessboard. According to the rules of the game, if the same position arises three times, meaning the players make the same moves back and forth for three turns in a row, a player can declare a draw. Just as in the "stalemate" tax example above, a draw always trumps a loss. As such, go for a draw if it means you can escape a loss.

In the following example, which looks like a sure loss for White, notice how White can create a "perpetual check" and ultimately claim a draw. If it was Black's turn, Black could move its queen to g2# and win the game. But it's White's turn. Where can White move to check the black king?

White can move the queen over to a1+. Traversing the long diagonal of the board, the queen would then put the black king in check. With the king unable to flee, the rook would have to act as bodyguard and intercept the attack by moving to g7.

White can again threaten check by moving the queen all the way up the "a" column to a8+. Since the black king has no escape route, it will once more call upon the rook to block, by moving it back to g8.

White can then ferry the queen back and forth between a1 and a8 until the same exact position occurs three times and the game ends in a draw. Given that White was down a rook, it really had no chance to win the game. If the player with the white pieces had tried a hardline attack, he would have surely lost. However, by going for the perpetual check, he got his half point for the draw.

Moving a piece to and from the same spot might seem like putting money in and out of a certificate of deposit (CD). It doesn't make much profit, but at least it's predictable. Compare that with the seventy-year-old who decides that he wants to buy a portfolio of high-yielding junk bonds since he's not happy with the interest rate that the bank pays him. That would be like White trying to launch an all-out attack on Black in this sample game. Unless Black totally messes up, something White cannot count on, then White would lose its king. When you can't win a game, or when the investment markets don't offer what you want, look for compromise positions that allow you to come back and play another day.

64. Leverage your strongest piece

Many examples throughout this book have illustrated the importance of sending your pieces into battle rather than leaving them stuck at the back of the board.

 Consider this potentially devastating decision: Develop your queen early. In the 36th Olympiad in 2004, Susan Polgar vs. Maia Chiburdanidze, here's how the board looked at the end of the third move:

Then, White placed the queen on c2.

Though such openings for White do occur (check out Vladimir Kramnik vs. Anatoly Karpov in 1997, which looked exactly like this game for the first eight moves), players normally opt for openings that keep the queen safe on the back row until much later in the contest.

Susan: When I was playing this game against Maia, I wanted to avoid permanent damage to my pawn structure. If I hadn't moved my queen out, I would have had to capture her bishop with a pawn which would have resulted in double pawns (when one pawn is directly in front of the other), a weakness that I wanted to prevent. This was an exceptional game, and an exception from the general principle of not bringing a queen out early. However, I understood the great potential that my queen had in this situation as well as the significant possibilities that it would have later on if I positioned it well at the outset. I am not a believer in the glib phrase that "rules are meant to be broken." Quite the opposite. Everyone should closely adhere to a set of principles, including the idea that you should not bring your queen out early in the game. Just don't follow rules blindly. Study them so you know the models inside and out, and then apply them in combination with your analysis of the current situation.

What is the strongest piece in your financial arsenal? *You.* Regardless of how much you know about investing, the surest way to build your wealth is to get the most out of yourself. More than any other wealth-building tool, your own earning capacity will determine whether you will succeed in becoming as "rich as a king."

In order to maximize your career opportunities, get out of your comfort zone. Just as the queen in the above example took a firm step at the outset of the game, you also need to earn what you're worth. Among the many tools that can help you to change your career paradigm, consider the following ideas from internationally acclaimed business consultant Brian Tracy[13]:

♟ Don't look at yourself as a worker for someone else, but as a "personal service corporation." See yourself as someone who is self-employed, and who takes responsibility for your position. Act as if you own the company where you work.

♟ Develop relationships. They are the cornerstone of your success.

♟ Become a problem solver. To develop this skill, think like a chess player. Instead of concentrating on the negative aspect of a difficulty, focus on the positive solution. Switch your mindset from worrying about who is to blame and instead ask, "What should we do now?"

If you work on improving your own earning potential, you will become like the queen that came out early in the game: strong and effective.

64+. Don't miss these fabulous free resources

Though you've come to the end of the book, take advantage of the ongoing information that we provide by signing up for some or all of our free lists. We've got blogs, Twitter feeds (@RichAsAKing), Facebook, and more that you can join at www.RichAsKing.com.

---

13   Tracy, Brian. *Earn What You're Really Worth: Maximize Your Income at Any Time in Any Market.* Vanguard Press, 2012.

CONCLUSION

How to Beat a Grandmaster

Doug: Towards the end of writing this book, I asked Susan if she wanted to play one more game of chess with me. She agreed, and I said I'd set up the pieces. When she came to the table, she laughed because I had given her only a king, but on my side, I had a king and a queen. She dodged my attacks for a number of moves, but eventually I pushed her to the wall – checkmate! What was my strategy? I used an approach from financial planning and applied it to chess, in the same way that this book has applied chess ideas to finance. I told myself that in order to win in personal finance, people need to take control of every aspect of their situation, from their budgets to their portfolios. The more power they have over these areas, the better they will do. They just need to internalize how much they can actually control. Likewise, since I set up the board in this game, I directed the situation. By making sure that I had a solid asset base, I dictated the pace of the game. And even though I was playing against a world champion, I set everything up to my advantage and came out ahead.

Though *Rich As A King* provides both the strategies and tactics required to handle your money, you need the willpower to set up your pieces to win. Every step of the financial game, like a grandmaster-level chess match, has different characteristics, risk levels, and opportunities. By honing your skills, you can learn to identify and act appropriately at each stage. People win and lose in both worlds, but those who get right back into the game after a defeat are the true grandmasters in their field.

Susan: When I was about four years old, playing chess against my father, I made a mistake. "Can I take that move back, Dad?" I asked. He smiled at me and said, "From now on, Zsuzsa, no more take-backs." Though I lost that game, I determined from that point on never to make a move without first thinking through all the consequences. That decision has served me well, not only on the chessboard, but in managing my career, my money, and my foundation. Now when I'm the coach, I don't let my young players move the pieces around the board to test different ideas. Rather, I require them to think through all of the steps in their heads before they even touch a piece. Forced to plan in advance, they become much better players, many of them later earning the grandmaster title themselves.

With the goal to succeed and the determination to always think through your moves, you can get ahead in chess, money, or whatever pursuit you choose. It's true that obstacles may slow you down or even stop you temporarily. It happens to everyone. In life, like in chess, you can't control everything. But that doesn't mean you can't be a winner. Follow the financial planning strategies and the investment tactics from these pages and you, too, can become as "rich as a king."

About the Authors

All too often, "about the author" pages mention the credentials of the writers without giving a sense of who the people really are. So rather than just listing our accomplishments and licenses here, we'd like to share a story about our professional development. By describing our paths to you, we hope you'll see who we are and why writing this book was so important to us.

SUSAN POLGAR

Photo by Paul Truong

Though I've been known as a chess player my whole life, I find that characterization of me to be somewhat paradoxical. On the one hand, I'm a very social person, with family and friends representing the cornerstone of who I am. On the other hand, however, playing chess is often seen as a solitary activity. After all, when I face my competitors with the clock ticking and money at stake, it's just me, all by myself.

I reconcile those two opposing attributes by considering how I have approached chess differently from many other serious players. I always liked being part of a group. It made me feel invigorated when I participated on the Olympic teams, for example, and thus greatly encouraged me along the way to becoming a five-time Olympic Champion, never once losing a game. Beyond that, I've always felt part of the team of women players as a whole, and have endeavored to show the world that at the chessboard, women are a force to be reckoned with. In fact, I broke the gender barrier in 1986 to qualify for the men's world championship cycle, and in 1991 when I earned the highest honor in the sport, the grandmaster title, I was the first woman to do it using the same criteria as the men. Since then, many female chess players have followed suit. I'm

261

proud of how women have advanced in the field, and have even set up my charitable foundation, The Susan Polgar Foundation, which has given out millions of dollars in grants to aspiring students, with one of its main missions being to encourage girls to excel in the game. Toward this goal, Doug and I and our publisher, too, have all decided to donate 10% of our income from this book to the foundation.

When I first spoke with Doug, I saw that the greatness of teamwork could also be applied to personal finance. Just as I teamed up for years with my sisters to compete in chess matches, I work with my husband as well to succeed in our financial challenges. And along with all of the *Rich As A King* team members who helped Doug and me as we worked on this book, I hope that we'll help our readers find their own paths to success.

DOUGLAS GOLDSTEIN

Photo by Yehoshua Halevi

When I started on Wall Street, my favorite client was my grandmother. She, in fact, had been a stock broker many years earlier, having been one of the first women to earn the license. Following in her footsteps, my mother also became an investment advisor, helping clients plan and build wealth. I joined my mother as her partner in 1992, and the #1 lesson that I learned from her was the importance of educating clients about handling their money wisely. Though we could guide them, they ultimately needed to make the final decisions themselves.

I obtained the licenses that allowed me to advise clients on trading not only stocks, bonds, and mutual funds, but also options, commodities, and futures. Eventually, I earned the license to supervise other advisors and received the designation of Certified Financial Planner™. Even with all of these professional accreditations to trade securities, and having started my own international investment company, Profile Investment Services, Ltd., I view myself more as a financial educator. I write extensively, using easy-to-understand language so everyone can realize that investing isn't only for the professionally trained. I write newspaper columns and books, teach college courses, and even host a personal finance radio program, *The Goldstein on Gelt Show*, which is what led to this book, since Susan was a guest of mine in 2010.

The idea to use chess as a metaphor to illustrate financial concepts began when I listened to my kids' chess coach teach them the philosophy of the game and I saw that he was using the same ideas that I used when speaking with clients. I brought up the idea with Susan when I interviewed her on the radio and she started coming up with more and more comparisons, too. We began a correspondence and quickly felt that we were onto something great. We started examining how we could employ chess strategies, the very same ones that had propelled Susan to championship status, to improve investment portfolios. As we both have had decades of experience in our fields along with a love for teaching, we decided to begin the task of researching and writing *Rich As A King*.

Index

A

active investing and trading
    certificates of deposit (CDs),
        44–45
    overconfidence and, 18–19
    understanding, 42–43, 45, 230
activity (chess goal), 27, 41, 43–44
advantage accumulation (chess
    principle), 167–171, 175, 186–
    187, 226
aggressive strategy
    in chess, 68
    in finance, 66–68, 153
Alekhine, Alexander, 185, 230
Alexander the Great, 26
alternative minimum tax (AMT), 136
Amazon, 17
American Airlines, 246
American Depository Receipts (ADRs),
    127–128
American Funds, 158
amnesty program, tax, 254
analysis tool for investing, 60–65
Anand, Viswanathan, 32, 38, 81
Anand vs. Carlsen, 38
Anand vs. Gelfand, 38, 81
Anderssen, Adolf, 184
annuities, 200, 219–220

architect's strategy, 195
Ariely, Dan, 17, 18–19
Art of Learning, The (Waitzkin), 104,
    149
assault preparedness, 36–37, 69,
    190–191
asset allocation. *See also specific types*
    by age, 66–73
    confidence and, 19–20
    long-term *vs.* immediate, 16
    model, 57–60, 66, 71, 83–86
    mutual funds and, 49
    review of, 11–14, 54–55, 173–
        175, 180
    theory, 66
attacks
    avoiding surprise, 235–238
    back-rank, 241–244
automobile insurance, 190
average annual returns statistics,
    60–64, 95

B

back-rank attacks, 241–244
backup plans as defense, 244–248
bad investment solutions, 174, 200–
    202
Baidu, 127

balanced funds, 153

balance of strategy, 5–6, 53, 56, 183–185

Banco Santander, S.A., 127

bank failures, U.S., 201–202

Bank of America, 247

Barber, Brad, 19

barriers to achieving goals, 5, 6, 81–83, 227

Barron's, 160

Barry, Dave, 251

Battle of Gaugamela, 26

bear market, 62, 125

Bear Stearns, 11, 152, 238

behavioral finance, 5, 7, 8, 12, 212

behavioral psychology, 16–22

Bell, Alexander Graham, 232

Berra, Yogi, 28, 176

bishop, 42–44, 58–59, 173

Blink (Gladwell), 110–111

blitz chess games, 51, 237

blocking obstacles (chess principle), 227

Boeing Company, 247

bonds

    bond funds, 154–156

    bond ladder, 70, 145–147, 222

    buy-sell-trade of, 133–135

    calculator, 139

    convertible bonds, 193–194

    discovered check, 113–114, 220–223

    high-yield, 140–145

    junk, 140–145, 256

    par value of, 136, 137–138, 139, 140, 156, 193

    portfolio of, 70, 84, 133

    premium, 140

    private activity, 136

    ratings of, 140–141

    U.S. government, 135

    yields of, 138–139

    zero-coupon, 136–137

books on chess

    Art of Learning, The (Waitzkin), 104, 149

    How Life Imitates Chess (Kasparov), 36

    Immortal Game, The (Shenk), 184

books on finance

    Blink (Gladwell), 110–111

    Invisible Gorilla, The (Chabris and Simons), 13–14, 19, 173

    Predictably Irrational (Ariely), 17

    This Time Is Different (Reinhart and Rogoff), 203

Borders Books, 152

Botvinnik, Mikhail, 43, 77

Browne, Walter, 115

Buckle, Henry Thomas, 29

budgeting, 105, 112–113, 114–117

Buffett, Warren, 22, 42, 131, 174, 202

bull market, 61–62, 125

business ownership. *See* company ownership

buy-and-hold investment strategy, 19, 125–126, 145, 161

buying mutual funds, 159–160

buy-sell-trade activity, 11–12, 156–159

C

calculators, online, 40, 86, 89, 139, 213

call options, 191–192, 197

call provisions of bonds, 139, 193–194

Capablanca, José Raúl, 22, 51

capital gains, 134, 136, 158, 202–203

career earning potential, 54, 67–69, 258

car insurance, 190

Carlsen, Magnus, 28, 32, 38, 48, 66, 203

Carnegie, Andrew, 150

Cash Available for Distribution (CAD), 129

cash *vs.* credit card, 117, 176–177

castling, 25–26, 38, 40, 189

Caterpillar Tractor Company, 247

certificates of deposit (CDs), 44–45, 56, 69, 144–145, 176

Certified Financial Planner, 66, 230, 262

Chabris, Christopher, 13–14, 19

chasing a piece (chess tactic), 248–250

chasing returns, 6, 159, 238

checkmate symbol (#), 180

Chernev, Irving, 230

chess pieces. *See specific ones*

Chiburdanidze, Maia, 24, 85, 143, 256–257

children and money management, 243–244. *See also* family money management

closed games, 84

Coca-Cola Company, The, 42

commissions and fees, 18, 42, 186, 203, 234, 241

commodities, 56, 130, 154. *See also* asset allocation

common stocks, 126–127

communication and budgeting, 105–106. *See also* family money management

company ownership, 122–123, 126–127, 130–131, 133

compromise over loss, 251–256

computer *vs.* human behavior, 22, 98, 99, 166–167, 175

concentration, sustaining, 231–232

conservative investment strategy, 70–71

consolidating forces (chess principle), 194–195

consumer price index (CPI), 95

convertible bonds, 193–194

Coolidge, Calvin, 208

core asset protection, 37–38. *See also* asset allocation

cornering the market, 59

corporate bonds, 134. *See also* bonds

Cortes, Hernando, 30

cosigning loans, 232–233
cost of living adjustment (COLA), 220
Council for Disability Awareness, 39
coupon rate, 137, 138
credit card
    balance transfers, 110
    vs. cash, 117, 176–177
    debt, 112, 183, 228, 239
current yield of bonds, 138

D
Dalbar, Inc., 125
death and financial changes, 91. *See also* life insurance
debentures, 134
debt, personal, 112, 183, 228–229, 239–241
debt securities, 55, 133
decision-making strategy, 15–16, 166–167, 224–226
decision paralysis, 225–226
decision trees strategy, 24
decoy (chess tactic), 239–241
Deep Blue, 22
defensive money management, 183–185, 211–212, 227, 244–248
Desprez, Marcel, 178
Desprez Opening, 178
develop with purpose (chess principle), 167, 198–200
disability insurance, 38–39, 190
discovered check, 113–114, 220–223
Disney, Walt, 225

disposition effect, 7–11
diversification. *See also* asset allocation
    in chess, 58–60
    with foreign investments, 126–127
    with mutual funds, 150, 151, 159–160
    with real estate, 128–129
diversified commodities fund, 56
dividends from company stocks, 123, 126–127, 130–131, 204–205
division of labor and budgeting, 105
dollar cost averaging, 151
double check (chess tactic), 223–224
draw (chess tactic), 188, 208, 254–255
Dvoretsky, Mark, 174

E
Earnings Per Share (EPS), 129
economic crises, 5–6, 181, 183
economies of scale, 151, 156
Einstein, Albert, 92, 203
Elo, Arpad, 48
Elo system of ratings, 36, 48, 140
emergency fund, 83, 175, 185, 190, 230, 244
Emerson, Ralph Waldo, 210
emotional decision-making, 6–8, 18–22, 182–183, 186
Employee Benefit Research Institute, 37
endgame strategy, 72–73, 99
energy company investments, 131
English Opening, 85

Enron Corporation, The, 238
envelope system of budgeting, 116
equity investments, 124, 125
equity REITs. *See* Real Estate
    Investment Trusts (REITs)
Euwe, Max, 167
exchange traded funds (ETFs), 130,
    178, 198

F
face value of bonds, 136, 137–138,
    139, 140, 156, 193
failure, learning from, 224–225
Fama, Jr., Gene, 126
family money management
    balance in, 177
    coordination of professional
        consultants, 234–235
    risk management in, 57
    strategies for, 13, 14, 53–54, 113,
        114–115, 183–184
    tactical skills of, 105–108
    teaching children, 243–244
family-owned businesses, 217
fantasy stock market, 111–112, 213
Federal Deposit Insurance Corporation
    (FDIC), 144–145, 202
Federal Trade Commission, 233
Fédération Internationale des Échecs
    (FIDE), 36, 48, 68
fees and commissions, 18, 42, 186,
    203, 234, 241

Financial Industry Regulatory
    Authority, Inc. (FINRA), 123
financial plan
    by age, 67–68, 71–73
    creating and maintaining a, 53–56,
        75–87, 92–94, 207
    professional, 76–77, 86, 93, 98
Financial World, 160
first-move advantage, 27
Fischer, Bobby, 48, 66, 176, 185–186
fish bowl paradigm, 64–65
fixed annuities, 219–220
fixed-income security, 133, 145–146
flank openings, 84
flipping study, 5
focus, sustaining, 231–232
Forbes, 160
Ford, Henry, 33, 225
foreign investments, 127–128, 153–
    154
forking (chess tactic), 213–216
Fortunoff, 152
401(k) retirement funds, 67, 71, 171,
    175, 213, 238
Franklin, Benjamin, 77, 165
fraud protection, 73–74
free strategies, 16–18, 74, 108–110,
    176, 212
Funds From Operations (FFO), 129

G
Gates, Bill, 225
Gelfand, Boris, 38, 81, 207

Gelfand vs. Polgar, 207
General Motors Corporation, 247
Genius in All of Us, The (Shenk), 231
Getty kouros statue, 110–111
Gladwell, Malcolm, 110–111
Global Crossing, 152
global market investments, 127–128,
    153–154
goal-setting
    in chess, 82
    in finance, 23–25, 28–36, 75–76,
        81–83
Goldstein, Douglas
    advice from, 92–93, 228
    chess games with Polgar, 227, 259
    client lessons from, 20, 73–74,
        106, 173, 218, 235
    financial background of, 104–105,
        262–263
grading system for bonds, 141–142
grandmasters. *See also specific persons*
    behaviors of, 11, 22
    planning strategy of, 53
    title requirement of, 48, 212
Growth Fund of America (American
    Funds), 158
growth investments, 130–131, 153

H
Hanes, 172–173
Hannibal, 77
Hardicsay, Peter, 179–180

healthcare planning, 72, 73, 91, 96,
    190
hedge funds, 45, 112, 218
Heisman, Dan, 123
high-risk investment schemes, 67
high-yield bonds, 140–145
historical *vs.* modern chess, 26, 69,
    165, 177, 184
home ownership, 38–40, 55, 181, 183,
    190
Horowitz, Israel, 53
housing crisis, U.S., 181, 183
How Life Imitates Chess (Kasparov), 36
human *vs.* computer behavior, 22, 98,
    99, 166–167, 175
Hungarian Chess Federation, 3, 68

I
illiquid investments, 45, 53, 218, 220
illusion of attention, 13–14
illusion of confidence, 19–22
illusion of knowledge, 19
Immortal Game, The (Shenk), 184
implementing *vs.* planning, 75, 104,
    115, 117–118, 196
income tax. *See also* tax considerations
    filing mistakes, 251–254
    refunds, 171
index funds, 156, 185, 250
Individual Retirement Accounts
    (IRAs), 71, 137, 171, 211
inflation, 55, 75, 78, 91, 95, 230
information overload, 14–15

initiative
    in chess, 27, 41, 48, 49
    in finance, 48–49, 228–229
insurance, 37–41, 57, 72, 79, 175, 189–190, 219–220
interest rates on investments, 91, 137, 145–146, 156, 241
intermediate-term bonds, 69
Internal Revenue Service (IRS), 251–254
international investments, 127–128, 153–154
International Master, Polgar as, 94
internet games. *See also* software
    for chess, 70, 99, 111
    for finance, 111–112, 213
intuition, 110–111
investment firms, 133–134
investor behavior, 4–8, 17–18, 228. *See also specific behaviors*
Invisible Gorilla, The (Chabris and Simons), 13–14, 19, 173
Ioseliani, Nana, 92
IRAs (Individual Retirement Accounts), 71, 137, 171, 211
IRS (Internal Revenue Service), 251–254

J
Jagger, Mick, 94
JDS Uniphase, 152
Johnson, Kelly, 89
J. Paul Getty Museum, 110–111

Jun, Xie, 8–9
junk bonds, 140–145, 256

K
Kahneman, Daniel, 5, 6, 18, 166
kamikaze attacks, 186–187
Karpov, Anatoly, 69, 257
Kasparov, Garry
    advice of, 36, 111, 181, 183
    games of, 22, 184, 191
    as Olympiad coach, 87, 107
    opening strategies of, 66
    rating of, 48
Kasparov vs. Deep Blue, 22
Kasparov vs. Tal, 191
Keres, Paul, 76
Kieseritzky, Lionel, 184
king, 12, 38, 40, 168–169, 173
KISS acronym, 89, 92
knight, 46–47, 173, 210–211
Korchnoi, Victor, 32
Kotov, Alexander, 51
Kramnik, Vladimir, 32, 69, 257
Kramnik vs. Karpov, 257

L
Landers, Ann and Abigail, 172
Lasker, Emanuel, 72, 75, 93, 103
L'eggs, 172
Lehman Brothers, 11, 152
life expectancy, 56–57, 91, 97
life insurance, 37–38, 39–41, 79, 190
limited partnerships, 45

limit orders, 248, 250
Lincoln, Abraham, 81
Lipper Mutual Fund Performance Analysis, 160
liquidation of company stocks, 127
liquidity of investments, 45, 218
load mutual fund, 161
loans, cosigning, 232–233
longevity. *See* life expectancy
long-term *vs.* short term strategy, 15–16, 30–31, 202–204
loss, moving on from, 224–225
loss aversion, 5–6
Lynch, Peter, 131, 172

M
Madl, Ildiko, 3
Madoff, Bernard, 176
Magyar Telekom, 127
man *vs.* computer behavior, 22, 98, 99, 166–167, 175
margin call, 241
margin trading, 47, 240–241
marketability of funds, 45
marketplace. *See* stock market
Mason, James, 181
material advantage. *See* advantage accumulation (chess principle)
measurable goals, 30–31
media response, 14–15, 16
memorization *vs.* understanding, 99
men, overconfidence of, 19
mental accounting, 12–13, 14

Merrill Lynch, 11
Michelangelo, 179
mid-game strategies, 70–71
mistakes
  capitalizing on other's, 187, 204
  fixing financial, 251–254
  learning from, 224–225
mitigating risk. *See* risk reduction
modern *vs.* historical chess, 26, 69, 165, 177, 184
money communication and relationships, 105–106, 108
money diary, 115
Monte Carlo simulation (MCS), 60, 62–65, 98
Moody's rating system, 140, 141–142
Morningstar, 160
mortgage REITs, 130
move with purpose (chess principle), 165–167, 179, 234
municipal bonds, 135, 136
Murey, Jacob, 212
music and chess strategies, 43
mutual funds. *See also* asset allocation; *specific types*
  benefits of, 125, 149–152, 185
  buying and selling, 150–152, 156–160
  classifications of, 153–156
  ETFs, 130
  formats of, 156
  load, 161
  mistakes, 159–160

prospectus of companies, 160–161
saving goals and, 49
specialization of, 151
taxes on, 161–162

N

Napoleon Bonaparte, 210
net worth statement, 175
New York Stock Exchange, 134
Nimzo-Indian Defense, 191
Nimzowitsch, Aron, 209
no-load mutual fund, 161
norm, grandmaster, 212
Nortel (Northern Telecom Limited),
    152

O

Odean, Terrance, 8, 19
offensive money management, 184–
    185. *See also* aggressive strategy
older people and finance. *See*
    retirement planning
online calculators. *See* calculators,
    online
online training. *See* internet games
open games, 84
opening-game strategies
    in chess, 15, 25–27, 66, 67, 84,
        177–178, 185, 229
    in investing, 27–29, 67
out of book game, 15, 84
overconfidence, 18–22, 67, 166, 173
overseas investments, 127–128,
    153–154
overtrading, 87, 234

P

paper trading, 111
par value of bonds, 136, 137–138,
    139, 140, 156, 193
passed pawn, 10
patience, 92–94, 108–109, 174–175,
    182–183, 188. *See also* success,
    strategy for
pattern recognition, 51–52
Patton, George, 30
Paulson, John, 131
pawn, 173, 181, 189, 192, 205–206,
    232
Penney, J.C., 29
pension changes, 91, 95, 246–247. *See
    also* retirement planning
periphery moves (chess principle),
    186–187, 207
perpetual check (chess tactic), 254–255
persistence, 207–208. *See also*
    aggressive strategy
petty cash, 107
pharmaceutical company investments,
    126, 131
pin (chess tactic), 216–217
planning *vs.* implementing, 75, 104,
    115, 117–118, 196
point system (chess), 6, 188
poised-to-attack strategy, 36–37, 182–
    183. *See also* aggressive strategy
Polgar, Judit, 3, 15, 32, 231
Polgar, Sophia, 3, 32, 231
Polgar, Susan
    becoming Grandmaster, 212, 261
    becoming International Master, 94

childhood lessons of, 32–33, 107, 118, 231, 260
    disposition effect and, 8–11
    family of, 3, 15, 32, 231
    FIDE score intervention, 36
    foundation of, 260, 262
    simultaneous chess games by, 54
    style of chess, 185–186
Polgar vs. Boguszlavszkij, 214
Polgar vs. Chiburdanidze, 24, 85, 143, 256–257
Polgar vs. Goldstein, 227, 259
Polgar vs. Hardicsay, 179–180
Polgar vs. Ioseliani, 92
Polgar vs. Jun, 8–11
Polgar vs. Karpov, 25–26, 194–195
Polgar vs. Kiss, 199
Polgar vs. Murey, 212
Polgar vs. Smyslov, 43
Polgar vs. Vanheste, 189
Ponzi scheme operators, 176
portfolio management. *See* asset allocation
positional *vs.* tactical chess, 69, 84
postmortem, 224–225
Predictably Irrational (Ariely), 17
preferred stocks, 126–127
premium bonds, 140
private activity bonds, 136
professional management, financial coordination of, 234–235
    for mutual funds, 161
    services of, 66, 76–77, 85–86, 92–93, 98, 151
prospectus of mutual fund companies, 160–161

publicly-traded stocks, 122–123
purposeful moves (chess principle), 165–167, 179, 234

Q
quantifiable goals, 30–31
queen, 48, 168–169, 173, 181, 192, 256–257

R
Ramsey, Dave, 208
rating systems
    in chess, 36, 48, 140
    in stock market, 124, 140, 141–142, 157, 160
real estate investments, 97–98, 128–130, 181
Real Estate Investment Trusts (REITs), 128–130
reducing risks. *See* risk
Regulation T, 47
Reinfeld, Fred, 217
Reinhart, Carmen, 203
reinvestment risk, 222
relationships and money, 80, 105–106, 108, 109
repetition *vs.* understanding, 99
research strategies
    for chess, 69, 84, 85, 111, 160
    for investing, 14, 70, 73, 98–99, 111, 160–161, 212–213
Reshevsky, Samuel, 117
Réti, Richard, 51–52
retirement planning, 36–37, 70–74, 175. *See also* pension changes
401(k) plans, 71, 171, 238

benefits, 80
bonds and, 222
defensive, 246–248
IRAs, 71, 137, 171
software for, 97
spending changes and, 96
returns. *See* average annual returns
reversion to the mean, 238
rigorous goal attributes, 32–33
risk
    in chess, 6
    insurance and, 38–41
    in investing, 6, 55–56, 86, 159,
        204, 222, 237–238
    margin trading and, 47–48
risky stocks, 187–188
Rogers, Jim, 131
Rogers, Kenny, 196
Rogoff, Kenneth, 203
rook, 25–26, 173
Rowling, J.K., 208
Royal Dutch Shell Plc., 127

S
salary increase, 170
saving strategies, 35, 49, 67, 78,
    113, 114–115, 170–172. *See also*
    spending
Searching for Bobby Fischer, 149
secret to success falacy, 176
sector funds, 154
sectors, major market, 126
Securities and Exchange Commission
    (SEC), 123
security portfolio, 84
selling investments, 156–159, 197, 202

Shefrin, Hersh, 7
Shenk, David, 184, 231
short-term *vs.* long-term, 15–16,
    30–31, 202–204
Simon, Herbert, 52
Simons, Daniel, 13–14, 19, 173
simultaneous chess games by Polgar, 54
skewer (chess tactic), 235–237
S&L bailouts, 5
Smyslov, Vasily, 43, 67
Smyslov vs. Botvinnik, 43
Social Security, 97, 136
Social Security Administration, 38, 80,
    95–96, 246
software. *See also* internet games
    for chess, 65
    for investing, 95, 96–99
Soros, George, 131
S&P 500. *See* Standard & Poor's
    Corporation
spending. *See also* saving strategies
    behavior, 103, 114–115, 116
    changes after retirement, 96
    goals, 30, 33, 170
Spielmann, Rudolph, 73
stalemate, 169, 251–253
Standard & Poor's Corporation, 124,
    125, 140, 141–142, 157, 160, 204
statistical modeling, 60–61
Statman, Meir, 7
stealth tax, 136
Steinitz, Wilhelm, 93, 121, 229
Steve Miller Band, 201
stock market
    company ownership, 122–123,
        126–127, 130–131

counsel for, 112

jargon, 56

oversight of, 123

simulations of, 111–112, 213

volatility of, 5–6, 61–62, 91, 131, 140–143, 159

stocks

common *vs.* preferred, 126–127

publicly-traded, 122–123

risky, 187–188

story, 172

story stocks, 172

STRATegic goal system, 29–35, 81

strategy *vs.* tactics, 52–53, 117–118, 195, 207

stress and finances, 15, 149, 150, 152, 183, 186, 188

success, strategy for, 4, 30, 65, 93, 230–232. *See also* patience for success

surprise attacks (chess principle), 235–237

Syms, 152

Szecsenyi, Istvan, 192

Szecsenyi vs. Polgar, 192–193

T

tactical skills. *See also specific tactics*

in chess, 113, 117–118, 196, 210

in finance, 52–53, 106–108, 117–118, 196

vs. positional, 69, 84

Tal, Mikhail, 69, 184, 191

Tarrasch, Siegbert, 103

Tartakower, Savielly, 179

tax amnesty program, 254

tax considerations

with bonds, 135–136

income tax and, 171, 251–254

with mutual funds, 158, 161–162

planning software, 97

savings and, 170

trading investments and, 197

tax-loss harvesting, 197–198

teamwork mentality, 234–235, 261–262

technology company investments, 154, 181

telecommunications company investments, 131

temperament and money, 108, 109

tempo (chess), 174

tempting goal attributes, 34

1035 exchange, 200

1040x form, 253

Teva Pharmaceuticals, 127

30-day-wash-sale rule, 197

This Time Is Different (Reinhart and Rogoff), 203

threats, identifying (chess principle), 208–210

time-bound goal attributes, 29–31

time management, 107–109

TOTAL S.A., 127

tournament point system (chess), 6

Tracy, Brian, 81, 258

trade orders, 49

trading fees and commissions, 241

trading strategy

behavior studies of, 5, 7, 8, 123–125

in chess, 196

in investing, 197–198, 228
traditional strategy for success, 230–231
training
    in chess, 99, 111
    in finance, 111–112, 213
transfers, credit card balance, 110
transparency of stock market, 152, 176, 187, 228
traps
    in chess, 217–218
    in finance, 175–177, 187, 217–220
trusts, 71, 72, 78, 175, 235
turnover ratio of mutual funds, 161

U

under-promoting (chess principle), 205–206
underwriters, 133–134
United Airlines, 247
U.S. Chess Federation, 3–4
U.S. government bonds, 135
U.S. Navy SEALs, 103
U.S. Postal Service, 247
U.S. Treasury Inflation Protected Securities (TIPS), 55
utility company investments, 130

V

Vanheste, Jeroen, 189
victory, celebrating, 30
volatility of stock market, 5–6, 61–62, 91, 131, 140–143, 159

W

Wachovia Corporation, 152
waiting moves (chess principle), 166
Waitzkin, Josh, 104, 149
Wall Street. *See* stock market
Wall Street Journal, 14, 77, 121, 160, 231
Walton, Sam, 112
Washington Mutual, Inc., 152, 201–202
Washington Redskins, 247
weak pawn, 232
Williams, Robin, 177
wills, 71, 175, 196
Winfrey, Oprah, 33
win-lose-draw, 6
women in chess, 36, 261–262
World Chess Federation. *See* Fédération Internationale des Échecs (FIDE)
WorldCom, 152

Y

yield to call (YTC), 139
yield to maturity (YTM), 139
young investors portfolio strategy, 66–68
Yusupov, Artur, 174

Z

zero-coupon bonds, 136–137

Don't Miss Out
on Any New Ideas

It's impossible to become as "rich as a king" overnight.

Picking up this book and implementing the strategies and tactics suggested is an excellent way to begin your journey to greater financial security. But it's only a starting point. Join the *Rich As A King* community by subscribing to our blog and podcasts for periodic tips and encouragement on how to use strategies of the chess elite to become a grandmaster of investing.

How to Get the *Rich As A King* Resource Guide

 To thank you for signing up for our list, we'll send you a free copy of our resource guide called *The Grandmaster's Toolbox*. This e-book includes links to some of the best finance and chess tools that we have found on the internet.

If you'd like to keep up with hot-off-the-press chess and investment news and ideas, and get a free copy of *The Grandmaster's Toolbox*, sign up at www.RichAsAKing.com.

CPSIA information can be obtained at www.ICGtesting.com
Printed in the USA
LVOW07*1027270415

436242LV00005BA/7/P